Science Versus Idealism

An Examination of "Pure Empiricism" and Modern Logic

By

MAURICE CORNFORTH

M.A.

To the Memory of David Guest

LONDON

LAWRENCE & WISHART

THIS BOOK IS PRODUCED IN COMPLETE CONFORMITY
WITH THE AUTHORIZED ECONOMY STANDARDS

MADE AND PRINTED IN GREAT BRITAIN
AT THE CHAPEL RIVER PRESS
ANDOVER, HANTS
12.46.

Acknowledgments

I wish to acknowledge with gratitude :

(1) The help of my wife, Kitty Cornforth, in the writing and revision of all parts of this book ;

(2) The help of Professor J. B. S. Haldane in the preparation of the second and third sections of Chapter 12. In particular, his very valuable suggestions on questions of theories of time and of the use of alternative " languages " in science. But, of course, he is not responsible for any errors I have made in carrying out these suggestions.

M. C. CORNFORTH.

London, *January*, 1946.

CONTENTS

INTRODUCTION

This book examines a particular trend in modern philosophy—the trend of "empiricism" or more precisely of "pure empiricism." I have tried to trace the process of the development of such theories, to show where they go wrong, and to suggest the right way of dealing with the questions at issue.

More specifically, the purpose of this book is to examine and to criticise that tendency of modern philosophical thought which, taking its origin in the materialism of Bacon and his successors, Hobbes and Locke, turned from materialism to subjective idealism, gave rise to the various subjectivist theories of Berkeley, Hume, Mach and the agnostics, and is still alive today, giving rise to fresh philosophical theories in the same tradition.

In the first part of this book I have surveyed the main line of development from Bacon to Mach.

This same line of development—though in some respects it seems to have ceased to develop and to have reached a complete theoretical dead-end—has been continued in the present century with the theories known as "Logical Analysis" and "Logical Positivism."

The peculiar and "new" characteristic of this philosophy today is that it has now turned to formal logic for its basis and justification. It has developed a system of logic and methods of "logical analysis." This "logical analysis" was first formulated by Bertrand Russell, beginning with his books, *The Principles of Mathematics* and *Principia Mathematica.* Then it was further taken up in Wittgenstein's *Tractatus Logico-Philosophicus.* And its latest form is to be found in the works of the school of Logical Positivists, founded by Rudolf Carnap, who base their views on what is called the study of "logical syntax" and "the logical analysis of science."

The examination of these "logical" schools is unfortunately an involved and difficult process, as compared with the relative simplicity and straightforwardness of the ideas of their predecessors. The second and longest part of this book is devoted to unravelling them.

Today these particular theories pass themselves off as the very last word in scientific enlightenment. But I believe that, far from representing the summit of scientific philosophy, they are rather a barrier standing in the way of the progress of scientific thought. In trying to get to grips with them, it is important not to take them at their face value. They did not appear suddenly out of the blue, as their authors themselves sometimes seem to think, as the long-sought solution of all the problems of philosophy. They have an historical background, and are only descendants of certain earlier tendencies of philosophy. And so I have approached them historically, to find out both where they came from and whither they are leading. (The answer to the first question is that they derive from the idealist theories of George Berkeley. The answer to the second question is—nowhere.)

While the purpose of this book is mainly critical, criticism can have little value unless it is directed from some positive standpoint. In that case, criticism of rival points of view helps to develop and test the validity of the standpoint from which it is directed. My own standpoint is that of philosophical materialism, which in its modern form is known as Dialectical Materialism.

This standpoint contains a very definite criterion whereby one may attempt to judge the value of any philosophy. The value of any philosophy must be judged by how far it helps to understand and to solve the practical problems facing humanity. This is a test, not merely of its social utility, but of its truth.

I would say that the outstanding problem of life today arises from the contrast between the enormous new powers of production at the disposal of society and our apparent lack of ability to control them. This in turn reflects the basic contradiction between the growing power of social production and the social organisation which places it at the disposal of a small privileged class as their private property. It is this which impedes productive development, and even leads to productive powers being used to destroy nations in warfare, instead of for lightening the labour and increasing the material prosperity of mankind.

Now the development of the means of production, and the

discovery and use of new sources of productive power, has depended on the advance of the natural sciences, of scientific knowledge. The growth of science, extending to all spheres of phenomena, and building up more and more a unified scientific picture of the world we live in, has been the outstanding theoretical fact of the present age.

Philosophy, therefore, has today above all the task of enabling us to understand the significance of science, and its meaning for us ; and to understand the nature of the tasks which face us in harnessing this knowledge, and the power it confers, for the purposes of human progress.

In this sense, philosophy must be a matter of deep concern, not merely to "professional philosophers," but to every thinking man and woman. And we find, too, that the whole of modern philosophy, and of contemporary philosophy in particular, tends to become more and more engrossed with questions of the significance and interpretation of the sciences. Thus modern "logical analysis" becomes above all "the analysis of science."

But contrary tendencies exist in the sphere of philosophical ideas. There are philosophical tendencies which are helping forward the advance of science, and are helping us to understand it and its significance in the modern world ; and there are contrary tendencies. The former are serving the interests of the forces of progress—that is, the forces working for the fullest development of our productive powers for the welfare of mankind ; and the latter are not. Clearly, therefore, the positive work of pressing forward philosophical truth must be combined with the negative task of criticism and controversy. Indeed, progress and truth in any sphere is only won in the midst of the struggle against reaction and error.

It is my contention that philosophical progress is in the main represented by the development of materialist ideas and by the contradictions and controversies between materialist and idealist theories.

Such a fundamental division of philosophy into materialist and idealist trends reflects the fact that the development of scientific knowledge comes into conflict at every stage with various traditional supernatural ideas, and in particular with the ideas of religion. The religious explanation of life and of the world is very deep-rooted, and it arises from a stage prior to the winning of scientific knowledge. As scientific knowledge is won it continually contradicts and oversets the accepted notions of religion.

Materialism is that trend in philosophy which champions scientific knowledge as against supernatural beliefs. On the other hand, idealism is that trend which, in a direct or indirect way, defends supernatural beliefs against scientific truth.

As science extends our knowledge of nature and society, and lays the basis for a new mode of living for humanity, so does idealist philosophy hasten to the rescue of the threatened traditional ideas. And by so doing it serves to obscure the understanding of the significance of science and of the possibilities which the utilisation of science opens up for the people.

The materialist philosopher Frederick Engels gave the following well-known characterisation of the theoretical difference between materialist and idealist trends of philosophy :—

"The great basic question of all philosophy, especially of modern philosophy, is that concerning the relation of thinking and being. . . . The answers which philosophers have given to this question split them into two great camps. Those who assert the primacy of spirit to nature, and, therefore, in the last instance, assume world creation in some form or other, comprise the camp of idealism. The others, who regard nature as primary, belong to the various schools of materialism."[1]

Thus materialist philosophy holds, in one way or another, that all events have a natural explanation. Idealism, on the other hand, postulates ultimate spiritual or supernatural causes.

Materialism, therefore, whether in an open or in a disguised and apologetic form, challenges the whole standpoint of religion. Idealism, on the other hand, though it may not take a theistic form, is an apology and justification for the religious outlook.

Thirdly, while materialist philosophy encourages the outlook that men can learn to control nature by gaining knowledge and understanding of the material world, and thereby can become masters of their own destiny, idealism tends to preach dependence and subjection to the supernatural.

When philosophical inquiry, as distinct from theology based

---

[1] Engels, *Feuerbach*, Ch. 2.

on the elaboration of accepted religious notions, first arose in ancient Greece, it took the form of philosophical materialism. It was the attempt of Thales of Miletos to find a natural, though purely speculative, explanation of the whole world, by the theory that everything had evolved through the changes and differentiations of one Primary Substance, that gave the first impulse to the development of philosophical thought.

But very soon the materialist philosophy of Thales and his followers in the ancient world was met by the counter-development of idealist theories (first elaborated in the philosophy of Pythagoras), which taught that the cause of all things was spiritual and that knowledge was to be obtained by the inner light of the soul and not through sense and experience.

The rapid and brilliant development of modern natural science seems definitely to confirm and justify the materialist view of the world. The natural explanation of all things, which such ancient thinkers as Thales or Democritus or Epicurus could establish only speculatively and in very general outline, is being established scientifically and in ever growing detail and comprehensiveness by the advance of natural science during the past three hundred years.

The advance of science, then, and the development of new processes and techniques associated with it, have not only revolutionised methods of social production and created the basis for great social transformations. At the same time modern natural science from its inception has represented a challenge and a threat to all old-established ideas, particularly the ideas of religion, and so laid the basis for a great transformation of ideas. It was inevitable, therefore, that it should give rise to a reaction. This reaction was expressed in new forms of idealist philosophy, whose tendency was to justify religious ideas in the face of the challenge of science.

Thus with the rise of natural science, materialist philosophy had begun, with the philosophy of Bacon, to develop a materialist theory of knowledge, as a justification of science and a contribution to the understanding of scientific methods. It was particularly on the ground of the theory of knowledge that modern idealism made its most effective challenge to materialism. A marked tendency of modern idealism has been to retreat from a position where it would challenge natural science on its own ground, formulating supernatural as distinct from natural explanations of phenomena. Instead, it has concentrated attention more and more on the theory of knowledge. And its method has been to declare that science is after all not knowledge of the objective material world, but only of the subjective world of ideas; and that therefore, while science may be valid in its own sphere, religion and idealism nevertheless represent the ultimate truth.

This form of idealism was first clearly formulated by George Berkeley, in the year 1710. Its theory of knowledge took the form of empiricism—recognising with science that knowledge could only be reached through the means of the senses and experience, but maintaining that sensation nevertheless cannot give us knowledge of the real external material world.

It was further developed by Hume, in another way by Kant, and then by the neo-Kantians, Machians, positivists and agnostics in the 19th century.

In our own day it is carried on by the schools of "logical analysis" and "logical positivism." In essentials, indeed, these schools are lined up in the camp of philosophical idealism in opposition to philosophical materialism. It will be shown that the principle, first vaguely foreshadowed by Wittgenstein, and then formulated as a rigid methodological dogma by Carnap, that we cannot compare thoughts with things, propositions with facts, but only thoughts with thoughts, propositions with propositions, most decisively ranges these schools within the idealist camp.

It is interesting, too, to note that "logical analysis" began with Russell affirming what is known as "a correspondence theory of truth," that is, that truth consists in the correspondence of propositions with facts, in opposition to the idealists who held that there were no objective facts and that truth consisted simply in the "coherence" of ideas within a total system of ideas. But the development of "logical analysis" finally leads back again to a "coherence theory" of truth. With Carnap, the correspondence of our ideas with facts of any sort vanishes altogether, and we are left with nothing but the system of our ideas.

For materialism, on the other hand, every idea must be tested by comparison with objective reality; and that test is in the last analysis provided by practice.

At the same time it is to be remarked that these theories—essentially lined up with idealism in the struggle against a scientific materialist view of the world and of life—claim to be very revolutionary, ultra-scientific, and Carnap even calls himself " a materialist." They claim to be based on the strictest logic, on the most empirical empiricism. They claim to de-bunk all superstitions. But the principal " superstition " and " metaphysical illusion " that they set out to overthrow, is that of the real existence of the objective material world.

But I believe that in opposition to such theories, and to all the conundrums and confusions produced by idealism, philosophical progress today is represented, and can only be represented, by the progress of materialist theories. And in proof of this may be cited the whole great development of natural science over more than three hundred years, and the ensuing development of philosophical theory through the English materialists of the 17th century, the French materialism of the 18th century, together with the all-embracing dialectical logic of Hegel, to the philosophical standpoint of contemporary dialectical materialism.

In a popular book entitled *The Evolution of Physics*, Einstein and Infeld wrote : " Our intention was to sketch in broad outline the attempts of the human mind to find a connection between the world of ideas and the world of phenomena. We have tried to show the active forces which compel science to invent ideas corresponding to the reality of our world."[1]

I quote this remark as an example of a thoroughly materialistic account, by scientists, of the significance of science. Science establishes " a connection " between ideas and the real world, it " invents ideas corresponding to reality." Therefore on the basis of science we reach an ever-expanding and deepening *knowledge* of the objective world and of our place in it, which banishes all superstitions, ghosts and supernatural forces, and which is a weapon for the liberation of mankind and for the control of both natural and social forces in the interests of humanity.

This is in accord with the further definitions of materialism which Lenin gave, continuing the work of Engels, in his book, *Materialism and Empirio-Criticism* :—

[1] Einstein and Infeld, *The Evolution of Physics*. Preface.

"The fundamental premise of materialism is the recognition of the external world, of the existence of things outside and independent of the mind. . . . The recognition of objective law in nature, and that this law is reflected with approximate fidelity in the mind of man, is materialism. . . . Our consciousness is only an image of the external world, and the latter exists independently. . . . Matter is the objective reality which is given to man by his sensations, and which is reflected by our sensations while existing independently of them."[1]

But anti-materialist philosophy, the same with "modern logic" as with older philosophies, will have none of this materialism. It has the greatest respect for science. But it will not allow that science establishes "a connection" with the objective material world. By no means. It establishes a connection only between ideas. And it will not allow that science "invents ideas corresponding to reality." Science only invents ideas. To talk about objective material reality, about the connection between ideas and the external world, is said to be quite "unscientific"; it is nothing but "meaningless metaphysics." That was the standpoint of Berkeley over two hundred years ago, and it is the standpoint of Logical Positivism today.

And so what do such anti-materialist theories amount to? They are theories which try to limit the scope and power of our minds. From the standpoint of materialism, we see in science a great weapon of enlightenment and emancipation—increasing our knowledge of the real world and therefore our power to live well in that world, and destroying the superstitions and illusions which fog the mind, debase the dignity of the human race, and uphold oppression, exploitation and backwardness. But these theories try to disarm science. Therefore future progress demands that these theories should be shown up, refuted, discredited.

That is what I have tried to do in this book. And at the same time I have tried to indicate some of the ways in which materialism can tackle problems raised by modern science and by the philosophy of science.

---

[1] Lenin, *Materialism and Empirio-Criticism,* Selected Works, Vol. 11, pp. 148, 216, 136 and 192.

PART ONE

MATERIALISM AND EMPIRICISM

CHAPTER I

ENGLISH MATERIALISM IN THE 17TH CENTURY

1. *Materialism and the Scientific Outlook—Francis Bacon*

" ENGLAND," said Marx, " is the original home of all modern materialism, from the 17th century onwards."[1]

Two Englishmen, Francis Bacon, and after him Thomas Hobbes, inaugurated modern materialism. A third, John Locke, continued the work they had begun.

Their main contention was that all knowledge is furnished through the senses. That is to say, we can know nothing except what we can learn through our senses, we can form no significant ideas that are not derived from experience, and theories which cannot be experientially verified are worthless.

" The real progenitor of English materialism," Marx continued, " is Bacon. To him natural philosophy is the only true philosophy, and physics, based upon the experience of the senses, is the chief part of natural philosophy. . . . According to him the senses are infallible and the source of all knowledge. All science is based upon experience, and consists in subjecting the data furnished by the senses to a rational method of investigation. Induction, analysis, comparison, observation, experiment, are the principal forms of such a rational method."

This materialist doctrine set up the scientific view of the world, as against the previous traditional philosophy.

Thus for instance Thomas Aquinas, who was a traditionally recognised philosophical authority, would agree that knowledge *begins* with experience, and that the senses provide the data for the system of human knowledge. But for him Reason then stepped in (duly instructed by the Church as to what it was required to prove) and, by arguing from empirical data to " first causes," constructed a body of theoretical propositions which could not possibly be submitted to any test of experience.

If science was ever to flourish, then this traditional philosophy

[1] Quoted by Engels in the Introduction to ***Socialism, Utopian and Scientific.***

had to be destroyed. For, as Bacon pointed out, such reasonings to first causes " are indeed but remorae and hindrances to stay and slug the ship from further sailing ; and have brought this to pass, that the search of the physical causes hath been neglected and passed in silence."

The materialist doctrine inaugurated by Bacon was of a rather *specialised* sort. It did not formulate any all-embracing materialist theory of the world, but was *limited* to a materialist theory of knowledge and scientific method.

This theory of knowledge, however, revolutionised philosophy.

Bacon's two chief philosophical works, *The Advancement of Learning* and *Novum Organum* (or *New Logic*), were not philosophical treatises on the nature of things, but were treatises on the *method* whereby *knowledge* of the nature of things might be secured.

In the First Aphorism of *Novum Organum*, Bacon propounded the leading principles of his whole thought, as follows :—

" Man, the minister and interpreter of nature, does and understands so much as he may have discerned concerning the order of nature by observing and meditating on facts ; he knows no more, he can do no more."

And again, in the *Advancement of Learning* :—

" All true and fruitful natural philosophy hath a double scale or ladder, ascendent and descendent ; ascending from experiments to the invention of causes, and descending from causes to the invention of new experiments."

In the *Novum Organum*, Bacon went on to compare this view of knowledge with the views of his predecessors.

" They who have handled the sciences," he wrote, " have been either empirics or dogmatists. The empirics, like the ant, amass only and use ; the dogmatists, like spiders, spin webs out of themselves. But the course of the bee lies midway—she gathers materials from the flowers of the garden and the field, and then by her own powers changes and digests them. Nor is the true labour of philosophy unlike hers. It does not depend entirely, or even chiefly, on the strength of the mind, nor does it store up in the memory unaltered the materials provided by natural history and mechanical experiments—but changes and digests them by the intellect."

Bacon had not the slightest doubt that knowledge thus gained by correct scientific method was *objective*, that is to say, referred to the really existing material world, and gave a true, though of course always incomplete, account of that world.

Thus in the *Novum Organum* he spoke of: " Knowledge which is the image or echo of existence." And in the *Advancement of Learning* he said :—

" God hath framed the mind of man as a mirror or glass, capable of the image of the universal world, and joyful to receive the impression thereof, as the eye joyeth to receive light ; and not only delighted in beholding the variety of things and the vicissitude of times, but raised also to find out and discern the ordinances and decrees, which through all those changes are infallibly observed."

Thus in brief Bacon's new doctrine asserted :

(1) That science is the highway to knowledge.

(2) That scientific knowledge is based on observation. On the basis of observations, scientific theories are worked out, which must always be *tested* by fresh observations, which in turn suggest further theoretical developments—and so on.

(3) That scientific knowledge is objectively true, and that no other means of attaining objective truth exists.

(4) Bacon contrasted the method of science, not only to the unscientific amassing of " undigested " facts, but to the method of " dogmatism." By this he meant the propounding of theories a-priori, that is, not based on observation, not tested by observation, but derived from principles which are supposed to be given in some way without reference to experience.

Bacon's materialism, as Marx observed, " pullulates with inconsistencies imported from theology." But nevertheless such a materialist doctrine, which attacked and destroyed the old scholastic philosophy, was no less destructive of the theology of which that scholasticism was the philosophic foundation.

For Bacon not only asserted the importance and value of the natural science which was growing up in his time. He was not content merely to assert that this science established many interesting and useful truths about the constitution of the created world. But he asserted that the methods of natural science were the *only* methods of obtaining knowledge ; that theories which could not be scientifically verified were worthless ; and that on the basis of natural science a sufficiently complete picture of the world of nature and society could be built up, which would require no supplementation from any philosophy standing above the sciences.

This was the materialist and revolutionary content of Bacon's philosophy. And the scientific view of the world, for which Bacon argued, must in the end say of God, as of all theological and supernatural principles, " I have no need for that hypothesis."

2. *A Materialist System of Metaphysics—Hobbes*

Bacon's doctrine was developed by his pupil, Thomas Hobbes, into a systematic theory of metaphysical materialism.

" Hobbes," said Marx, " is the man who systematises Baconian materialism."[1]

But " in its further evolution, materialism becomes one-sided." Where Bacon had expounded the principles of scientific method, and had left it to the future development of science to elaborate the theory of the constitution of the universe and the nature of man, Hobbes laid down a system of hard and fast metaphysical principles.

With Hobbes, wrote Marx, " knowledge based upon the senses loses its poetic blossom, it passes into the abstract experience of the mathematician ; geometry is proclaimed as the queen of the sciences. Materialism takes to misanthropy. If it is to overcome its opponent, misanthropic fleshless spiritualism, and that on the latter's own ground, materialism has to chastise its own flesh and turn ascetic. Thus, from a sensual, it passes into an intellectual entity ; but thus too it evolves all the consistency, regardless of consequences, characteristic of the intellect."

Hobbes took as his starting point Bacon's principle that all knowledge is furnished through the senses.

" Concerning the thoughts of man," he wrote, " . . . the original of them all is that which we call sense ; for there is no conception in a man's mind which hath not at first, totally or by parts, been begotten upon the organs of sense. The rest are derived from that original."[2]

---

[1] Quoted by Engels in the Introduction to *Socialism, Utopian and Scientific*.

[2] Hobbes : *Leviathan*, I, 1.

"The cause of sense," he continued, "is the external body, or object, which presseth the organ proper to each sense, either immediately, as in the taste and touch, or mediately, as in hearing, seeing and smelling."

The action of external objects upon the sense organs produces in the mind what Hobbes called variously "seemings" or "apparitions" or "fancies"—the sensations of light, colour, sound, odour, hardness, softness, etc.—"all which qualities called *sensible* are in the object that causeth them but so many several motions of the matter by which it presseth our organs diversely. Neither in us that are pressed are they anything else but diverse motions, for motion produceth nothing but motion. But their appearance to us is fancy, the same waking as dreaming."

Thus: "Whatsoever accidents or qualities our senses make us think there be in the world, they be *not* there, but are *seeming* and *apparitions* only; the things that really *are* in the world without us are those motions by which these seemings are caused."[1]

So for Hobbes that which really exists, and which *appears* to us through our senses as clothed in the appearance of sensible qualities, is *matter—body*. Nothing else exists. The world consists of bodies, their motions and mechanical interactions.

Hobbes defined body, or matter, with reference to the property of existing objectively in space, external to and independent of our consciousness. Our consciousness, indeed, was for him only an "appearance" or "apparition" arising from the interactions of bodies.

"The word body," he wrote, "signifieth that which filleth or occupieth some certain room or . . . . place; and dependeth not on the imagination, but is a real part of that we call the universe. For the universe, being the aggregate of all bodies, there is no real part thereof that is not also body; nor anything properly a body, that is not also part of that aggregate of all bodies, the universe."[2]

From this standpoint he went on to develop some theories about the nature of knowledge, and of thought.

All knowledge must relate to the properties and motions of

[1] Hobbes: *Human Nature*, 2.

[2] Hobbes: *Leviathan*, II, 34.

bodies, derived from what we can learn about them through the medium of the senses.

Thought is impossible without a body that has sensations and thoughts, and it consists in a train of ideas derived from sense-impressions. More exactly, thought consists in the significant conjunction of *words*. We attach different words to the different bodies and properties of bodies that we perceive, and so by joining words together in sentences and strings of sentences we signify various facts about the motions and properties of bodies.

From this follow important consequences about the significance and insignificance of thoughts, or sentences. For when we join words in a way that contradicts the nature of the things signified, the result is not *untrue* thoughts, but *insignificant* thoughts, or nonsense—as " round quadrangle," " immaterial substance," or " free will."[1]

For instance, to make assertions about " immaterial substance " or " free will " is not to speak untruth, but rather to speak insignificant nonsense—just as it is obviously nonsense to speak of a " round quadrangle." Hobbes here developed a powerful weapon of criticism against all previous dogmatic, spiritualist or idealist philosophy. " Substance and body," he wrote, " signify the same thing ; and therefore substance incorporeal are words which when they are joined together destroy one another, as if a man should say an incorporeal body."[2]

From all this immediately follows further the openly anti-religious and atheistical character of Hobbes' materialism. Religion was explained as the mechanical product of human ignorance and fear ; and God—a being " incorporeal," " infinite," " omnipotent," etc.—was absolutely incomprehensible.[3]

3. *The Proof that Knowledge derives from Sense—Experience—Locke*

The work of Bacon and Hobbes was further continued by John Locke, the third great English materialist.

---

[1] Hobbes : *Leviathan*, I, 5.

[2] Ibid., II, 34.

[3] Ibid., I, 12.

" Hobbes had systematised Bacon," Marx wrote, " without however furnishing a *proof* for Bacon's fundamental principle, the origin of all human knowledge from the world of sensation. It was Locke who, in his *Essay on the Human Understanding*, supplied this proof."[1]

Locke began his Essay by attacking all theories that knowledge is derived from some inner light and not exclusively from sensation and experience. He opened with an onslaught against " innate ideas "—the doctrine that certain ideas, such as God, substance, cause, etc., are innate in the human mind, not derived from experiential sources, and self-evidently true. As against the doctrine of innate ideas, he tried to show in elaborate detail how the whole of human knowledge is built up through the action of external material objects upon the bodily sense organs.

" Let us suppose," Locke wrote, " the mind to be, as we say, white paper, void of all characters, without any ideas ; how comes it to be furnished ? . . . To this I answer in one word, from experience ; in all that our knowledge is founded, and from that it ultimately derives itself. Our observation employed either about external sensible objects, or about the internal operations of our minds, perceived and reflected upon by ourselves, is that which supplies our understandings with all the materials of thinking. These two are the fountains of knowledge, from whence all the ideas we have, or can naturally have, do spring."[2]

According to Locke, the action of external objects upon our sense organs produces, in the first place, " simple ideas," the elementary sense-data supplied by each of the special senses. These simple ideas are the atoms, so to speak, from which the whole complex of knowledge is built. They form " the materials of all our knowledge."[3]

" When the understanding is once stored with these simple ideas," wrote Locke, " it has the power to repeat, compare and unite them, even to an almost infinite variety ; and so can make at pleasure new complex ideas. But it is not in the power of the most exalted wit, or enlarged understanding, by

---

[1] Quoted by Engels in the Introduction to *Socialism, Utopian and Scientific.*

[2] Locke : *Essay on the Human Understanding*, II, 1, 2.

[3] Ibid., II, 2 2.

any quickness or variety of thought, to invent or frame one new simple idea in the mind."[1]

Locke then distinguished simple ideas which, as he asserted, were exact resemblances of qualities really inhering in the bodies which evoked those ideas ; and simple ideas to which nothing in the external world exactly corresponded.

The former he called ideas of *Primary Qualities ;* the latter he called ideas of *Secondary Qualities*.

Thus our ideas of solidity, extension, figure, motion or rest, and number, were ideas of primary qualities, corresponding exactly to the real solidity, extension, figure, motion or rest, and number, of the objects of the external material world.

But our ideas of colour, taste, smell, sound, were ideas of secondary qualities only, not corresponding to any real colour, taste, smell, sound, inhering in external material objects.

" The ideas of primary qualities of bodies," Locke wrote, " are resemblances of them, and their patterns do really exist in the bodies themselves ; but the ideas produced in us by these secondary qualities, have no resemblance to them at all. There is nothing like our ideas existing in the bodies themselves. They are in the bodies we denominate from them, only a power to produce those sensations in us ; and what is sweet, blue, warm in idea, is but the certain bulk, figure, and motion of the insensible parts in the bodies themselves, which we call so."[2]

It will be seen that in all this what Locke was doing was to elaborate the basic principles of his materialist predecessor, Hobbes. Locke's " theory of ideas," therefore, represented the highest elaboration of the English materialism of the 17th century, and was not (as it is often misrepresented as being in works on the history of philosophy) the beginning of an entirely new trend of thought. (Writers on philosophy evidently make this misrepresentation because they like to pretend that materialism has no significant place in the history of modern thought, and they would like to dispose of materialism by ignoring it.)

---

[1] Locke : *Essay on the Human Understanding*, II, 2, 2.

[2] Ibid., II, 8, 15.

4. *What is the Object of Knowledge?*

In proceeding to the further elaboration of his theory, Locke made an assumption which proved to be of the very greatest importance.

Namely, he maintained that when we perceive, think, understand, judge, know, in other words, when we carry out any act of cognition from the simplest sort of sense-perception to the most complicated thought, then the *objects* of our cognition are not external objects themselves, but are rather *our own ideas* which are called up in our minds by the action of external objects.

This assumption is made in his initial definition of the term " idea," which he defined as " that term which, I think, serves best to stand for whatsoever is the *object* of understanding when a man thinks."[1]

In dealing with the development of knowledge, Locke proceeded to say : " Since the mind, in all its thoughts and reasonings, hath no other immediate object but its own ideas, which it alone does or can contemplate, it is evident that our knowledge is only conversant about them. Knowledge, then, seems to me to be nothing but the perception of the connexion and agreement, or disagreement and repugnancy, of any of our ideas. In this alone it consists."[2]

The perceptions, thoughts and knowledge of man, therefore, are confined within the circle of his own ideas. It is ideas, not things, that we " contemplate " or are " conversant about."

But since ideas were originally caused through the action of real external objects, Locke thought that nevertheless knowledge *does* relate to the objective world, in so far as ideas are *copies* of things. " It is evident that mind knows not things immediately, but only by the intervention of the ideas it has of them. Our knowledge therefore is real only so far as there is conformity between our ideas and the reality of things."[3]

But this means that our knowledge of the nature of things is necessarily very limited. Thus because we can be " conversant " only with our ideas of bodies, and not with bodies

---

[1] Locke : *Essay on the Human Understanding*, I, 1, 8.

[2] Ibid., IV, 1, 1–2.

[3] Ibid., IV, 4, 3.

themselves, " therefore I am apt to doubt, that how far soever human industry may advance useful and experimental philosophy in physical things, scientifical will still be out of our reach ; because we want perfect and adequate ideas of those very bodies which are nearest to us, and most under our command."[1]

In particular, as to what is the *substance* of real things, we must remain for ever ignorant.

Gone is Hobbes' easy assurance that in saying that the universe consisted in bodies, he had expressed the general nature of the universe. According to Locke, when we repeatedly find a group of simple ideas associated together, then " we accustom ourselves to suppose some substratum wherein they do subsist, and from which they do result ; which therefore we call substance."[2] But what the nature of this substance is, our ideas do not inform us. They only indicate to us that substances exist, which are the ultimate cause of our ideas. " If anyone will examine himself concerning his notion of pure substance in general, he will find he has no other idea of it at all, but only a supposition of he knows not what support of such qualities, which are capable of producing simple ideas in us."[3]

" The secret, abstract nature of substance " is necessarily unknown to us. " The idea of corporeal substance or matter is as remote from our conceptions and apprehensions, as that of spiritual substance or spirit."[4]

Thus with Locke a position was reached, which he derived from the original materialist principle that all knowledge is based upon experience, according to which the object of our knowledge is not the objective external material world, but the subjective world of our own ideas.

The scope of our knowledge is limited to the perception of the order and arrangement, agreement and disagreement, of our own ideas. Behind our ideas, so to speak, and causing them, is the real material objective external world. But of the nature of the objects that constitute this world, we can

[1] Locke : *Essay on the Human Understanding*, IV, 3, 26.

[2] Ibid., II, 23, 1.

[3] Ibid., II, 23, 2.

[4] Ibid., II, 23, 5.

know nothing. They are, to use a phrase coined a hundred years after Locke, unknowable " things in themselves."

At the same time, and certainly inconsistently, Locke maintained that, to a certain extent, our ideas are true copies of real things, and to that extent we do know what " things in themselves " are like ; namely, our ideas of solidity, extension, figure, motion and number are true representations of the real solidity, extension, figure, motion and number of objective things.

(Incidentally, it is interesting to note that Locke used his doctrine of the unknowability of substance—a thesis which has often since his time been used as a basis for all manner of idealism and mysticism—as an argument in favour of a materialist view of the world. In one passage he argued against the dogma that " spiritual substance " must have an existence independent of matter, by saying that, since we do not in any case know what the real nature of matter is, therefore it is perfectly possible " that matter thinks.")[1]

5. *A Parting of the Ways*

With Locke, English materialism reached a parting of the ways.

On the one hand, his insistence that the object of knowledge is the world of our own ideas, and that the substance of objective things is unknowable, led away from materialism, to subjective idealism and agnosticism.

On the other hand, his insistence that all knowledge is the product of sense-experience ; that sensation is caused by the action of external objects on the bodily sense organs ; that our ideas, at least of primary qualities, are copies of real things ; led to the further development of materialism. And this further development was principally undertaken by the great French materialists of the 18th century, whose heritage was in turn studied and developed in the 19th century by Marx and Engels.

Locke's doctrine of ideas was in fact inconsistent, and so led to contradictory results according to which side of his inconsistency was stressed, and which side was criticised.

---

[1] Locke: *Essay on the Human Understanding*, IV, 3, 6.

On the one hand, he could be criticised in that, having said that knowledge was limited to the world of our own ideas, he nevertheless allowed ideas to be represented as the product of the action of external objects, and to be copies of such objects. For if only our own ideas are the objects of our knowledge, how can we possibly know whence those ideas arise, or what they are copies of?

On the other hand, he could be criticised in that, having said that our ideas are the products of the action of external objects and are copies of such objects, he nevertheless maintained that knowledge is limited to the relations between ideas, and that the substance of objective things is unknowable.

How did Locke's theory come to involve such inconsistencies, leading to such contradictory lines of criticism, and contradictory tendencies of future development arising—which were certainly not apparent in the work of his materialist predecessors, Bacon and Hobbes?

As has been shown, Locke was the man who first tried to develop in detail the fundamental materialist theory of knowledge of Bacon and Hobbes; and it was in the manner of this detail development that the inconsistencies arose.

In working out this detail theory, Locke made certain rigid and hard and fast distinctions. In particular:—

(1) He rigidly distinguished the sensation or idea produced in the mind, from the external object on the one hand, and from the act of cognition on the other hand; so that for him "ideas" seemed to exist as a set of sensible or mental *objects* standing between the knowing mind and the external material world.

(2) He rigidly distinguished the substance of a thing from the totality of its properties, so that while the properties might be known, the substance remained as some unknown "support" of such properties. The substance or being was abstracted from the thing's life-history, and set up as a separate unknowable existence distinct from the totality of happenings, relationships and properties.

(3) He rigidly distinguished theory from practice, knowing from doing, so that it appeared that while a man might in his practical life be busily engaged with material things, in his theoretical activity he was not engaged with material things at all, but with his own ideas.

It was from such rigid distinctions and abstractions, that the difficulties and inconsistencies arose.

The setting up in thought of such hard and fast antitheses which do not exist in fact is what, since the time of Hegel, has come to be called the " metaphysical " mode of thought. Locke inherited this habit of thought from the whole previous development of both philosophy and science. And where it led him in the development of English materialism shows that the whole subsequent forward development of materialism has to be along the lines of overcoming such narrow metaphysics. It was Marx and Engels who subsequently succeeded in finally freeing materialism from metaphysics.

CHAPTER 2

MATERIALISM AND THE RISE OF CAPITALISM—SCIENCE, PHILOSOPHY AND RELIGION

1. *Social Roots of 17th Century Materialism.—Materialism as the Vindication of Science*

This materialist movement of philosophy did not arise and flourish on British soil through any accident. On the contrary, it was the early rise of capitalism in Britain, and the break-up of every form of feudal institution and ideology through the irresistible growth of capitalist relationships within the old system, that provided the soil for this materialist philosophy.

This philosophy absolutely smashed the old scholastic forms of thought, which had to be overcome if the spirit of science, invention and discovery, so necessary for the development of capital, was to hold sway. It smashed the world-outlook of feudal rulers and monks, in order to establish the world-outlook of the owners of capital and of scientists.

It was directly out of the development of natural science that the English materialism of the 17th century arose. Essentially it was a product of the growth of natural science.

Its function was to justify the methods of natural science, which it did by showing how all knowledge must arise from experience and be tested by experience, and how on this basis a systematic and verifiable account of the nature of things, including the human mind, could be reached.

Thus this philosophy did not present any comprehensive cosmological theory, as was the manner of ancient philosophies and also of the contemporary Cartesian theories on the Continent—but it confined itself *mainly* to the elaboration of a theory of knowledge.

The rise of natural science was one of the outstanding features of the period of the break-up of feudalism and the establishment of the foundations of the future capitalist order. It was called forth and conditioned by such factors as the development of navigation, the development of mining, and the use of artillery in warfare. Such fields of new activity necessarily called forth scientific researches, and demanded the aid of scientific research if they were to be successfully exploited.

The new science met with the most bitter opposition from the established Church philosophy. More than that, scientists were often met with persecution by Protestant no less than by Catholic authorities. Nevertheless science was able to triumph over this opposition and persecution. And this triumph was inevitable, because science was serving the needs of expanding social production and of the new rising social class, the capitalists.

The new capitalist forms of production and trade developed within the social framework of feudalism. In the course of a long series of revolutions the capitalists first established their right to live and to expand their capital and activities within feudal society, and finally destroyed feudal society altogether, and set up their own class rule.

In this struggle they not only disrupted feudal forms of property and feudal forms of government, in order to establish capitalist property and capitalist government ; but they brought about the destruction of the whole complex of religious and philosophic beliefs associated with feudalism, in order to establish the dominance of new religious and philosophic beliefs that accorded with the requirements of capitalism.

The rise of natural science, and the adoption of scientific views about the world, was a most important part of the new culture created by the rise of capitalism. The expansion of capital necessarily created a new scientific culture, because it demanded the services of science to aid its expansion. And with equal necessity, science came into conflict with the dominant ideas of feudal philosophy and theology, fought them, and overthrew them.

" The revolutionary act," wrote Engels, " by which natural science declared its independence and, as it were, repeated Luther's burning of the Papal Bull, was the publication of the immortal work by which Copernicus, though timidly, and, so to speak, only from his deathbed, threw down the gauntlet to ecclesiastical authority in the affairs of nature. The emancipation of natural science from theology dates from this act, although the fighting out of the particular antagonistic claims has dragged out up to our day, and in many minds is still far from completion. Thenceforward, however, the development of the sciences proceeded with giant strides, and, it might be said, gained in force in proportion to the square of the distance (in time) from its point of departure. It was as if the world were to be shown that henceforth the reciprocal law of motion would be as valid for the highest product of organic matter, the human mind, as for inorganic substance."[1]

The philosophy of Bacon, at the start of the 17th century, constituted another " revolutionary act," whereby science was declared to be, not only independent of any ecclesiastical authority, but the one sure road to natural knowledge, all theories based on a-priori principles or on traditional authorities being declared worthless. And the philosophy of Locke, at the end of the 17th century, completed the revolutionary work of Bacon by its detailed examination of the sources of human knowledge.

To summarise, then. The English materialism of the 17th century was essentially a philosophical vindication of the claims of natural science, and an attack upon the claims of a-priori theorising and reliance on traditional authority in the interpretation of nature. This philosophy was a product of the rise of capital and the struggle of the capitalists for power—commencing with Bacon, when they were already a dominant social force, culminating with Locke, when they had attained to full political power.

2. *The Conflict of Science and Religion*

But while the rise of the capitalists called forth a scientific culture and led to the triumph of science over church authority, the capitalists at the same time clung to religion and their own reformed church.

The political struggles in the course of which the foundations of the capitalist order were established in England were fought under religious slogans—Protestants against Catholics, Presbyterians and Independents against High-Churchmen. Anything savouring of atheism was utterly abhorrent, and regarded as socially dangerous and disruptive to the highest

[1] Engels : *Dialectics of Nature*, Introduction.

degree. It is a noteworthy fact that atheistical theories made their appearance amongst the Levellers at the time of the Civil War in England, and were duly suppressed along with the whole Levellers' Movement. For while the owners of capital, in the most revolutionary way, set out to destroy feudal forms of ownership and feudal institutions and ideas, they took great care at the same time that the social position of privileged classes should remain secure. Church and State, they realised, must remain the pillars of society. And while for the short period of the Commonwealth both the Monarchy and the Church were abolished, they were very soon afterwards re-established, and moulded in the " glorious revolution " of 1688 into the form most in keeping with the interests and desires of big capital.

This consistent and deep-seated regard for religion on the part of the English capitalists had its inevitable reflection in the philosophic movement.

English philosophy set out to justify the claims of natural science. But the great social movement which produced it, set it also another task. The very same social forces which desired to extend the bounds of scientific knowledge, desired also to uphold religion and the Christian Church. And so the question arose of both upholding the independence of science as against religious authority, and at the same time of reconciling science with religion.

Thus philosophy had the dual task—on the one hand to uphold science as against the dogmas of Catholicism ; on the other hand to show that science gave no support for atheism, was not incompatible with belief in God and Immortality, and in general harmonised very well with the more liberal doctrines of the Church of England.

With Bacon there was as yet no hint of any awareness that scientific materialism must come into conflict with religion. Conflict with the " absurd " dogmas of the Catholic schoolmen there certainly was—but not with the essential beliefs of the Christian religion as preached by the reformed Church. As befitted his position as Lord Chancellor under King James I, Bacon had to uphold science as an essential aid to commerce and manufacture, and to uphold religion as an essential element of social security—and that the two might conflict did not occur to him. Thus as Marx observed of Bacon, "the aphoristically formulated doctrine pullulates with inconsistencies imported from theology." Bacon did not pursue the detail development of his philosophy sufficiently far to come upon any conflict between science and theology.

But with Hobbes, the existence of a real and fundamental conflict became immediately obvious.

In the political part of his philosophy (which occupied the greater part of his main book, the *Leviathan*), Hobbes attempted to deduce from his materialist premises the necessity of (*a*) the Monarchy and (*b*) the Church, as indispensable elements in the organisation of civil society. Without these two elements, he said, government would be impossible.

But for all that, his philosophy was glaringly anti-religious. The universe consists of bodies ; everything that happens results from the mechanical interaction of bodies ; consciousness is merely " a fantasm " of material events ; to speak of God is to use a word utterly meaningless and incomprehensible ; there is no possible evidence for religion, which is merely a mechanical product of man's ignorance and fear. With such doctrines, Hobbes might deduce as convincingly as he liked that religion was politically necessary and desirable as a binding force in society, but his doctrines were destructive of religion. Religion cannot in practice be upheld as a political expediency if at the same time people are taught not to believe in its truth.

Hobbes had shown where Bacon's doctrine consistently led. A scientific view of the world, which explains everything through natural causes, must regard matter as the prior reality, and spirit as only secondary. It leaves no room for religious beliefs. It banishes the supernatural from the world, and reveals it as mere superstition.

The very consistency with which Hobbes developed the Baconian doctrine to its logical conclusion in atheistical materialism, completely alienated him from the rising capitalist forces, that is, from the main forces of progress. His philosophy was generally denounced, and won support only from those who were antagonistic to capital ; on the one hand, certain elements amongst the Levellers ; on the other hand, a few of the more cynical and disillusioned of the old aristocracy.

3. *The Problem of Reconciling Science and Religion*

Hobbes, however, had raised a problem which had to be solved.

The new capitalist society then in process of formation could no more do without science than it could do without religion. Hobbes had apparently shown that the acceptance of the principles and methods of science led to a view of the world in which religious beliefs had no place. This challenge had to be answered. And it was Locke's *Essay on the Human Understanding*, published at the very moment when the capitalists finally rose to supreme power, which showed how to answer it. In working out in elaborate detail just how human knowledge was founded on sense-experience, Locke showed how you could both accept science and at the same time leave plenty of room over for religious beliefs.

Locke was, indeed, very well aware of this problem which he had to answer. " The motive of Locke's philosophy is explained by him as follows. ' Five or six friends ' used to meet regularly, while he was staying at Exeter House, to discuss the ' principles of morality and religion. They found themselves quickly at a stand by the difficulties that arose on every side.' It consequently occurred to him ' that before we set ourselves upon enquiries of that nature, it was necessary to examine our own abilities, and see what objects our understandings were or were not fitted to deal with.' "[1]

The solution which Locke found to the conflict between science and religion lay precisely in his insistence, which we have already noted, that the immediate object of knowledge consists in our own ideas, not the objective world external to consciousness.

How did this principle supply a basis for the solution of the conflict between science and religion?

Precisely because it *limited* the sphere of possible scientific knowledge, and denied that scientific knowledge could penetrate to the *substance* of things. If that is so, then the immortality of the soul, its salvation, and its relationship with God, cannot possibly be discovered by any possible application of scientific observation and inference—but nor can they be

[1] A. Wolf : *History of Science, Technology and Philosophy in the 16th and 17th Centuries*, p. 656.

overthrown. Scientific knowledge and religion each has its own proper sphere, and they do not encroach on one another. Science deals with the agreements and disagreements which we observe in the order of our own ideas ; religion deals with transcendent truths, which cannot be either demonstrated or refuted by methods of scientific observation, experiment and inference.

Locke, however, rather stumbled upon this ingenious mode of reconciling science and religion, than consistently and systematically developed it. On the contrary, in one chapter of his Essay he tried to develop a scientific "proof" of the existence of God ; and at the same time his philosophy continued to embody strong materialist elements taken straight from Hobbes, according to which all our thoughts were the mechanical results of the action of external material things on our sense organs, and our sensations were copies of a real world consisting of solid extended particles.

The reconciliation of science and religion, therefore, as it was worked out by Locke, rested on a very shaky basis. And the comfort to religion derived from the doctrine that science "only" deals with what we can observe of our own sensations and can establish nothing of the substance of the real world, was continually disturbed by the contrary doctrine that our sensations are copies of things, that science therefore does after all relate to the real world and is continually finding out more about it, and that science thereby presents a picture of the world in which the objects of religion have no place.

Locke's doctrine of ideas, however, had started a train of thought which was destined resolutely to cast off all such materialist impediments. George Berkeley, then a young student at Trinity College, Dublin, seized upon the vaguely formulated suggestions contained in Locke's Essay, and from them formulated a set of philosophical principles which in the most direct and simple way proclaimed that henceforth science and religion could coexist in harmony.

CHAPTER 3

FROM MATERIALISM TO PURE EMPIRICISM: BERKELEY

1. *Does " the External World " exist?*

The full title of Berkeley's principal philosophical work was: *A Treatise concerning the Principles of Human Knowledge, wherein the chief causes of error and difficulty in the sciences, with the grounds of scepticism, atheism and irreligion, are inquired into.*

Thus in the very title of his work Berkeley proclaimed, with the clarity and simplicity that was characteristic of him, that his purpose was to deal with the relations of science and religion, and to remove those " errors " in the concept of science which appeared to involve anti-religious consequences. The reconciliation of science and religion was his first avowed object.

In pursuit of this object, Berkeley proceeded to make a frontal attack upon the Lockean conception of matter.

Locke had maintained:

(*a*) That the " immediate objects " of knowledge are our own ideas.

But (*b*) that these ideas are produced by the action upon us of external material things, and that at least our ideas of " primary qualities " are copies of the qualities of external bodies.

Berkeley accepted the first proposition (*a*), and then set out to prove that the materialist addition (*b*) was absurd.

" It is evident to any one who takes a survey of the objects of human knowledge," he wrote, " that they are either ideas actually imprinted on the senses; or else such as are perceived by attending to the passions and operations of the mind; or lastly, ideas formed by the help of memory and imagination. . . ."[1] And he continued: " That neither our thoughts, nor passions, nor ideas formed by the imagination, exist without the mind is what everybody will allow. And to me

[1] Berkeley: *Principles of Human Knowledge*, 1.

it seems no less evident that the various sensations or ideas imprinted on the senses, however blended or combined together (that is whatever objects they compose) cannot exist otherwise than in a mind perceiving them."[1]

Figure, extension and solidity, no less than colour, sound and smell, are, Berkeley argued, presented to us as sensations of the mind ; and when we perceive any sensible object, what we are actually aware of is nothing but the existence in our consciousness of a certain combination of such sensations, which " cannot exist otherwise than in a mind perceiving them."

What can be meant, then, Berkeley asked, by the existence of a material object, external to the perceiving mind, corresponding to our sensations ?

" The table I write on," he said, " exists ; that is, I see and feel it : and if I were out of my study, I should say it existed ; meaning thereby that if I was in my study I might perceive it, or that some other spirit actually does perceive it. There was an odour, that is, it was smelt ; there was a sound, that is, it was heard ; a colour or figure, and it was perceived by sight or touch. That is all that I can understand by these and the like expressions."[2]

" It is indeed an opinion strangely prevailing amongst men," he continued, " that houses, mountains, rivers, and in a word all sensible objects, have an existence, natural or real, distinct from their being perceived by the understanding. . . . For what are the forementioned objects but the things we perceive by sense ? and what do we perceive besides our own ideas or sensations ? and is it not plainly repugnant that any one of these, or any combination of them, should exist unperceived ?"[3]

Berkeley went on to argue against the Lockean materialist conception that our ideas are copies of the qualities of external material things.

" I answer," he said, " an idea can be like nothing but an idea ; a colour or figure can be like nothing but another colour or figure. . . . Again, I ask whether these supposed

[1] Berkeley : *Principles of Human Knowledge*, 3.

[2] Ibid., 3.

[3] Ibid., 4.

originals, or external things, of which our ideas are the pictures or representations, be themselves perceivable or no? If they are, then *they* are ideas, and we have gained our point; but if you say they are not, I appeal to any one whether it be sense to assert a colour is like something which is invisible; hard or soft like something that is intangible; and so of the rest."[1]

Berkeley was able very soon to dispose of the distinction of "primary" and "secondary" qualities, that is, of Locke's doctrine that extension, figure, solidity, etc., inhere in material things independent of the mind, whereas colour, sound, smell do not.

"I desire anyone to reflect," he said, "and try whether he can, by any abstraction of thought, conceive the extension and motion of a body without all other sensible qualities. For my own part, I see evidently that it is not in my power to frame an idea of a body extended and moving, but I must withal give it some colour or other sensible quality, which is acknowledged to exist only in the mind. In short, extension, figure and motion, abstracted from all other qualities, are inconceivable. Where therefore the other sensible qualities are, there must these be also, to wit, in the mind, and nowhere else."[2]

The supposition of the existence of sensible material objects, external to the mind and independent of being perceived, was then for Berkeley an altogether meaningless abstraction. "For can there be a nicer strain of abstraction," he asked, "than to distinguish the existence of sensible objects from their being perceived, so as to conceive them existing unperceived? Light and colours, heat and cold, extension and figures—in a word the things we see and feel—what are they but so many sensations, notions, ideas or impressions on the sense? and is it possible to separate, even in thought, any of these from perception? For my part, I might as easily divide a thing from itself."[3]

As for Locke's conception of Matter, or Material Substance, as the really existing "substratum" which "supports" the

[1] Berkeley: *Principles of Human Knowledge*, 8.
[2] Ibid., 10.
[3] Ibid., 5.

various qualities of material things, Berkeley asserted that this was a completely meaningless and incomprehensible abstraction.

"If we inquire into what the most accurate philosophers declare themselves to mean by material substance, we shall find them acknowledge they have no other meaning annexed to those sounds but the idea of Being in general. . . . The general idea of Being appeareth to me the most abstract and incomprehensible of all other. . . . So that when I consider the two parts or branches which make the signification of the words material substance, I am convinced there is no distinct meaning annexed to them."[1]

Here, incidentally, the tables are indeed turned upon Hobbes' assertion that "substance incorporeal" is a meaningless expression: it is "material substance" that is now asserted to be a meaningless combination of words. In this assertion Berkeley first formulated the contention, which has been repeated so many times since, that "matter," "the external material world," "the existence of real material things and events which cause our sensations," etc., are meaningless abstractions; and that to use such words is to use expressions to which "there is no distinct meaning annexed." Materialism is asserted to be a doctrine based on unintelligible abstraction, confused, meaningless, nonsensical.

Finally, Berkeley asserted: "If there were external bodies, it is impossible we should ever come to know it; and if there were not, we might have the very same reasons to think there were as we have now."[2] For since all we can perceive are sensible objects, or combinations of sensible qualities, which have no existence outside the mind, there can be no possible grounds for inferring from the existence of these to the existence of other unknown things external to the mind.

2. *Berkeley's Conclusion—Religion vindicated, Atheism destroyed*

From all this, the conclusion follows: "Some truths there are so near and obvious to the mind that a man need only open his eyes to see them. Such I take this important one to be, viz., that all the choir of heaven and furniture of earth,

---

[1] Berkeley: *Principles of Human Knowledge*, 17.
[2] Ibid., 20.

in a word all those bodies which compose the mighty frame of the world, have not any subsistence without a mind ; that their being is to be perceived or known ; that consequently so long as they are not actually perceived by me, or do not exist in my mind, or that of any other created spirit, they must either have no existence at all, or else subsist in the mind of some Eternal Spirit : it being perfectly unintelligible, and involving all the absurdity of abstraction, to attribute to any single part of them an existence independent of a spirit."[1]

Berkeley hastened to defend himself against the imputation that there is anything paradoxical, or contrary to common sense and experience, about this conclusion.

"Ideas imprinted on the senses are real things, or do really exist : this we do not deny ; but we deny that they can subsist without the minds that perceive them. . . . It were a mistake to think that what is here said derogates in the least from the reality of things. . . . We detract nothing from the received opinion of their reality, and are guilty of no innovation in this respect. All the difference is that, according to us, the unthinking things perceived by sense have no existence distinct from being perceived. . . . Whereas philosophers vulgarly hold that the sensible qualities do exist in an inert, extended unperceiving substance which they call Matter, to which they attribute a natural subsistence, exterior to all thinking beings, or distinct from being perceived by any mind whatsoever, even the Eternal Mind of the Creator."[2]

But while the concept of Matter has no basis in experience, its chief use is as an aid to the enemies of religion.

"How great a friend Material Substance has been to Atheists in all ages were needless to relate. All their monstrous systems have so visible and necessary a dependence on it, that when this corner-stone is removed, the whole fabric cannot choose but fall to the ground ; insomuch as it is no longer worth while to bestow a particular consideration on the absurdities of every wretched sect of Atheists."[3]

On the other hand, the articles of the Christian faith can

---

[1] Berkeley : *Principles of Human Knowledge*, 6.

[2] Ibid., 90, 91.

[3] Ibid., 92.

be much more readily accepted, once the prejudice of the existence of matter is removed.

" For example, about the Resurrection, how many scruples and objections have been raised by Socinians and others? But do not the most plausible of them depend on the supposition that a body is denominated the same, with regard not to the form or that which is perceived by sense, but the material substance, which remains the same under several forms? Take away this material substance—about the identity whereof all the dispute is—and mean by body that which every plain ordinary person means by that word, to wit, that which is immediately seen and felt, which is only a combination of sensible qualities and ideas: and then their most unanswerable objections come to nothing."[1]

Indeed, " Matter being once expelled out of nature drags with it so many sceptical and impious notions, such an incredible number of disputes and puzzling questions, which have been thorns in the sides of divines as well as philosophers, and made so much fruitless work for mankind, that if the arguments which we have produced against it are not found equal to demonstration (as to me they evidently seem) yet I am sure all friends of knowledge, peace and religion have reason to wish they were."[2]

3. *A Philosophy of Pure Empiricism*

Berkeley reached these idealistic conclusions, viz.: " That all the choir of heaven and furniture of earth . . . have not any subsistence without a mind," by means of an apparently very strict adherence to the original principle of his materialist predecessors, that sensation is the source of all knowledge.

He was as much opposed to a-priori speculations, and as much convinced that knowledge advances through experience, observation and experiment, as were Bacon, Hobbes and Locke. Only he argued that the objects of knowledge being our own ideas, dependent upon the mind, there is no such thing as the external material world—and if there were, we could still know nothing whatever about it.

---

[1] Berkeley: *Principles of Human Knowledge*, 95.

[2] Ibid., 96.

The doctrine that sensation is the source of all knowledge is denoted by the name Empiricism. Thus, just like Bacon, Hobbes and Locke, Berkeley was an empiricist.

But the former three thinkers went beyond Empiricism. They were materialists. For in its views about knowledge, Materialism includes the empirical standpoint, but goes beyond it.

Materialism holds that knowledge is derived from sensation, but it does not accept sensation as merely " given." For Materialism, sensation arises from the action of external material objects upon the sense-organs ; and so our ordinary perceptions, and the knowledge gained by tested scientific methods, give a true objective account of what is going on in the external material world, and of the laws of motion of material things, and are by no means limited to the subjective world of ideas.

Thus for Materialism, in the last analysis, knowledge arises from the interaction between man and the material objects that surround him.

Berkeley threw over all such materialist views about knowledge, such as were held by his predecessors. He upheld Empiricism, pure and simple. He purged away all the materialist elements of the theory of knowledge of Locke—and what remained was Pure Empiricism.

Berkeley retreated from Materialism into Pure Empiricism, an anti-materialist idealistic doctrine.

By Pure Empiricism, therefore, I mean adherence to the doctrine that sensation is the source of all knowledge, while denying that sensation and knowledge have any objective reference to a material world outside the circle of our own sensations and ideas.

This distinction, taking its origin from Berkeley, between Materialism and Pure Empiricism, was commented on by Lenin, in his *Materialism*, where he said : " All knowledge comes from experience, from sensation, from perception. That is true. But the question arises, does *objective reality* belong to perception, i.e., is it the source of perception ? If you answer yes, you are a materialist. If you answer no, you are inconsistent and . . . the inconsistency of your empiricism, of your philosophy of experience, will in that case lie in the fact that you deny the objective content of experience, the objective truth of your experimental knowledge."[1]

It is the purpose of the rest of this book to trace the development of Pure Empiricism from Berkeley, and to criticise it from the standpoint of Materialism.

4. *The Reconciliation of Science and Religion by Pure Empiricism*

Berkeley arrived at his doctrine of pure empiricism with the object of combating those " errors " in the conception of science which gave support to materialist and atheistic conclusions.

How, then, does pure empiricism square science with religion? It achieves this object in an extremely neat and simple way, which can be briefly summarised as follows.

Scientific results are true, valid and useful—but we must not overestimate their significance. They only deal with the order of our sensations. For sensations come to us in certain orders and in certain combinations, in which invariable rules and laws can be discerned. And science discovers and systematises these rules.

Science is therefore not a materialist theory of the world, it is only a set of rules and predictions of the order of human sensations.

Science is therefore circumscribed within its own limited sphere, and has no bearing at all on the nature of things. Therefore nothing that science can establish can possibly contradict the main tenets of religious faith.

Or to put the issue in another way—

We accept science. We welcome scientific discoveries. We take up " a scientific attitude." But we recognise that science is not about what it appears to be about.

Science appears to be about the objective material world, its constitution and laws, which are absolutely independent of human thought, will or sensation. When so interpreted, science is materialistic, and seems irreconcilable with any idealistic or religious conclusions.

But science is really concerned with predicting the order of sensations, and discovering the rules of invariable sequence

[1] Lenin: Selected Works, vol. 11, p. 190.

and combination of sensations, and with nothing else. And so the position is reversed. Nothing that science can establish can, rightly interpreted, any more possibly contradict the main tenets of religion and idealism.

The clear and concise formulation of the position of pure empiricism by Berkeley was a philosophical event of the first importance.

It provided the most satisfactory means of solving the great problem which the rise of capitalist society had set for philosophy, namely, of reconciling the development of science with adherence to religion. Berkeley's pure empiricism so exactly corresponded with the ideological needs of the developing capitalist society—and in Britain, the most " advanced " country, especially—that it took the deepest roots, and has flourished, in one form or another, ever since.

Berkeley laid down the guiding principles, and set the tone, so to speak, for the whole subsequent British philosophy, and for a good deal of philosophy on the Continent as well. The most modern " logisticians " and " logical positivists " have hardly, as I shall show, advanced a step beyond Berkeley ; and they still run round and round in the circle of ideas which Berkeley so expertly mapped out.

CHAPTER 4

FROM MATERIALISM TO PURE EMPIRICISM: HUME

1. *Some Inconsistencies of Berkeley*

BERKELEY'S circumscription of science, and reconciliation of science and religion, had, however, its negative features. In attempting to solve one problem, it gave rise to many others. Indeed, since science and religion are in fact absolutely incompatible, not even the British bourgeoisie, those masters of compromise, could be expected to produce a completely satisfactory reconciliation.

And so it came about that Berkeley's effort to remove " the grounds of scepticism, atheism and irreligion " almost immediately gave rise to the very sceptical and apparently irreligious philosophy of Hume.

Not content with showing that science could not overthrow religion, Berkeley, it must now be remarked, tried to develop his philosophical principles as a *justification* of the fundamental tenets of religious faith.

Having made out that matter does not exist, and that our sensations are therefore not caused, as most philosophers " vulgarly hold," by the action upon us of external material objects, Berkeley was led to speculate upon the real origin of our sensations, and of the rational order and combination which is observable amongst them.

The origin, he maintained, must be God.

And following up this line of speculation, he was led to postulate a third mode of cognition in addition to sense-impressions and ideas derived from sense-impressions, namely, cognition through what he called " Notions," particularly the " notions " of God and the human soul.

Now in this he was obviously inconsistent.

For if it is illegitimate to infer an unperceived material world as the ground of our experience, it must be equally illegitimate to infer an unperceived " infinite spirit " as that ground.

If all knowledge is derived from sense, how can knowledge through transcendental " notions " of God and the soul be allowed?

If it is permissible to have a " notion " of the soul and of God, why is it absurd to have another " notion " of matter?

Or if the words " material substance " represent a meaningless expression and unintelligible abstraction, surely the same applies to " infinite spirit "?

These sorts of inconsistencies, or deviations from pure empiricism, of which Berkeley was guilty, were corrected by Hume, who took it upon himself to develop Berkeley's empirical principles with greater consistency.

But I would point out how intellectually inevitable it is that pure empiricism should lapse into such inconsistency.

For if you hold it " absurd " that sensations are produced by the action of external material objects, you are still faced with the question—*Whence comes our experience?* A materialist philosophy answers this question very simply in material terms. But for pure empiricism it is a question that cannot possibly be answered in any empirical and scientific way—for pure empiricism cannot go " beyond " sensations.

Thus life, and experience, and the reason why " I am," is as much a mystery for the pure empiricist as for the most obscurantist religious mystic.

It presents a question which—inside the limits of the philosophy of pure empiricism—science cannot even attempt to answer.

Here is my experience—there is a rational order of events within it, but it has no material basis. What does it mean? Whence comes it? What lies " beyond "?

And so it comes about that, in 1710, Berkeley said that experience was directly called forth in us by God; and after more than two hundred years we find a leading figure of " modern " philosophy, the Professor of Logic and Metaphysics at the University of Cambridge, L. Wittgenstein, saying what amounts to exactly the same thing in the mystical conclusion to his *Tractatus Logico-Philosophicus:* " We feel that even if all possible scientific questions be answered, the problems of life have still not been touched at all. . . . There is indeed the inexpressible. This shows itself; it is the mystical."[1]

Now we see, incidentally, why Lenin said that pure empiricism was "inconsistent." Through its rejection of materialism it inevitably leads beyond itself into its very opposite, religious mysticism. But I shall proceed to Hume's efforts to create a *consistent* empiricism.

2. *The Consistency of Hume: Atomism and Solipsism*

Hume began his *Treatise of Human Nature* with the proposition: "All the perceptions of the human mind resolve themselves into two distinct kinds, which I shall call *impressions* and *ideas*."[2] This was an improvement on the somewhat ambiguous use of the general term "idea" by Locke, which was also followed by Berkeley, to denote *any* "object" of the mind, from sense-impressions to thoughts. What Hume meant by "impressions" included sensations of colour, sound, smell, touch, pleasure and pain, etc., while "ideas" included images, memories, thoughts.

Hume thought he could distinguish between impressions and ideas simply in terms of "the degrees of force and liveliness with which they strike upon the mind, and make their way into our thought or consciousness. Those perceptions which enter with most force and violence, we may name *impressions*. . . . By *ideas*, I mean the faint images of these in thinking and reasoning."[3]

Hume then went on to say: "There is another division of our perceptions, which it will be convenient to observe, and which extends itself both to our impressions and ideas. This division is into *simple* and *complex*. Simple perceptions, or impressions and ideas, are such as admit of no distinction nor separation."[4]

And from this he proceeded "with establishing one general proposition, That all our simple ideas in their first appearance, are derived from simple impressions, which are correspondent to them, and which they exactly represent."[5]

[1] Wittgenstein: *Tractatus Logico-Philosophicus*, 6·52.
[2] Hume: *Treatise of Human Nature*, I, I, 1.
[3] Ibid.
[4] Ibid.
[5] Ibid.

Thus, with far greater strictness than Berkeley, Hume limited " *all* the perceptions of the human mind " to " simple," that is, indivisible, " impressions "; plus " complex impressions " which are merely combinations of " simple impressions " ; plus " simple and complex ideas," the " simple ideas " being merely " faint images " of simple impressions, and the " complex ideas " being formed by combining simple ideas together.

From this Hume went on to draw the inevitable conclusion : " We may observe, that 'tis universally allowed by philosophers, and is besides pretty obvious of itself, that nothing is really present with the mind but its perceptions or impressions and ideas, and that external objects become known to us only by those perceptions they occasion. . . .

" Now, since nothing is ever present to the mind but perceptions, and since all ideas are derived from something antecedently present to the mind ; it follows, that 'tis impossible for us so much as to conceive or form an idea of any thing specifically different from ideas or impressions. Let us fix our attention out of ourselves as much as possible ; let us chase our imagination to the heavens, or to the utmost limits of the universe ; we never really advance a step beyond ourselves, nor can conceive any kind of existence, but those perceptions, which have appeared in that narrow compass."[1]

Thus the objects of the mind being strictly limited to our own impressions and ideas, any external reality " beyond " the circle of impressions and ideas is absolutely inconceivable.

In other passages Hume tried to show in some detail how the " illusion " that external material things exist, which occasion our perceptions, and which they represent, arises solely from the persistence and recurrence in actual experience of certain groupings of impressions. Such groupings dispose us to believe that corresponding permanent external things exist. But in fact we have no evidence that anything exists beyond impressions and ideas ; and when submitted to strict analysis the supposition of such existence turns out to be nonsensical and meaningless.

So far Hume agreed with Berkeley, though he had developed Berkeley's empirical principles with somewhat greater precision

---

[1] Hume : *Treatise of Human Nature*, I, II, 6.

and accuracy. But he went on to point out that, on the same principles, not only do external material objects disappear, but the knowing mind, or the soul, disappears as well.

"Self or person," Hume wrote, "is not any one impression, but that to which our several impressions and ideas are supposed to have reference."[1]

And so he asked: "After what manner therefore do they belong to self, and how are they connected with it? For my part, when I enter most intimately into what I call *myself*, I always stumble on some particular perception or other, of heat or cold, light or shade, love or hatred, pain or pleasure. I never can catch *myself* as any time without a perception, and never can observe anything but the perception. . . . If anyone, upon serious and unprejudiced reflection, thinks he has a different notion of *himself*, I must confess I can reason no longer with him. . . . But setting aside some metaphysicians of this kind, I may venture to affirm of the rest of mankind, that they are nothing but a bundle or collection of different perceptions, which succeed each other with an inconceivable rapidity, and are in a perpetual flux and movement."[2]

And so just as permanent external material objects are reduced to collections of fleeting impressions, the same applies to the permanent self, or soul, or mind. "We may observe, that what we call a *mind*, is nothing but a heap or collection of different perceptions, united together by certain relations, and supposed, though falsely, to be endowed with a perfect simplicity and identity."[3]

So much, therefore, for Berkeley's "notion" of the soul. It has gone the same way as external bodies—been reduced to an illusion, and nothing remains but the series of fleeting impressions and ideas.

Here it may be incidentally remarked that the train of empirical thought which led from Locke, through Berkeley, to Hume, was a train of thought which relentlessly reduced the extent and content of the objects of our knowledge. Thus Locke had allowed three circles of being, so to speak, amongst the objects of our knowledge, viz. (1) Impressions and Ideas,

---

[1] Hume: *Treatise of Human Nature*, I, IV, 6.
[2] Ibid., I, IV, 6.
[3] Ibid., I, IV, 2.

(2) the Self, to which these belong, and (3) External Material Objects, which they represent. Berkeley reduced these three circles to two, viz. (1) Impressions and Ideas, and (2) the Self, to which they belong. Hume finally reduced the two circles to one only, viz. (1) Impressions and Ideas, which belong to nothing and represent nothing.

Having arrived at this position, Hume went on to develop it further, with the same relentless consistency. He next attacked the idea of Causality.

He pointed out, as indeed Berkeley had pointed out before him, but without drawing the inevitable conclusion—that sense-impressions are quite "inert," and do not contain any element of "power" or "efficacy" or "necessary connection," whereby one can produce or cause another. They simply follow one another, or co-exist together, without any causal connection.

From this Hume concluded that, since our knowledge is limited to the world of such sense-impressions, the popular idea of causality must be, like the popular idea of the external world, an illusion. Each event is absolutely independent of every other. The world we know consists of atomic sensible events, between which there is no necessary or causal connection.

"All events," he wrote, "seem entirely loose and separate. One event follows another, but we never can observe any tie between them. They seem *conjoined*, but never *connected*."[1]

What we take to be causality is merely a habitual conjunction of sensible events, which we can sum up in a scientific law or hypothesis, but about which there is no causal necessity whatever.

"A cause," Hume defined, "is an object precedent and contiguous to another, and so united with it that the idea of the one determines the mind to form the idea of the other, and the impression of the one to form a more lively idea of the other."[2] Causality has no other significance than this.

Finally, Hume went on to the conclusion that, the objects of knowledge being limited to fleeting impressions and ideas, the knowledge of any one person at any moment is strictly speaking

[1] Hume : *Inquiry concerning Human Understanding*, 7.
[2] Hume : *Treatise of Human Nature*, I, III, 14.

limited simply to the existence of his own impressions and ideas at the moment of knowing. So that pure empiricism, developed consistently, leads to a " solipsism of the present moment."

It is " experience " and " habit " alone, Hume said, which dispose us to believe that permanent external objects exist, that other people exist, that our memory affords us a true picture of our own past existence, and so on. But such beliefs, though we are bound to indulge in them, have no sort of rational or empirical justification.

" Without this quality, by which the mind enlivens some ideas beyond others (which seemingly is so trivial, and so little founded in reason), we could never assent to any argument, nor carry our view beyond those few objects which are present to our senses. Nay, even to these objects we could never attribute any existence but what was dependent on the senses, and must comprehend them entirely in that succession of perceptions which constitutes our self or person. Nay, farther, even with relation to that succession, we could only admit of those perceptions which are immediately present to our consciousness ; nor could those lively images, with which the memory presents us, be ever received as true pictures of past perceptions."[1]

Of all philosophical conclusions, solipsism is the most absurd, and most obviously condemns the premises from which such a conclusion could be derived. However, Hume maintained that there was no need to cavil at his solipsistic conclusions.

" I am first affrighted and confounded," he wrote, " with that forlorn solitude in which I am placed in my philosophy. . . ." But " most fortunately it happens, that since reason is incapable of dispelling these clouds, Nature herself suffices to that purpose, and cures me of this philosophical melancholy and delirium, either by relaxing this bent of mind, or by some avocation, and lively impression of my senses, which obliterate all these chimeras. I dine, I play a game of backgammon, I converse, and am merry with my friends ; and when, after three or four hours' amusement I

[1] Hume : *Treatise of Human Nature*, I, IV, 7.

would return to these speculations, they appear so cold, and strained, and ridiculous, that I cannot find in my heart to enter into them any farther. Here, then, I find myself absolutely and necessarily determined to live, and talk, and act like other people in the common affairs of life."[1]

Thus, starting from the basis of pure empiricism, that is, from the standpoint that all knowledge derives from sense-experience and relates solely to the objects contained in sense-experience, and developing this pure empiricism in an absolutely consistent way, Hume arrived at the paradox that his conclusions were such that the whole of his life and experience compelled him to ignore them.

These conclusions I will now briefly summarise :—

The known world consists of atomic sensible events.

We can, for our convenience, study the order and combinations of such events experimentally, and formulate scientific laws giving the rules observed in such order and combination. But we cannot discover any necessary causal connection between events. Nor can we discover any permanent ground for the passing phenomena of sense—no objective external material world, nor any permanent self or soul that knows.

My own knowledge is moreover limited to the present events in my own experience. My knowledge cannot penetrate to anything outside the limits of that experience, either in the present, the past or the future.

From this consistent standpoint of pure empiricism, Hume launched a determined attack upon all " metaphysics "—by which he meant any theory without an empirical foundation, and which dealt with ideas not definable in terms of the objects contained in sense-experience.

" When we run over libraries, persuaded of these principles, what havoc must we make ? " he asked. " If we take in our hand any volume, of divinity or school metaphysics, for instance, let us ask, Does it contain any abstract reasoning concerning quantity or number ? No. Does it contain any experimental reasoning concerning matter of fact and

---

[1] Hume : *Treatise of Human Nature*, I, IV, 7.

existence? No. Commit it then to the flames; for it can contain nothing but sophistry and illusion."[1]

3. *Hume's Philosophy in its bearings on the Problem of Science and Religion*

Is it not the case that, unlike Berkeley, the philosophy of "the infidel Hume" (as he was called) was thoroughly anti-religious, anti-idealist? Far from reconciling science and religion, is not this philosophy utterly destructive of religion?

No, this is not the case. And in proof of this contention it is possible to cite Hume himself.

At the end of his *Inquiry concerning Human Understanding*, Hume remarked:

"The sciences which treat of general facts, are politics, natural philosophy, physics, chemistry, etc., where the qualities, causes and effects of a whole species of objects are inquired into. Divinity or theology, as it proves the existence of a deity and the immortality of souls, is composed partly of reasonings concerning particular, partly concerning general facts. It has a foundation in reason, so far as it is supported by experience. But its best and most solid foundation is *faith* and divine revelation."[2]

Again, of the immortality of the soul:

"By what arguments or analogies can we prove any state of existence, which no one ever saw, and which no way resembles any that ever was seen? Who will repose such trust in any pretended philosophy as to admit upon its testimony the reality of so marvellous a scene? Some new species of logic is requisite for that purpose, and some new faculties of the mind, that they may enable us to comprehend that logic. Nothing could set in a fuller light the infinite obligations which mankind have to Divine revelation, since we find that no other medium could ascertain this great and important truth."[3]

Again, at the end of the *Dialogues concerning Natural Religion*:—

"A person seasoned with a just sense of the imperfections of natural reason, will fly to revealed truth with the greatest

[1] Hume: *Inquiry concerning Human Understanding*, 12.

[2] Ibid., 12.

[3] Hume: *Essay on the Immortality of the Soul.*

avidity ; while the haughty dogmatist, persuaded that he can erect a complete system of theology by the mere help of philosophy, disdains any further aid, and rejects this adventitious instructor. To be a philosophical sceptic is, in a man of letters, the first and most essential step towards being a sound believing Christian."[1]

Now I am well aware that in passages such as these, Hume had his tongue in his cheek. He himself did not care a fig for religion, whether "natural" or "revealed." In several passages of his books he pointed out how utterly impossible it was to adduce any proofs or evidence of any kind for the existence of God or the immortality of the soul, and in other passages, like those just quoted, he adopted a weapon of polished sarcasm against religion.

But nevertheless, he did bring out the fact that his philosophy was *not* destructive of religion. It *was* destructive of a certain sort of dogmatic theology, which seeks to base religion on metaphysical proofs of the existence of God and the immortality of the soul. But it was perfectly compatible with religious *faith*—religion not based on reasonings or proofs or metaphysics of any kind, but simply on faith and inner experience.

For just as Hume's philosophy limited the sphere of possible scientific knowledge to the very "narrow compass" of one's own sense-impressions, so it necessarily left open the whole question of the why and wherefore of life to non-scientific and non-rational modes of consciousness—to religion, faith, divine revelation, mystical experience, etc.

Hume himself had no religion, no faith, he did not believe in divine revelation, he had no mystical intuitions. But his philosophy was one of "live and let live" so far as religion was concerned. Scientific knowledge had one sphere, religion another—and there was an end of the matter.

Hume was, in fact, the first of the British "agnostics."

It is specially important to notice the significance of Hume's views about causality in this connection. One of the chief bugbears of religion is the notion that science establishes a view of the world in which everything can be explained from natural causes, and which therefore leaves no place for creation,

---

[1] Hume : *Dialogues concerning Natural Religion*, 12.

divine intervention, or any of the beliefs of the religious consciousness. Hume's analysis of causality completely disposed of any such notion of the significance of science. He explained that any idea of causal *efficacy*, of any causal *connection* between events in nature, of the natural *production* of the whole succeeding state of affairs from that which preceded it by the operation of causes and effects, was a complete illusion. By so doing he rendered natural science quite innocuous as presenting any sort of challenge to the validity of religious consciousness.

Hume's views about causality have had the very greatest influence on subsequent philosophy. Apart from the materialists, and Hegel, *all* subsequent philosophers have adopted, in one form or another, the view that the existence of objective causal connection in nature is an illusion.

So therefore Hume essentially continued and *completed* the work of Berkeley in the matter of the reconciliation of science and religion.

Hume corrected Berkeley. Berkeley had tried to make science itself preach religion. But that would not do.

Hume simply showed that, if science is concerned solely with the order of events in one's own experience, then it cannot possibly conflict with religion. A scientist can be religious or not as he chooses—scientific knowledge simply throws no light at all on the truth or otherwise of religious faith. On the other hand, the religious man has no cause to fear or to quarrel with science.

What does this amount to in relation to the progress of scientific knowledge?

It renders science virtually innocuous in relation to religion. Science makes no claims, it presents no challenge, as against established religion.

In the first period of the development of modern natural science, in the days of Copernicus and Galileo, science took up arms against religious obscurantism. It took up arms in the struggle for human enlightenment, and began to demolish the various dark superstitions which clustered under the banner of religion. But now science is to be disarmed. It is to lay aside the claim to represent a true and expanding picture of the real nature of things, of the natural history of the world, the forces at work in the world, and the explanation of events.

Moreover, in the first period of the development of modern natural science, science served as an ideological weapon in the struggle to overthrow the old feudal order of society, that is, to destroy the ideas which helped to bolster up that old order and to establish the programme and beliefs of a new society. But now science is to adopt a non-partisan standpoint. It is to busy itself in formulating useful rules and laws governing the probable sequence and combination of events, which will aid the development of mechanical inventions and discoveries, but it is not to challenge the established ideas or formulate any programme for a radical transformation of human life.

The disarming of science in the struggle for enlightenment and progress, the disarming of science in the struggle against superstition, oppression and exploitation—such, therefore, is the meaning of the reconciliation of science and religion effected by pure empiricism.

CHAPTER 5

THE AGNOSTICS, KANT, AND MACH

1. *Agnosticism*

BERKELEY and Hume may be said to have given to the world the classical form of bourgeois " scientific " philosophy.

But this expression perhaps needs some explanation. By calling their philosophy a " scientific " philosophy, I mean that it was apparently founded on and tested by empirical principles, unmixed with a-priori speculations ; clear, logical, consistent ; and that it clearly recognised the value of natural science as the way to the understanding and interpretation of nature. By calling it a " bourgeois scientific " philosophy, I mean that it harmonised perfectly with the mood and intellectual requirements of the cultured members of the middle class, was progressive and scientific strictly within limits, suggested no revolutionary ideas, left alone the foundations of Church and State, and in general was in no way dangerous to the established and developing capitalist order of society. And by calling it " the classical form " of bourgeois scientific philosophy, I mean that it served as the type and model for all subsequent bourgeois scientific philosophy.

With this achievement, the great movement of British philosophical thought of the 17th and 18th centuries came to an end. In the 19th century all that occurred of any philosophic importance in Britain was the elaboration of the work of Berkeley and Hume—an elaboration often for the worse rather than for the better, the main advances achieved being in the specialised sphere of Logic.

" About the middle of this century " wrote Engels, " what struck every cultivated foreigner who set up his residence in England, was, what he was then bound to consider the religious bigotry and stupidity of the English respectable middle class. . . . But England has been ' civilised ' since then. . . . Anyhow, the introduction and spread of salad oil (before 1851 known only to the aristocracy) has been accompanied by a fatal spread of continental scepticism in matters religious, and it has come to this, that agnosticism, though not yet considered 'the thing' quite as much as the Church of England, is yet very nearly on a par, so far as respectability goes with Baptism, and decidedly ranks above the Salvation Army."[1]

In other words, during the course of the 19th century, the ideas of Hume made their way in England, and took the popular form of "agnosticism."

Engels went on to give a well-known characterisation of agnosticism :—

"What, indeed, is agnosticism but, to use an expressive Lancashire term, 'shamefaced' materialism ? The agnostic's conception of nature is materialist throughout. The entire natural world is governed by law, and absolutely excludes the intervention of action from without. But, he adds, we have no means of ascertaining or of disproving the existence of some Supreme Being beyond the known universe. . . .

"Again, our agnostic admits that all our knowledge is based on the information imparted to us by our senses. But, he adds, how do we know that our senses give us correct representations of the objects we perceive through them ? And he proceeds to inform us that, whenever he speaks of objects or their qualities, he does in reality not mean these objects and qualities, of which he cannot know anything for certain, but merely the impressions which they have produced on his senses."[2]

It would be very wearisome and unnecessary to particularise about the different brands of empirical agnostic philosophy in England in the 19th century—Mill, Huxley, Pearson and the rest. All alike had this in common, that they tried to assimilate the great scientific advances of the 19th century, while maintaining the standpoint that scientific knowledge extends no further than the limits of one's own sense-impressions.

In contrast to Hume, all these later agnostics were extremely muddled.

For Hume boldly and with clarity drew the consequences of pure empiricism, which the agnostics embraced, namely, solipsism of the present moment, denial of causality and

[1] Engels : *Socialism, Utopian and Scientific*, Introduction.

[2] Ibid.

objective causal connection in nature. But on the other hand, the 19th century agnostics tried *both* to assert the limitation of scientific knowledge to sense-impressions, *and* at the same time to affirm that consciousness has a material origin, that man evolved from the animals, and that the universe itself, prior to any mind or consciousness coming into existence, had its beginning in some primordial nebula.

This was no doubt a very scientific philosophy. But they never noticed that if science establishes such propositions as these, and if these propositions are going to be accepted as philosophical truths about the world, then both science and philosophy are certainly venturing far beyond the bounds of any individual's sense-impressions.

Hence the philosophy of the agnostics was indeed of a muddled, half-hearted, inconsistent kind—" shamefaced," as Engels expressed it.

Since Hume, incidentally, the main empirical philosopher who has *consistently* drawn the consequences of pure empiricism, is L. Wittgenstein. " What solipsism means is quite correct," Wittgenstein affirms. And again, of scientific theories : " The Darwinian theory has no more to do with philosophy than has any other hypothesis of natural science." With Wittgenstein, moreover, the rôle of pure empiricism as a means of smuggling religion past science is also very clearly expressed. It is an " illusion," says he, " that the so-called laws of nature are the *explanations* of natural phenomena." And he goes on to say : " The *feeling* of the world as a limited whole " (i.e., the limitation of knowledge to the circle of my own immediate experience, the limitation of " the world " to " my world ") " is the mystical feeling." " There is indeed the inexpressible ; this shows itself ; it is the mystical."[1]

But between the thorough-going sceptical empiricism of Hume, and the (as we may express it) mystical empiricism of our contemporary, Wittgenstein, went the half-hearted empiricism of the " shame-faced " agnostics—people who at one and the same time took science at its face value as giving a materialist picture of the objective world, and also denied the objectivity of scientific knowledge.

---

[1] Wittgenstein : *Tractatus Logico-Philosophicus*, 5.62, 4.1122, 6.371, 6.45, 6.522.

2. *The Agnosticism of Kant, and its criticism from two angles*

In the meantime, the philosophy of Hume was followed, in Germany, by another sort of agnosticism—the agnosticism of Kant.

But Kant was not an empiricist. He could not agree that all knowledge was derived from sensations. But at the same time he was profoundly influenced by Hume, who, as he expressed it, " first awoke me from my dogmatic slumbers."

Hume had argued that there can be no empirical basis for the supposition of the objective existence of permanent " substances," or of " causality." Therefore, he concluded, we possess in fact no objective knowledge of substances or causes. Our knowledge is limited to the world of our own sense-impressions.

But, Kant replied, we *do* possess such knowledge—for instance, we *do know* that every event has a cause, and that this is a necessary law of nature. And therefore, since Kant agreed with Hume that such knowledge could not have an empirical origin, that is, could not be derived simply from what is given us in sensation, he came to the conclusion that there must exist non-empirical sources of knowledge.

For take the proposition : " Every event has a cause." We know this to be true—but since Hume has shown that it cannot be proved from experience, we must know it independently of all experience. Such knowledge is not empirical knowledge, it is a-priori knowledge.

How is this possible ? Kant asked. In his own words : " How is synthetic a-priori knowledge possible ? "

To this he replied that the sense-impressions which the mind receives from without are not just accepted ready-made by our consciousness, but are " worked up " and arranged by the mind according to principles of its own. Hume had said that the mind was in fact nothing but just " a bundle " of sense-impressions. But this, said Kant, was wrong. The mind is rather furnished in advance with all sorts of innate theoretical principles, so that as soon as sense-impressions are received, it gets busy with them, and begins to change them.

Thus sense-impressions are first perceived as spatio-temporal, arranged by the mind itself in a spatio-temporal order. Thus from the " crude " (very crude, as in themselves they have not even a spatio-temporal order) impressions of sense, the mind begins from its own powers to create the " representation " of a world in space and time.

The mind then produces further from its own resources such ideas—Kant called them "categories"—as Substance and Causality ; so that it creates, out of the crude impressions of sense, the "representation" of a world in space and time, consisting of various substances, which act causally on one another.

We *know*, therefore, that every event has a cause, etc., because it is *we ourselves* who have arranged for every event to have a cause.

Thus, Kant explained, what we call the objective world—the world which science studies—does not really exist in the form in which it appears to us. The world as we perceive it and know it is a creation of the mind, according to principles innate in the mind itself. It is simply a " representation " or " phenomenon " ; a world which we, with our own mental resources, create from the crude impressions of sense.

Where these original impressions come from, we do not know. And what the *real* world is like we do not know—" *things in themselves* " are necessarily unknowable. Our knowledge is limited to the world of " phenomena."

Thus it seems clear that with Kant we merely reach the same essential conclusion as before, though by another road. Scientific knowledge is valid " within its own sphere." It is valid of " phenomena." But " things in themselves " transcend all possibility of scientific knowledge. Does God exist? Is the soul immortal? Is the will free? We cannot know. Such questions transcend the limits of scientific knowledge. They are matters of *faith*, rather than knowledge. They concern things in themselves, whereas knowledge relates only to phenomena.

Thus both Engels and Lenin rightly treat Kantianism as a species of agnosticism. For instance, " The distinction between the Humean and Kantian theories of causality," Lenin wrote, " is only a secondary difference of opinion between agnostics who are basically at one, viz., in their denial of *objective* law in nature."[1]

[1] Lenin : *Materialism and Empirio-Criticism,* Selected Works, 11, p. 225.

It must not be concluded from the obscurity, muddle and ambiguity of Kant's philosophy, that it did not play a profoundly important part in the history of modern thought. The exceptional importance of Kant in the history of modern philosophy is in fact rather like that of a railway junction in the economic system of a country—it is a place where many lines meet and diverge again.

"The principal feature of the philosophy of Kant," said Lenin, "is an attempted reconciliation of materialism and idealism, a compromise between the claims of both, a fusion of heterogeneous and contrary philosophic tendencies into one system. When Kant admits that something outside of us—a thing in itself—corresponds to our perceptions, he seems to be a materialist. When he, however, declares this thing in itself to be unknowable, transcendent, 'trans-intelligible'—he appears to be an idealist. Regarding experience as the only source of our knowledge, Kant seemed to be turning towards sensationalism (i.e., empiricism) and by way of sensationalism, under certain special conditions, towards materialism. Recognising the a-priority of space, time and causality, etc., Kant seems to be turning towards idealism."[1]

Indeed, materialism and idealism, empiricism and rationalism, science and theology, dogmatism and scepticism—all meet and have their place within the puzzling ramifications of Kant's philosophy.

For this reason Kant could be, and was, criticised from a variety of contradictory standpoints. In particular, two main lines of criticism of Kant emerge :—

On the one hand, there is the criticism that Kant was wrong to separate the phenomenon from the thing in itself—that we are not each shut up in his own phenomenal world. but that we do have objective knowledge of the real world.

This was the line of criticism taken up by Hegel, and after him by Marx.

But Hegel regarded the world as still being the creation of spirit. Only for him the nature of the world was determined, not, as Kant had said, by the categories employed by the particular individual mind, but by the universal categories of the universal mind.

[1] Lenin: *Materialism and Empirio-Criticism,* Selected Works, 11, p. 257.

Marx, however, pointed out that the world exists on its own ; that ideas are the reflections of real things, and not the other way round ; that "universal mind" has no meaning ; that only particular minds exist, which arise from the organisation of matter at a certain stage of development. "To Hegel," said Marx, "the life-process of the human brain, i.e., the process of thinking, which, under the name of 'The Idea,' he even transforms into an independent subject, is the demiurgos (creator) of the real world, and the real world is only the external, phenomenal form of 'The Idea.' But with me, on the contrary, the ideal is nothing else but the material world reflected by the human mind and translated into forms of thought."[1]

It is clear that Hegel and Marx criticised Kant in the same way, namely, they criticised his denial of the objectivity of knowledge. It was Marx who developed this line of thought *consistently*, as a *materialist* line of thought.

On the other hand, a quite opposite criticism was made of Kant ; namely, the criticism that he should not even have mentioned things in themselves as the ultimate source of our knowledge ; that our knowledge is entirely confined to the sensible elements of experience ; that Kant's theory about the a-priori origin of the "categories" of causality and substance (his so-called "transcendental deduction of the categories") conceded too much to the reality of objective law in nature, whereas in actual fact all that the use of such "categories" amounts to is a convenient mode of describing the order and combinations of our sense-impressions.

Thus on the one hand, Kant was criticised for not allowing enough objectivity to knowledge ; on the other hand for allowing too much.

Lenin expressed this by contrasting "the criticism of Kant from the left and from the right"—the criticism "for not being more of a materialist," and "for being too much of a materialist."[2]

It will be noticed that this two-sided criticism of Kant was a repetition, at a new and more advanced stage, of the two-sided criticism which I previously remarked as arising from the philosophy of Locke. The same two-sidedness was in

[1] Marx : *Capital*, Preface to the Second Edition.

[2] Lenin : *Materialism and Empirio-Criticism*, Selected Works, vol. 11, p. 259.

Kant as in Locke ; on the one side, the restriction of knowledge to the world of our own ideas ; on the other side the recognition of the existence of the outside world. But in Kant this dilemma was expressed in a new, richer and more complicated form. And now again the first line of criticism led *forward* to something new, namely, Hegel and Marx, whereas the second now only led *back*—to a new edition of the old empiricism of Berkeley and Hume.

3. *From Kant, back to Pure Empiricism—Ernst Mach*

The "neo-Kantian" movement, that is, the movement which went backwards from Kant to pure empiricism, produced, as its perhaps most readable exponent, the "scientific" philosopher, or "philosophical" scientist, Ernst Mach.

Mach called his main philosophical book, *The Analysis of Sensations.* In it he affirmed that the "elements" of the known world are sensations. All our knowledge, he said, refers to the order and arrangement of such "elements," that is, to the order and arrangement of sensations.

Therefore scientific theories and scientific laws are to be understood as simply statements that "the elements," i.e., sensations, occur in such and such an order.

Thus : "Bodies do not produce sensations, but complexes of elements (complexes of sensations) make up bodies.

"If, to the physicist, bodies appear the real, abiding existences, whilst the 'elements' are regarded merely as their evanescent, transitory appearance, the physicist forgets, in the assumption of such a view, that all bodies are but thought-symbols for complexes of elements (complexes of sensations). . . .

"For us, therefore, the world does not consist of mysterious entities, which by their interaction with another, equally mysterious entity, the ego, produce sensations, which alone are accessible. For us colours, sounds, spaces, times, are provisionally the ultimate elements, whose given connection it is our business to investigate. It is precisely in this that the exploration of reality consists."[1]

Again :

"In conformity with this view the ego can be so extended

[1] Mach : *Analysis of Sensations*, I, 13.

as ultimately to embrace the whole world. . . . The antithesis between ego and world, between sensation (appearance), and thing, vanishes, and we have simply to deal with the connection of the elements."[1]

But this theory, Mach asserted, is not " subjective idealism." Quite the contrary.

The " elements," he explained, are not mental, but neither are they material. What are they, then? They are " neutral." When we deal with one sort of " order " of the " elements," that is the science of psychology, and we call them " mental." When we deal with another sort of " order," that is the science of physics, and we call them " physical " or " material." But really they are " neutral "—just " elements " ; and all our knowledge and all science has the same objects, namely, the " elements " which we are acquainted with in experience ; and which in one order make up a mind, and in another order, a body.

It is not difficult to see that this theory differs in no important respect from the pure empiricism of Hume. The main difference is in terminology.

But there is also another difference.

Hume clearly admitted that his philosophy meant solipsism. Mach, on the other hand, tried to dodge this conclusion, by the device of calling his sensations by the name of " elements," and describing them as " neutral." But yet, " a rose by any other name will smell as sweet."

Mach said he did not deny the existence of external material objects. A table, for instance, is real enough, he argued. It is a real set of " elements," which, considered in one relation, is my sensation of a table, but which, considered in another relation, is the table itself.

Again, he tried to make out that all we say and know about, for instance, other minds, and similarly about other times and places, and about the past, and about the state of matter even before any living beings with their sensations ever existed, is literally true, as science teaches, because appropriate arrangements of " neutral elements " correspond to all such statements.

But all this was a painful muddle.

---

[1] Mach : *Analysis of Sensations*, I, 7.

For what evidence is there for the existence of all these "elements," floating and combining in the void?

Mach asserted that ordinary bodies, considered as "real abiding existences," were "mysterious entities." But if there is a "mystery," what about the "neutral elements"? These surely are the product of the metaphysical imagination? They really *are* "mysterious entities."

Moreover, the mere use of the word "neutral" tacked on to "elements," to denote sensations, does not make "my" sensations any less "my own," and "mine" exclusively. Still less can it conjure forth sensations which "belong" to nobody. But when Mach imagined arrangements of "neutral elements" corresponding to all the statements of science, it was precisely that absurdity which he was imagining.

But in truth it must be said that he did not succeed even in imagining such a thing; for no one can imagine the unimaginable, or conceive of the inconceivable. He was tacking new-fangled words together; but the statements produced were in fact meaningless.

Hence it must be admitted that Mach and his followers, no more than the English agnostics, advanced a step beyond Berkeley and Hume. But on the other hand, they did succeed in obscuring the classical clarity of Berkeley's and Hume's philosophy with a great many "new" muddles.

Besides Mach, and besides the English agnostics, there were dozens of other philosophers of the neo-Kantian, Machian, positivist and agnostic variety; the differences between whom seemed of great importance to themselves, but were of secondary importance in the history of thought.

Remarking on this, Lenin said: "It should be noted that an eclectic combination of Kant and Hume, or Hume and Berkeley, is possible, so to speak, in various proportions, by laying principal stress now on one, now on another element of the mixture."[1]

The important feature, which is in common between all these systems, is the denial of the objectivity of scientific knowledge, the pure empiricist theory that all knowledge derives from sensations and cannot extend beyond the limits of sensations.

---

[1] Lenin: *Materialism and Empirio-Criticism*, Selected Works, vol. 11, p. 266.

4. *The Appeasers in the Camp of Scientific Thought*

I think it will be clear from the whole of this exposition, that the agnosticism and Machism of the 19th century fulfilled exactly the same philosophical role as the philosophy of Berkeley and Hume in the 18th century, that is, to produce a philosophy which would enable would-be scientific minds to avoid "dangerous thoughts" by appearing to "accept science," without overthrowing religion.

But since the science of the 19th century was far more advanced, far richer in content, and covered a far wider field, than the science of the 18th century, it followed that this philosophical task became much more difficult, and the philosophy accordingly became involved and muddled.

"Three great discoveries," said Engels, "enabled our knowledge of the interconnection of natural processes to advance by leaps and bounds ; first, the discovery of the cell as the unit from whose multiplication and differentiation the whole plant and animal body develops. . . . Second, the transformation of energy, which has demonstrated that all the so-called forces operative in the first instance in inorganic nature . . . are different forms of manifestation of universal motion. . . . Finally, the proof . . . that the stock of organic products of nature surrounding us today, including mankind, is the result of a long process of evolution from a few original unicellular germs, and that these again have arisen from protoplasm or albumen which came into existence by chemical means.

"Thanks to these three great discoveries and the other immense advances of natural science, we have now arrived at the point where we can demonstrate as a whole the inter-connection between the processes of nature not only in particular spheres but also in the inter-connection of these particular spheres themselves, and so can present in an approximately systematic form a comprehensive view of the inter-connection in nature by means of the facts provided in empirical natural science itself."[1]

In other words, 19th century science had advanced to a point where it already began to present, at least in general

[1] Engels : *Feuerbach*, ch. 4.

outline, a scientific materialist picture of the world, including the physical and mental life and experience of mankind. This picture was further developed by the demonstration provided by Marx, that human history and the movement of society and ideas had likewise a natural scientific explanation. Scientific knowledge remained, it is true, as it always must remain, in many respects incomplete and provisional. But the development of science held out the promise that there was no sphere of nature or human experience which was not susceptible of scientific treatment, and which could not be included in the general unified scientific picture of the world.

In face of this tremendous advance of scientific knowledge, extending to every aspect of nature and society, the "philosophers of science" set themselves to prove that knowledge cannot extend beyond the limits of sensations; that all science can do is but to work out an elaborate system for describing and predicting the order of our sensations; and at the same time they tried to maintain the standpoint of people who "accepted" all the discoveries of science.

No wonder they got into a muddle.

Their philosophy turned out to be, therefore, one whose mission it was to add to all the discoveries of science a big "BUT." Science has discovered the truth of the evolution of life from the lower forms of organisms to the higher: *but* this discovery only relates to the order of our sensations. Science has formulated the laws of the conservation and transformation of energy: *but* this really relates only to the order of our sensations. And so on.

The significance of this "but" is that it denies that science presents a true, or approximately true, picture of the objective material world and of our place in it. The "but" destroys science as a picture of the objective world.

By so doing, this philosophy clearly gives leave to the exponents of anti-scientific views of the world to claim credence for *their* world-picture—and then to keep pulling to pieces, blotching and smudging the scientific picture of the world.

The whole history of modern science from the time when Galileo fell into the hands of the Holy Inquisition has been the history of struggle against anti-scientific ideas. It has been the history of the uprooting of dogmas, mysteries and superstitions from one field after another ; of the victory of enlightenment ; and of the winning of men's free control over nature and their own destiny in place of acceptance of things as they are and worship of the unknown.

Machism and similar theories are therefore with some justice accused of being theories that disarm science in this struggle for enlightenment. Their " but " is a gesture of appeasement of the enemies of scientific knowledge and of scientific culture. It gives way to them, lets them get on with the dissemination of anti-scientific views, and renounces the aim of the scientific explanation of the whole world.

And just as appeasement in any sphere always leads to the disruption of one's own camp in the interests of the enemy, so it is with the philosophy of science. It leads to the disruption of scientific thought by many obscurities and muddles, the importation into scientific thought of nonsensical and meaningless terms. It leads to the presentation, not of a picture of the objective world we live in, its laws of motion and our own place in it, but to a picture of what Sir James Jeans later called " the mysterious universe." Everything becomes doubtful and obscure ; and strange shadowy entities—" elements " and so forth—take the place of material and controllable facts and processes.

This theoretical confusion has more than a merely theoretical significance.

Our ideas arise from our material mode of living, but they govern our material mode of living too. If the human race is to be emancipated from poverty and oppression, then our struggle for progress must be guided by a clear scientific theory, in politics in particular, but in every other sphere of human activity as well. Unscientific and anti-scientific notions are at best a hindrance to progress. But most often they are used by those whose interests are opposed to progress as a means of helping to oppose it.

The theoretical activity, therefore, of those philosophers and scientists who are engaged in adding " buts " to science is not something independent of the social struggle. Whether the philosophers intend this to be so or not, it plays its part in giving aid and comfort to the enemies of progress.

A philosophy which sets limits to science by denying its

reference to the objective world, necessarily has its counterpart in the flourishing of superstition and ignorance amongst the people. For if people do not learn to understand the world scientifically, then they must remain victims of faith, tradition and authority. And so, great as may be the gulf, intellectually and socially, between the academic philosopher and scientist and the common man, this type of philosophy plays its part in society as a barrier to the enlightenment of the people, and so far therefore as a help to reaction.

Above all, if we can only show how science reveals the true nature of the world in which we live, then we can understand how, by the social use and control of scientific discoveries, we can change the world and transform human life. But theories which deny the objectivity of scientific knowledge play into the hands of those who are opposed to any such change and transformation.

CHAPTER 6

CRITIQUE OF PURE EMPIRICISM

1. *How do we gain our knowledge?*

IN this chapter, before passing on to the examination of contemporary forms of empirical philosophy, I shall attempt to analyse the main theoretical mistakes made by the philosophy already passed under review.

What is wrong with it as a philosophy? Briefly, the answer is :

(A) That it is founded on premises which are obviously untrue.

(B) That its conclusions are in glaring contradiction with well-established facts.

The first line of refutation was particularly developed by Engels, and the second by Lenin.

(A)

I think it is clear from the whole preceding exposition that, at the basis of the philosophy of pure empiricism, in all its various forms, lie certain characteristic views about the nature of *knowledge*. Namely, knowledge is regarded as being derived from sense-perception, in the sense :

(i) That sense-perception is the original starting point of knowledge, and that the objects of sense-perception are our own sensations or sense-impressions, which therefore constitute the original given data from which the whole body of knowledge is derived.

(ii) That sensations being the ultimate given data of knowledge, then knowledge is derived through the mental activity of analysing, comparing, combining, ordering, etc., our sensations ; so that whatever results can be so obtained by contemplating sensations, constitute knowledge ; whereas propositions which cannot be so derived, and which in any way go beyond what can be so derived, do not constitute knowledge, but are mere baseless speculations, or are even entirely without meaning.

Naturally, the above view of knowledge can be expressed in many other ways, utilising various sorts of philosophical terminology ; but the above, I believe, constitutes the gist of the matter as concerns the fundamental view of knowledge taken by pure empiricism.

Now if this premise regarding the nature of knowledge is granted, then the rest of pure empiricism follows.

It is undeniably true that, taking sensation as the given ultimate basis of knowledge in this sense, then you cannot, by any conceivable species of logic, arrive at the knowledge of the existence of anything else except sensations. Sensations are the given ; we cannot know that anything exists whose existence cannot be known through contemplating sensations, their combinations and orders—if that is granted, then we cannot know about the existence of anything else except sensations themselves.

But the point is—the premise is obviously untrue.

" Some truths there are," to quote Berkeley, " so near and obvious to the mind that a man need only open his eyes to see them." And " such I take this important one to be, viz." that our knowledge is *not* derived from sensations in the way described above. We do not gain our knowledge by simply accepting given sensations, and then analysing and comparing our sensations one with another. On the contrary, we gain our knowledge by doing things, acting on things, changing things, producing things, which involves far more than merely contemplating the sensations which happen to enter into our consciousness.

In order to convince oneself of this, one need not look further, indeed, than " one's own experience."

Furthermore, just as the pure empiricist, in his " analysis of sensations," usually introduces into his own sense-experience an atomism which as a matter of fact is not there at all, so he regards experience in general in an atomistic way. He treats the experience of each person, of each knowing subject, as a separate atom, totally exclusive ; and so each has only his own private knowledge, derived from his own private sensations, and has no grounds for inferring, or knowing, anything beyond what is contained in his own private experience. That is why pure empiricism, *consistently* carried out, must always lead to solipsism.

But again, such a view of the basis of knowledge is totally at variance with the manifest facts.

It is not the case at all that knowledge is the private property of each knowing mind. But just as knowledge is *not* gained by the mere contemplation on the part of each individual of his own private sensations, but *is* gained by practical activity directed upon surrounding objects; so also knowledge is gained by the co-operative practical activity of many people, and many generations of people, and is not separately built up by each person. Knowledge is public, not private; it is the common product and the common property of many people organised in society; and the sum of knowledge gained by their social co-operation could not possibly be gained by any one individual, even if he were the cleverest empiricist in the world.

Hence pure empiricism is based upon an obviously false premise—on the premise that the knowledge of each one of us is derived from the private contemplation of the private sensations of each one of us; whereas in fact there is common social human knowledge, derived from the co-operative activity of generations of people, directed upon, and in interaction with, surrounding objects.

2. *Does our Knowledge relate to the Objective Material World?*

Having laid bare this basic error of pure empiricism in its account of the nature of knowledge, it is possible to indicate the way out from some of the typical philosophical puzzles generated by pure empiricism, and also the general justification of the materialist postulate of the existence of the objective material world, to which all our knowledge must relate.

But before proceeding further, it will be well here to define what is meant by this expression, "objective material world." In a moment I shall have to deal again with the contention that such an expression is incomprehensible and meaningless, so it will be useful to establish in advance just what it does mean.

I will not define "world," I hope that word is understood. But in speaking of the "objective" world, I mean that that world is the same for everyone. Thus if my perceptions give me information about the objective world, that means they give me information about exactly the same world as your perceptions give you, and as everyone else's perceptions give them. And in speaking about the objective "material" world, I mean that that world exists in space and time independently of being perceived or known, and, indeed, independently of any sort of consciousness or mental or spiritual being or process.

Often the objective material world is referred to as being "external." This of course means external in relation to any individual's consciousness. My consciousness occurs within the totality of events which make up the world ; but the events which arouse my consciousness, and to which it relates, are external to my consciousness.

It is, then, a typical doctrine of all forms of pure empiricism and agnosticism that our knowledge cannot penetrate beyond sensations, or beyond the contents of our own experience. Sensations are the given data which we have to work with ; and therefore the idea of an *external* objective world, *independent* of our experience, *causing* our sensations, and *represented* by our sensations, is a purely "metaphysical" idea, absurd and incomprehensible.

We cannot know anything about such an external world. It is outside the limits of our knowledge, just because it is external to sense-experience. Indeed, we can attach meaning to our words themselves only in so far as they refer to given elements of sense-experience, and therefore we cannot even attach any meaning to our words when we talk about an external world.

Thus Berkeley said : "When I consider . . . the signification of the words 'material substance,' I am convinced there is no distinct meaning annexed to them." Again : "If there were external bodies, it is impossible we should ever come to know it." And : "You may, if so it shall seem good, use the word 'matter' in the same sense as other men use 'nothing.' . . ."[1]

Kant spoke of the external objective world as a realm of "things in themselves," unknowable and incomprehensible.

[1] Berkeley : *Principles of Human Knowledge*, 17, 20, 80.

Mach spoke of supposed real external objective things as " mysterious entities."

And so in general, it is everywhere asserted that the external objective material word, the system of material processes which in their interaction with our own organic bodies produce sensations, is a meaningless supposition, without any grounds in experience or reason, mysterious, incomprehensible, absurd —in a word, " metaphysical."

The answer to this line of empirical reasoning was worked out by Engels. His answer was in essence very simple. He pointed out that once a correct view is taken of the basis of our knowledge, in place of the distorted empiricist view, then it becomes obvious that external material objects, far from being unknowable and incomprehensible, are very easily known, and the validity of our knowledge of them is very readily tested.

" This line of reasoning," Engels wrote, " seems undoubtedly hard to beat by mere argumentation. But before there was argument, there was action. ' In the beginning was the deed.' And human action had solved the difficulty (i.e., the difficulty of securing knowledge of external objects) long before human ingenuity invented it. The proof of the pudding is in the eating. From the moment we turn to our own use these objects, according to the qualities we perceive in them, we put to an infallible test the correctness or otherwise of our sense-perceptions. If these perceptions have been wrong, then our estimate of the use to which an object can be turned must also be wrong, and our attempt must fail. But if we succeed in accomplishing our aim, if we find that the object does agree with our idea of it, and does answer the purpose we intended for it, then that is positive proof that our perceptions of it and its qualities, so far, agree with reality outside ourselves."[1]

Referring to Kant's statements about the unknowable " thing in itself," Engels further wrote : " To this Hegel, long since, has replied : If you know all the qualities of a thing, you know the thing itself ; nothing remains but the fact that the said thing exists without ; and when your senses have taught you that fact, you have grasped the last remnant of the thing in itself. . . . To which it may be added, that in

[1] Engels : *Socialism, Utopian and Scientific*, Introduction.

Kant's time our knowledge of natural objects was indeed so fragmentary that he might well suspect, behind the little we knew about each of them, a mysterious thing in itself. But one after another these ungraspable things have been grasped, analysed, and what is more reproduced by the giant progress of science ; and what we can produce, we certainly cannot consider unknowable."[1]

Again : " The most telling refutation of this as of all other philosophical fancies is practice, viz., experiment and industry. If we are able to prove the correctness of our conception of a natural process by making it ourselves, bringing it into being out of its conditions and using it for our own purposes into the bargain, then there is an end of the Kantian incomprehensible thing in itself."[2]

To all this it may be objected that the argument fails as a proof of the existence of external material things, because it all the while assumes their existence. Therefore, regarded as a proof of the existence of the objective material world, Engels' argument falls into the fallacy of arguing in a circle.

Such an objection must doubtless be urged by those who prefer to assume that they know only that themselves and their own subjective experience exist. But they fail to see that they also are arguing in a circle. For they too start with an assumption, namely, that the objects of our knowledge are restricted to sensations, sense-impressions, sense-data ; and if they make that assumption, then of course they can never show either that the objective material world exists, or that we can have any knowledge about it.

But the objection fails to grasp the purpose and force of Engels' argument. He was not trying to produce a proof from first principles, that the external world exists. There can be no such " proof," nor is one needed. The Cartesian philosophers in the 17th century used to bring forward what was called " the ontological proof " of the existence of God, which was a proof " that God necessarily exists." Engels was not trying to produce an ontological proof of the existence of matter, or of the objective material world. What he was trying to do (and I think, succeeded in doing) was to show

[1] Engels . *Socialism, Utopian and Scientific*, Introduction.
[2] Engels : *Feuerbach*, ch. 2.

how, given external material objects, with their action upon us and our action on them, we can come, through that interaction, to have verifiable *knowledge* about external material objects.

Now this *was*, first of all, a refutation of the arguments of the pure empiricists, subjective idealists, solipsists, etc. For they had all argued that we *cannot* be said to have knowledge of the objective material world, whereas Engels had shown just how we both can and do have such knowledge. Therefore they were refuted.

And therefore, too, the existence of the objective material world was established beyond all doubt ; for if we find that our knowledge relates to it, then of course it must exist. We may assume, and we ought to assume, in any philosophical account of knowledge, that the objective material world exists. For as soon as we begin to analyse the nature and grounds of our knowledge, we find that it does relate to the objective material world ; and if we try to relate it to anything else, then we falsify it.

What precisely, then, is contained in Engels' " most telling refutation " of pure empiricism ?

Simply this. That in life men enter into relations with the external world. Knowledge of external objects seems mysterious and impossible only when knowledge is regarded in abstraction from all other human activity. But when such a false abstraction is corrected, and knowledge is regarded concretely, as it exists in actual life and experience, in its relations to the totality of human activities, then there is nothing mysterious or impossible in the fact that it relates to external material objects. On the contrary, that relation, and the general principles of that relation, become very clear.

Consider human knowledge concretely, as it actually exists, comes into being, and develops. Is it gained as a result of our contemplating, analysing, comparing, our own inner subjective sensations ? No, it is not.

All knowledge is gained as a result of grappling with problems. And the sort of problems that face us in real life are not problems of how to analyse our sensations and describe their order and combinations, but they are problems of how to conduct ourselves in relation to surrounding bodies. It is the problems of practice that set the problems of knowledge.

The root problem of knowledge is to evolve ideas and theories corresponding sufficiently well with the real nature of things, as to enable us to handle them successfully. And as the problem is, so of course is the answer. If the problem relates to the properties of external objects, so must the answer relate to the properties of external objects. And when our ideas of the properties of things enable us—as they very frequently do, otherwise we would not survive—not merely to find our way about amongst surrounding objects and to avoid being harmed by them, but to change them, and to produce them for ourselves, then that is the test and proof that the ideas correspond to the objects.

As Francis Bacon remarked : " Knowledge of nature is the same thing as power over nature."[1] He realised very well that to know the properties of things is to know how to control and to produce them. But those who started from the same empirical standpoint as himself, forgot this important fact.

This account of knowledge, and of the mode of development and test of the validity of knowledge, is integrally related to the materialist scientific account of social development as a whole. For the sum of human knowledge is as much a social product as any other of the activities and products of men ; and it has the same roots. The basic social activity of men, which drives forward and conditions the whole of their social activity, is the activity of *production*, that is, wresting a living from nature, and producing for ourselves the products and results which we require. Knowledge arises from the effort of production ; increase of knowledge brings increased power of production ; and that increased power of production is the test of the objective validity of knowledge.

Thus in proportion as we know how to produce processes and to produce objects for ourselves, out of their constituents, so is our knowledge of those processes and objects the more complete. That which we cannot produce remains for us, to that extent, something indeed mysterious, unknown, a " thing in itself." But when we learn how to produce it, the mysterious becomes comprehensible, the unknown becomes known, the " thing-in-itself " becomes a " thing for us."

For instance, we have at the present time some idea of the

---

[1] Bacon : *Novum Organum.*

nature of life, namely, that it is the mode of existence peculiar to bodies with a certain chemical constitution. But until we can actually learn how to produce living matter, there remains something mysterious and unknown about the nature of life. On the other hand, vitamins were, up to recently, a very mysterious type of substances ; but now we can manufacture vitamins, the mystery is disappearing. (Of course from this it is clear that those biologists who say that not only we cannot now, but we never can, be able to trace the production of living matter, are people for whom the nature of life is not a relative but an absolute mystery. They renounce the search for more knowledge about life, and would prefer that it remains unknown.)

I am not here trying to set down, however, a complete theory of knowledge. I am merely trying to indicate the general grounds on which it can be maintained that our knowledge relates to the objective material world ; and to show in a general way *how* our knowledge relates to the material world, and how knowledge of external processes, objects and facts can be acquired and tested. In the light of this general approach much, very much more must be written, which would be outside the limited critical purpose of this particular book.

But this treatment of knowledge is a scientific treatment, as opposed to the views on knowledge given in so-called scientic philosophies. For it attempts to treat knowledge as it actually exists and develops. It treats knowledge as the product of a human activity amongst other human activities, and thereby shows its objects, its function, and the way in which it is tested and verified in actual life.

What is there unknowable about the objective material world, as here demonstrated ? There is nothing mysterious, nothing incomprehensible about external material objects. On the other hand, if we seek incomprehensible mysteries, it is in the writings of pure empiricists that we shall find them. What *they* affirm the objects of our knowledge to be is indeed something incomprehensible. A limited subjective world of colours, sounds, smells, tastes, feelings of hardness and softness, etc., existing nowhere, with no material basis—here indeed, as Wittgenstein truly said, we find " the mystical."

3. *The Objects of Sense-Perception*

I have tried to show the basis, and the meaning, of our affirmation of the existence of the external objective material world, and of knowledge about that world. But what of this other " world " of the pure empiricists, that is, the world of sense-impressions, sensations or sense-data ; to which, according to them, our knowledge relates ; which comprises the objects of our knowledge ; and which is—not objective—but a subjective world, different for me than for you?

Some investigation is evidently needed of sense-perception, to find out whether it does in fact have as its objects such subjective entities as the world of the pure empiricists is supposed to consist of. And while this is properly a question of experimental psychology, physiology and neurology, enough can perhaps be established of the matter here to show up the nature of the errors into which the pure empiricists have fallen.

Knowledge begins with sense, and sensation and sense-perception is the foundation of all the higher forms of knowledge —of this there can be no doubt.

The pure empiricists say, however, in one way or another, that sensation or sense-perception is not a means whereby we have direct knowledge of objective external things, but on the contrary, that sensation erects an opaque barrier between ourselves and external objects. The objects of sense are sensations, sense-impressions, " sense-data " ; and we cannot, so to speak, see through sensations to the external things which lie beyond them. From this some conclude that nothing lies beyond ; others, that something may exist there, but it is unknowable ; others again, like Mach, more ingenious, conclude that sensations and external objects are the same thing, and that external objects are just so many complexes of sensations ; or (as we shall see in the Second Part of this book) they give an analysis of the meaning of propositions about external objects according to which such propositions are really about the order and arrangement of sensations.

Since sensation is in fact the direct means whereby we become aware of the existence and properties of external objects, it is strange that so many philosophers should regard it as a barrier shutting out knowledge of the existence and property of external objects. But this strange conclusion arises from regarding sensation abstractly, and not in its relation to life. When sensations are regarded abstractly, as so many given data with which the mind has to work, then of course the conclusion follows that (as has already been pointed out), just by apprehending, analysing and comparing such sense-data, we cannot arrive at the knowledge of anything beyond.

But we have no right to take such an abstract view of sense-perception. After all, it has been studied in some detail by experimental science, and if we philosophise about it we must do so on the basis of the scientific results. Physical phenomena too have been studied by science ; and that being so, any philosophy which attempted to generalise about physical phenomena on philosophical principles—like, for example, the ancient Greeks—and ignored the results of physical science, would be regarded as entirely out-of-date and baseless. Just the same is true of sense-perception.

Sense-perception is an activity of a sentient organism, whereby that organism becomes aware of various features of its environment, and also of the state of its own body. And "becomes aware" does not simply mean "becomes conscious," but means that the organism moves and behaves appropriately. If I am aware of a table in the middle of the room, I am conscious of the existence of the table, and when I walk across the room I will take care not to bump into it. Thus it may also be said that in sense-perception the organism discriminates various features of its environment, in order that it can react appropriately to their presence. The whole environment is an immensely varied and complicated system of objects and processes. In sense-perception the organism discriminates some of the features out of the total mass.

The sense organs are the organs through which this discrimination begins, by reacting to effects transmitted from external objects—the eyes to light waves, the ears to sound waves, the skin to touch, and so on ; impulses are transmitted from the sense organs to the brain ; in the brain the separate impulses are integrated together (through a process that we do not as yet know much about) ; and there follows the sensible conscious representation of the surrounding objects according to the information about them picked up by the sense organs and co-ordinated by the brain. The organism is then able to behave in a manner appropriate to this representation of its surroundings.

In this way, incidentally, it is not very hard to account for some of the well-known phenomena of sense, which have been thought to be a great puzzle by some philosophers. For instance, if we look sideways at a round penny, it will look elliptical. The sun, which is a very big object, but a long way away, looks smaller than the fire in my own fireplace, which is a comparatively small object, but is very near. A stick half submerged in the water looks bent. And so on. Moreover, the senses sometimes mislead us altogether, by representing things as quite different from what they are, or even things which do not exist at all. Sometimes the senses mislead us, and this is not surprising when you consider how the senses work. But we can usually tell, if not at the time, then afterwards, whether the senses mislead us or not. For when we deal with things according to the information received through the senses, and we find that thereby we can get along in the world, then that is the sign that, so far at least, the representation of things made from our sense-perception is a true representation, corresponding to the nature of the objects.

Sense knowledge, or sense-perception, is therefore to be regarded concretely as a certain activity of sentient organisms, through which these organisms discriminate various features of their immediate surroundings, integrate those features into a single representation, and are thus enabled to react appropriately. From this it is clear that the *objects* of sense-perception, the objects *known* through the senses, are material objects, objects of the objective external world. There is nothing " mysterious " about those objects ; for we are always surrounded by them, always interacting with them, and always in our waking hours gaining knowledge about them through sense-perception. Indeed, each one of us is only ourself one amongst those objects, for we, too, have a material existence. From this point of view, what *does* seem mysterious is rather the supposition of a set of special non-material sense-objects, private to the sentient mind—whether these are called "sense-impressions," "ideas," "sensations," "elements," or whatever they are called by the philosophers who invented them.

But here the philosophers will cry—No, what you say does not follow. Consider the stick that looks bent in the water; consider the penny that looks elliptical when you see it sideways; the alleged objective stick is straight and the penny is round, but *what you see* is bent or elliptical. What you see, the object of your sense-perception, is not an alleged external material object, but is rather a sensation, a sense-impression, a sense-datum.

Now on this I would make three remarks:—

(1) Is what we see, or, not to confine ourselves merely to sight, what we are aware of in sense-perception, analysable into separately existing sensations or sense-data?

No, it is not. At the present moment, what I am sensibly aware of is the room in which I am writing, including within it the visual appearance of the tables and chairs, the sound of the ticking of the clock, the warm sensation from the fire, and so on. Is this the same as an awareness of a collection of different sensations, of simple and separate colours, sounds, sensations of warmth, etc.? Is it analysable into such separate sensations? Clearly not. If by an effort of abstraction, for instance, I can bring myself to see the table before me, not as a solid table, but as a brown sensation, or brown patch, then I am causing myself to see something different from what I saw before. Hence to regard what I am aware of as being a collection of sensations or sense-data, made up out of the separate impressions of the different senses, is to begin to invent constituents of sense-experience which have no real existence whatever.

Of course, my total sense-perception *is* the result of a fitting together of the data provided by the separate senses. But that fitting together is done in the course of the complicated integrative processes which take place inside my brain, when the impulses from the different senses are received. The data of each sense do not enter my consciousness separately at all, as if my consciousness were analysable, as Hume said, into "a bundle of sense-impressions"; what I am conscious of, is a whole integrated representation of my surroundings, in which the data derived from each sense have become blended, and have no longer any separate existence.

And these results, be it noted, are not the mere product of some philosophical speculation, but emerge from the work of experimental psychology, especially the work of the so-called Gestalt psychologists, and of modern physiology and neurology.

Hence, in the first place, whether a stick looks bent in the water or not, it cannot be correct to suppose that the object of our sense-perception is analysable into a collection of separate sense-impressions or sense-data. "Sense-impressions," "sense-data," considered as "objects," are a purely metaphysical invention. They have no real existence, and no place in any science.

(2) In this connection, it is specially noteworthy that the alleged sense-impressions or sense-data are entirely passive or, as Berkeley put it, "inert," and have no sort of inter-action whatever one with another.

In them we have an alleged set of completely immaterial objects, which have no sort of effect or influence on one another or on anything else.

There is an alleged sense-impression of colour, or a coloured sense-datum : but it exists absolutely without activity of any description ; it has no power to change, influence or affect itself or anything else.

What a strange mode of existence this is—how mysterious, incomprehensible and incapable of any sort of scientific study. Having postulated such a mode of existence, philosophers have proceeded to argue that, since only such-like objects are known to the human mind, therefore causality and the power of things to influence and change one another in the world, must be an illusion. But the argument should rather go the other way round. Since the alleged sense-impressions or sense-data are so entirely "inert" and powerless to change, therefore it is they which are the illusion.

(3) How, then, does the illusion of the existence of sense-data arise ?

Sense-perception is an activity of the bodily organism, carried on through the sense-organs and the brain. But being a *conscious* activity, it is not merely a matter of physical stimuli and responses, impulses and reactions, but in order to fulfil its function in the life of the higher organisms that possess it, it involves the conscious representation of its objects.

But this conscious representation, or in other words, my consciousness, is yet only a part or an aspect of the material processes in my brain which constitute the activity of sense-perception. My consciousness has no existence apart from my brain. For the grey matter in my brain has the unique peculiarity (and exactly how this happens we do not yet know) that its motion is not merely physical but also, as we say, mental, that is, it gives rise to consciousness, or has a conscious aspect. My consciousness can change, and enter into many different states—but it remains as merely the conscious aspect of something material, the processes in my brain ; and if I imagine it to exist independently, I am making an absurd mistake.

Further, when I am engaged in sense-perception, my consciousness has a certain *content* ; and the content is determined by what goes on in my brain. Thus I am seeing a stick, a penny, the sun, the inside of my sitting-room, and so on ; the content of my consciousness is very varied and changing. But obviously, no more than my consciousness in general, has the content of my consciousness got any independent existence.

For instance, I am looking at a stick half submerged in water, and it looks bent. There really is the conscious sense-representation of a bent stick. But that is not to say that there is a bent-shaped object, existing somehow in my mind, as well as or instead of the objective stick, which is straight. The *only* objects involved are the stick itself, the light waves, and the processes in my eyes, optic nerve and brain, the conscious side of which includes the sense-representation of a bent stick. Why the stick looks bent instead of straight is easily explained from the nature of the image formed on my retina.

Much more can be written, and needs to be written, in explanation of the nature of consciousness, and of its "objects." But I think it is now possible to indicate the kind of mistake which the pure empiricists, and many other philosophers as well, have made.

They base their theories, in the first place, purely on passive introspection. Thus they look inside their own consciousness, so to speak, and they find there that their consciousness has a most interesting, varied and changing content. But inside their own consciousness they are not aware at all that their consciousness is only an aspect of certain material processes, namely, the processes inside their brain. So they ignore this fact and pay no attention to it. And having done so, they then come to regard their consciousness, and the whole changing content of their consciousness, as being an independently existing " world " on its own.

This process of abstraction, based on the mental attitude of introspection, was rather vividly, if strangely, described by a German " phenomenologist," E. Husserl—whom I have not mentioned before in this book, and will not mention again. In a book called *Pure Phenomenology* he said that what was necessary was to consider our own consciousness, and in doing so to " bracket " or " disconnect," as he expressed it, both the objective world and the existence of our own selves ; that is, to ignore such factors altogether. What was left over after such disconnecting was " pure consciousness." And : " Consciousness, considered in its ' purity,' " he said, " must be reckoned as a self-contained system of Being, as a system of Absolute Being, into which nothing can penetrate, and from which nothing can escape ; which has no spatio-temporal exterior, and can be inside no spatio-temporal system. . . ."[1]

Having, then, arrived at the position where our consciousness, with its content, is regarded as something that exists independently, the introspective empirical philosopher then proceeds to try to " analyse " it into its parts. He tries to represent this " world " of consciousness or pure experience as being built up out of constituent atoms, just as the objective material world is considered to be composed of atoms ; he calls these atoms " sensations " or " sense-data " or " elements," or any other name that occurs to him ; and so invents a whole realm of objects, which he declares to be the true objects of knowledge ; and he ends by declaring that the objective material world does not exist at all.

As I have shown, such " atoms " are not actually to be found inside our consciousness, nor do they have any of the

[1] Husserl : *Pure Phenomenology*, 33–49.

characteristics of real objects, because they cannot influence or change anything. But the basic fallacy which led to the assertion of the existence of such objects can now be made plain. It is a fallacy which has been fairly common in the history of philosophy; namely, the fallacy of mistaking for an independently existing object, some mere aspect or part of a fact or process, which can be thought of in abstraction, but which can have no independent existence. These philosophers think of consciousness in abstraction, and then try to represent the content of consciousness as a world of independently existing objects.

4. *Is Pure Empiricism compatible with the results of Science?*

What, then, is the upshot of this whole discussion about the theory of knowledge of pure empiricism? It is that the theories of pure empiricism are without foundation, because they rest on false premises, that is, on an inaccurate account of knowledge involving false abstractions; and that there is every reason to presume the very opposite of what pure empiricism asserts.

(B)

But secondly, the conclusions of pure empiricism, which are based on this inaccurate and abstract account of knowledge, are moreover themselves at variance with the most well-tested racts established by the very scientific knowledge about which pure empiricism tries to philosophise. This becomes very obvious after the preceding discussion.

Criticising pure empiricism, Lenin asked: "*Does man think with the help of the brain?*"[1]

The answer, of course, is: Yes, he does. It is scientifically established that not only does man think with the help of the brain, but that thought is a function of the brain, and that without a brain there can be no sensation, no experience, no thought.

But the conclusion of pure empiricism is that the brain is really only a certain sort of combination of sensations. As Mach said, "bodies do not produce sensations, but . . .

[1] See Lenin: *Materialism and Empirio-Criticism*, Selected Works, Vol. 11, p. 151.

complexes of sensations make up bodies." Therefore, sensation does not depend on the brain, but the brain depends on sensations, namely, on sensations being combined in a certain way.

Therefore, sensation is not a function of the brain, but the brain is a function of sensations.

Or to put it in another way, the idea of "the brain," like the idea of all bodies, is only a convenient mode of describing and predicting certain sensations which we experience under certain circumstances.

Hence quite clearly this philosophy holds that the existence of sensations, and the faculty of thought based on sensations, is really absolutely *independent* of any brain, or any other material thing. It tells us that when it says "brain," it means only something about sensations; and hence quite clearly it in effect *denies* that sensation or thought is dependent on anything other than itself. My sensation, my experience, is absolute—absolutely independent.

But clearly such a doctrine is in hopeless contradiction with what we know to be the case as a result of scientific investigations, namely, that sensation and thought are dependent, dependent on a material thing, the brain.

Whatever interpretations or analyses this philosophy may give of scientific propositions about thought and the brain (and it has given many), they cannot conceal the fact that this philosophy asserts that sensation exists without sense organs, thought without a brain.

Again, Lenin asked: "*Did nature exist prior to man?*"[1]

Again the answer, of course, is: Yes, it did. It is a well-established fact that the human race is descended from other forms of organic life, that life itself has a chemical origin, and that for ages and ages the state of matter was such that no life, let alone such a complicated form of life as man, was possible.

But what has pure empiricism to say of all this? Simply that nothing exists beyond sensations, and that our knowledge can in the last analysis refer only to sensations. Therefore, when we say, "Nature existed prior to man," we really mean, or ought to mean, something very different from what we say.

---

[1] See Lenin: *Materialism and Empirio-Criticism*, Selected Works, Vol. 11, p. 140.

Perhaps, for example, we mean that in the past certain combinations of sensations existed, without those particular combinations existing which constitute the life of man. But that supposes that sensations exist without anyone to have those sensations, which of all the abstruse, mystical and metaphysical speculations ever imagined, is the most absurd.

Or perhaps its meaning is to be explained in another way, for instance : " If I imagine myself to have existed so many millions of years ago, then I must imagine myself to perceive only sequences of events which would render life impossible," or something of that sort. This again is absurd, because I cannot imagine myself existing, far less perceiving anything, under such circumstances.

Or perhaps, more ingenious still (and this is the interpretation put up by the most up-to-date empiricists), it is to be explained in terms of the principle that " the meaning of a proposition is its verification."[1] In that case it would mean something like this : " If I have the sensations of looking at stratified rocks, then in some strata I will see fossil remains, and in other (which I call ' earlier ') strata I will not," and so on—thus making the present perceptions, which would be brought forward as part of the evidence or verification of the existence of inorganic nature prior to life, themselves constitute the meaning of the proposition for which they provide the evidence.

All such interpretations are very ingenious ; but they cannot conceal the fact that, if nature *did* exist prior to man, then there was a time when there were *no* sensations, *no* thoughts, but only material things. And therefore the philosophy of pure empiricism *denies* that nature existed prior to man, *denies* the theory of evolution, and denies in fact more or less the whole body of established scientific truth.

Pure empiricists will protest against this, that it is an elementary misrepresentation, that they deny no scientific truths, but only analyse them and interpret them philosophically. But it is one thing to say that I have, under certain conditions, sensations which I conveniently describe in various scientific terms. It is quite another thing is say that the world has had a long process of evolution ; that only at a

[1] See below, ch. 9, section 4.

certain stage did life appear ; that the higher forms of life evolved from the lower ; that the highest form of organisation of matter is the human brain ; and that sensation and thought are functions of the brain. The second is what science says. The misrepresentation is all on the side of the pure empiricists. They misrepresent the meaning of the results of science.

In fact, what the pure empiricists are doing is to *reject* the results of science, in favour of what can only be termed medieval obscurantism. For to deny the reality of the dependence of thought on the brain, to deny the reality of evolution, to deny that life itself emerged only at one stage of the history of the world—what is this, indeed, but medieval obscurantism in the place of science ?

Thus just as the premises of pure empiricism, in its treatment of knowledge, are false, so also are its conclusions at variance with the most well-established scientific truths.

Thus this philosophy is no scientific philosophy, but a thoroughly anti-scientific philosophy.

It is not, however, openly anti-scientific. It is not openly reactionary. Its denial of scientific truth is not made openly, but in a roundabout way, while ostensibly accepting the scientific truths which it nevertheless rejects. This conclusion reinforces the conclusion I had already formulated at the end of the previous chapter, that this philosophy plays the part of an agency of appeasement within the camp of science, holding back the advance of materialist scientific enlightenment, and confusing and distorting the teachings of science.

PART TWO

LOGICAL ANALYSIS, LOGICAL POSITIVISM

CHAPTER 7

LOGICAL ANALYSIS AS A PHILOSOPHICAL METHOD

1. *A Galilean Advance; Unassailable and Definitive Truth*

I HAVE examined the empiricism of the past, and now approach its offspring, the empiricism of the present day.

This contemporary "scientific" philosophy—"logical analysis," "logical positivism," "radical physicalism"—puts forward the greatest possible intellectual claims. Its various exponents are indifferent to the history of philosophy. They claim to be the exponents of the only correct and moreover radically *new* method of philosophical thinking, in the light of which most previous philosophy turns out to be meaningless "metaphysics," and all philosophical problems are capable of solution.

Thus Bertrand Russell, who was the principal founder of the views I am now to examine, wrote of his own philosophy: "It represents, I believe, the same kind of advance as was introduced into physics by Galileo; the substitution of piecemeal, detailed and verifiable results for large untested generalities, recommended only by a certain appeal to the imagination."[1]

Russell's pupil, Wittgenstein, went even further:

"How far my efforts agree with those of other philosophers I will not decide," he wrote. But "the *truth* of the thoughts communicated here seems to me unassailable and definitive. I am therefore of the opinion that the problems have in essentials been finally solved."[2]

I propose, however, to examine these various Galilean discoveries, and unassailable and definitive truths, on their merits.

---

[1] Russell: *Our Knowledge of the External World*, p. 4.

[2] Wittgenstein: *Tractatus Logico-Philosophicus*, Preface.

2. *Logic as the Essence of Philosophy*

The central feature of the contemporary " scientific " philosophy is the principle, first enunciated by Russell, that " logic " is " the essence of philosophy."

It is useful to recollect that Russell put forward this " logical " conception of philosophy in the rather curious conditions of British philosophical thought at the beginning of the present century. These conditions arose from the fact that, whereas during most of the last century the main philosophic trend in Britain had been a form of agnosticism, towards the end of the century British academic circles suddenly became aware of the existence of Kant and Hegel. Previous to this certain literary " transcendentalists," such as Coleridge and Carlyle, had spoken darkly of the profundities of German " transcendental " philosophy ; but it was not for years after Kant and Hegel were dead that their writings broke through the insular prejudices of our official Victorian philosophers.

Then J. Hutchinson Stirling wrote a book on *The Secret of Hegel*, and Edward Caird and others unravelled Kant for English-speaking readers. Long after the great tide of classical German idealism had subsided, a kind of backwash reached these islands. The flotsam and jetsam of systems of " absolute idealism " were washed up in the British universities.

The philosophical writings of Russell and his associates (particularly G. E. Moore) first appeared as the protest of science and commonsense against these belated disciples of German idealism. This fact contributed greatly to the Galilean appearance of Russell's work ; for he seemed indeed a genuine champion of the scientific outlook, in comparison with his " absolute idealist " contemporaries.

Distinguishing his own philosophical outlook from that of what he called " the classical tradition " in philosophy, Russell found the essence of this tradition in the belief " that a-priori reasoning could reveal otherwise undiscoverable secrets about the universe, and could prove reality to be quite different from what, to direct observation, it appears to be. It is this belief," he added, " rather than any particular tenets resulting from it, that I regard as the distinguishing characteristic of the classical tradition, and as hitherto the main obstacle to a scientific attitude in philosophy."[1]

In opposition to this tradition, Russell held that philosophy does not and cannot establish or discover new facts, or new generalisations, about the world, or about particular things in the world. That is the task of science, and can only be done on the basis of empirical evidence and scientific method.

Therefore the problems of philosophy, and the philosophical propositions in which these problems are stated and answered, must be of another kind altogether to the problems and propositions of science.

" The consideration that philosophy, if there is such a study, must consist of propositions which could not occur in the other sciences, is one which has very far-reaching consequences," said Russell. He went on to illustrate this : " All the questions which have what is called a human interest—such, for example, as the question of a future life—belong, at least in theory, to special sciences, and are capable, at least in theory, of being decided by empirical evidence. . . . A genuinely scientific philosophy cannot hope to appeal to any except those who have the wish to understand, to escape from intellectual bewilderment. . . . It does not offer, or attempt to offer, a solution of the problem of human destiny, or of the destiny of the universe."[2]

Thus, incidentally, this conception of philosophy at any rate offers us an " escape " from any " intellectual bewilderment " arising from the grave " problem of human destiny," by offering us a means of " escape " from the problem of human destiny itself. But to proceed :—

From this follows the conclusion that philosophical problems " all reduce themselves, in so far as they are genuinely philosophical " (that is, not pseudo-problems, or problems which should be answered through empirical scientific investigation) " to problems of logic. This is not due to any accident, but to the fact that every philosophical problem, when it is subjected to the necessary analysis and purification, is found either to be not really philosophical at all, or else to be, in the sense in which we are using the word, logical."[3]

[1] Russell : *On Knowledge of the External World*, p. 5.
[2] Ibid., p. 17. [3] Ibid., p. 33.

Russell announced, then, a philosophical programme, which can be briefly summed up as follows :—

(1) Facts and generalisations about the world—in other words, positive knowledge—must be acquired empirically, partly through ordinary perception, partly by the more refined technique of natural science. Hitherto unknown facts and generalisations about the world cannot be discovered by a-priori reasoning.

(2) The task of philosophy is to subject the propositions established through ordinary perception and by science to a logical analysis.

(3) Such logical analysis cannot establish any new truths.

(4) But by analysing and making clear the logical form of truths already known, it imparts to positive knowledge a new clarity, and overcomes the confusion and " intellectual bewilderment " which results when the logical form of what is known is not itself understood.

Such is the Galilean discovery and the general programme of the new " logical " and " scientific " philosophy inaugurated by Russell.

At first sight this programme undoubtedly appears to be reasonable and progressive in the highest degree. For what could be more reasonable and more progressive than the view that our knowledge of the world derives from perception and is deepened and enlarged by the methods of science, and that the task of philosophy is to provide a logical clarification of such positive knowledge ?

But I would say that a further consideration reveals very soon that this " new " programme bears a suspicious resemblance to the very old philosophical programme of Berkeley and those who followed from him.

They said : We " accept " the results of science . . . BUT—we give them a certain interpretation. Now it is said : We " accept " the results of science . . . BUT—we submit them to logical analysis.

3. *The Meaning of Logical Analysis*

The idea of " logical analysis " has its roots in certain conceptions of pure mathematics and mathematical logic, which Russell thought could be generalised into a new method of philosophy.

Mathematicians have found it necessary to give a good deal of attention to the exact definition of the terms of which they make use. It is this mathematical type of exact definition which Russell thought could be generalised into a method for philosophy.

For instance, in the sphere of the differential calculus, the whole fundamental idea of the differential function was for a long time very obscure. Thus a differential function gives the velocity of a moving body at a given instant of time ; and this was thought to involve the very obscure conception of the infinitely small distance travelled in an infinitely small time. Yet obviously the whole idea of infinitely small quantities was impossible and contradictory, since all real quantities, however small, are necessarily finite. This difficulty was cleared up by mathematicians, by giving a more exact definition of the differential function. It was defined as the *limit* towards which the relation of the distance travelled to the corresponding period of time approaches as the distances and times considered get smaller and smaller. Thus this more exact definition got rid of the conception of infinitely small quantities, and employed only the conception of finite quantities approaching the limit of zero as they get smaller and smaller. Thus it gives an analysis of what is meant by expressions involving differential functions.

Again, take irrational numbers, such as $\sqrt{2}$, which were a puzzle to mathematicians for about 2,000 years. Rational numbers could be defined as ratios between integers, such as $\frac{1}{2}$, $\frac{1}{4}$, $\frac{1}{8}$, etc. ; but there is no rational number to be found such that its square is equal to 2. And yet mathematicians were constantly under the necessity of operating with irrational numbers such as $\sqrt{2}$, although they could not define them and their use seemed to involve a contradiction. This difficulty was avoided when it was found possible to define $\sqrt{2}$ and other irrational numbers in terms of rational numbers—just as it was found possible to define the relations between infinitesimal quantities in terms of relations between finite quantities. Thus a series of rational numbers can be defined, such that their squares approach nearer and nearer to 2 without limit, though there is no rational number whose square is actually equal to 2. All that had to be done was then to say that in referring to $\sqrt{2}$ we are simply referring to this series of rational numbers, and the " mysterious " irrational number was then defined in terms of the rational numbers. This gave an analysis of what is meant by expressions involving irrational numbers.

In his *Principles of Mathematics*, and in much greater detail in his *Principia Mathematica* (which was dignified by having its title in Latin), Russell thought he could show how all the different sorts of numbers which are used in mathematics could be defined in terms of the series of " natural " numbers, 0, 1, 2, 3, 4, 5, 6. . . . Thus rational numbers were defined as ordered pairs of natural numbers. Then the idea of series of rational numbers with an upper or lower limit could be defined ; and in terms of this, the real numbers, as series of rational numbers, which included both irrational numbers and rational real numbers. Then complex or " imaginary " numbers (such as $\sqrt{-1}$) were defined as ordered pairs of real numbers.

These definitions would show how all expressions involving rational, irrational or imaginary numbers are capable of an analysis in terms of natural numbers. Apart from this analysis, it might seem that rational, irrational and imaginary numbers all have, so to speak, an ultimate mathematical existence.

But Russell also tackled the analysis of the natural numbers themselves, and tried to show how they could be analysed in terms not properly mathematical at all, but rather logical. Thus the whole of pure mathematics could be derived from logic.

He thought that natural numbers could be defined in terms of the logical idea of a class. A class (in the logical sense used by Russell) consists of all individuals having a certain property ; and a class is characterised by a number, namely, the number of individuals which have that property, or are members of that class. Clearly two classes have the same number when a relation can be established between their members, such that to each member of the one class corresponds a member of the other class. So a number is a property or characteristic of a class. Just as all individuals having a certain property can be said to constitute a class (of individuals), so all classes having a certain property can be said to constitute a class of classes. The natural numbers are then defined as classes of classes.[1]

Thus just as all statements about higher forms of numbers are analysed as statements about natural numbers, so statements about natural numbers themselves are analysed as statements about classes. Thus the whole of mathematics, when submitted to analysis, turns out to be about classes.

This method of analysis which, in Russell's opinion, had so successfully elucidated the foundations of mathematics, could, he thought, be applied not only to mathematics but to every department of knowledge. By applying the method of logical analysis in every sphere of thought, obscurities and confusions could be dissolved, and clarity could be reached as to the real meaning and content of our knowledge.

4. *Russell on our Knowledge of the External World*

I will proceed, therefore, to the question of the application of the method of logical analysis to the problems of philosophy.

" I wish to apply the logico-analytic method," said Russell, " to one of the oldest problems of philosophy, namely, the problem of our knowledge of the external world." After warning the reader that, " What I have to say on this problem does not amount to an answer of a definite and dogmatic kind," Russell added : " But although not yet a definite solution, what can be said at present seems to me to throw a completely new light on the problem."

" In every philosophical problem," he continued, " an investigation starts from what may be called ' data,' by which I mean matters of common knowledge . . . commanding our assent as on the whole and in some interpretation pretty certainly true."[2]

---

[1] Russell gives a popular exposition of his theory of numbers in *Introduction to Mathematical Philosophy*. In Chapter 2, on the Definition of Number, he defines two classes as " similar " when they each have the same number of members, i.e., when a one-to-one correspondence can be established between the members of the one class and those of the other class. He then states : " The Number of a class is the class of all those classes that are similar to it " (p. 18) ; and : " A Number is anything which is the number of some class " (p. 19).

[2] Russell : *Our Knowledge of the External World*, p. 65.

He went on to say that the " data " are of three main kinds, namely: (1) facts known through current experience; (2) facts known through memory and the testimony of others; (3) the principles of science. " In the main," he said, " we may accept this mass of common knowledge as affording data for our philosophical analysis."[1]

Here is demonstrated the essence of the logical-analytic method in action. All philosophers who follow this method make such a beginning as this. They claim to accept the " mass of common knowledge," vouched for by common sense or common observation, and science, as the data of philosophy. They claim to take it for granted that all this is " on the whole and in some interpretation pretty certainly true." And they then submit this knowledge to logical analysis. In carrying out this analysis they try to discover the ultimate irreducible elements which the whole " mass of common knowledge "—all the typical propositions which they are analysing—refers to; and then to show how all statements are translatable or analysable into statements about these elements (just as, for instance, the ultimate elements of mathematics were found to be the natural numbers, which themselves could be analysed as classes of classes).

Russell went on to point out that the various data mentioned vary in respect of certainty. Some of the data, when submitted to criticism, can very well be doubted. But the degree of legitimate doubt must vary; and some cannot be doubted at all. The latter Russell called " hard data " and: " Let us confine ourselves to the hard data," he said, " with a view to discovering what sort of world can be constructed by their means alone."[2]

Thus Russell thought the ultimate terms or elements of the analysis of " the external world " should be the so-called " hard data." But so far, incidentally, " the completely new light on the problem " turns out to be nothing but the Method of Doubt enunciated by Rene Descartes in 1628. " Only those objects should engage our attention," wrote Descartes in that year, " to the sure and indubitable knowledge of which our mental powers are adequate." And, " our inquiries

[1] Russell: *Our Knowledge of the External World*, p. 66.

[2] Ibid., p. 71.

should be directed . . . to what we can clearly and perspicuously behold and with certainty deduce ; for knowledge is not won in any other way."[1] And just as Descartes set out to construct a world on the basis of a few principles which could not possibly be doubted, so, it seems, did Russell set out to " construct a world " on exactly the same basis.

But to continue. " Our data now," said Russell, " are primarily the facts of sense, i.e., of *our own* sense-data, and the laws of logic."[2]

Russell went on to interpret, or analyse, ordinary commonsense knowledge of the things about us, and scientific knowledge, in terms of " sense-data." " I think it can be laid down quite generally," he said, " that, in so far as physics or commonsense is verifiable, it must be capable of interpretation in terms of actual sense-data alone."[3]

Carrying out this " new " interpretation, Russell called a " sense-datum " which would commonly be said to be a sense-datum " of " a thing or external object, perceived by a certain person from a certain point of view, an " aspect " of the thing.

He then proposed " the task of reconstructing the conception of matter without the a-priori beliefs which historically gave rise to it. . . . For this purpose, it is only necessary to take our ordinary commonsense statements and re-word them without the assumption of permanent substance. . . . A ' thing ' will be defined as a certain series of aspects, namely, those which would commonly be said to be *of* the thing. To say that a certain aspect is an aspect *of* a certain thing will merely mean that it is one of those which, taken serially, *are* the thing."[4]

He added : " The above extrusion of permanent things affords an example of the maxim which inspires all scientific philosophising, namely, ' Occam's razor ' : *Entities are not to be multiplied beyond necessity*. In other words, in dealing with any subject matter, find out what entities are indubitably involved, and state everything in terms of those entities."[5]

---

[1] Descartes : *Rules for the Direction of the Mind*, 2 and 3.

[2] Russell : *Our Knowledge of the External World*, p. 72.

[3] Ibid., p. 81.

[4] Ibid., p. 105.

[5] Ibid., p. 107.

In this case, all that is " indubitably involved " in " our knowledge of the external world " is the fact that we perceive sense-data ; and so the external world is to be interpreted as consisting simply of certain series and combinations of sense-data, and objective permanent material things and processes are " extruded."

Just as numbers are " analysed " as classes of classes, so external objects are " analysed " as combinations of sense-data.

I do not think it is necessary to follow up this " analysis " any further. For the source of the " completely new light on the problem " is now itself fully illuminated.

The " method " itself is only a mixture of the method of Descartes and the even earlier method of William of Occam. The philosophical results turn out to be identical in absolutely every respect with the philosophy of Ernst Mach, which Russell reproduces almost down to the last detail.[1] And finally, the " re-wording of commonsense statements without the assumption of permanent substance " is only a re-wording—in fact, scarcely even that—of the Principles of Bishop Berkeley.

Criticism of Russell's philosophical conclusions is, therefore, unnecessary here. They are not new, and I have criticised them already. The results of the " logico-analytic method," at least in Russell's hands, represent only a re-statement of the old Berkeley-Humean empiricism.

5. *Logical Analysis as a Method of Unscientific Speculation*

I have examined Russell's application of the " logical-analytic method." Other philosophers, however, who have used this method, have reached results which (in their opinions) differed in important respects from those of Russell. It may be claimed, therefore, that because exception can be taken to Russell's conclusions, it does not follow that the method as such should be rejected, but only that Russell had made a wrong use of it.

I shall therefore devote a little attention to the logical-analytic method as such, as a method of philosophy.

Once again, what is the logical-analytic method ?

---

[1] In later works, particularly his *Analysis of Matter* and *Analysis of Mind*, Russell succeeded in adding a lot more subtle complications, without adding anything essentially new.

It is a method which claims to reveal philosophical truth by the logical analysis of typical propositions of " science and common sense." Its exponents claim that by its means philosophy becomes scientific, and that it puts an end to arbitrary system-building and speculation.

The general features and assumptions of the logical-analytic method have already been defined. Summarising once again, the method may be said to be based on two postulates. On the one hand, it postulates that the body of propositions which are vouched for by normal experience and by scientific method, are true. In other words, what we would ordinarily call knowledge really *is* knowledge. And on the other hand, it postulates that such propositions do not, in their ordinary form of expression, exhibit the *ultimate* data or subject matter to which they refer, and so stand in need of a logical analysis.

For instance, propositions expressing facts of ordinary perceptual or commonsense knowledge contain such expressions as " table," " chair," " mountain " ; or again such expressions as " person," " nation " or " State." Scientific propositions contain such expressions as " atom," " electron," " gene," etc., etc. . . . But such " objects " and their properties and relations are not *simple*, and so are not the *ultimate* constituents of the world. Such expressions will therefore *disappear in analysis*. And when the propositions containing such expressions are analysed, then they will be expressed in terms of the *ultimate* constituents. In other words, ordinary unanalysed knowledge seems to be about such things as tables, chairs, electrons, and so on ; but analysis will make clear the ultimate constituents of knowledge.

Mr. J. Wisdom (an analytic philosopher who once made it his main business to analyse analysis) has expressed this by saying that " the philosopher asks, What is the Self? What is the State? What is Time? . . . The philosopher is asking for a certain kind of definition of the Self, of the State."[1] These questions are to be answered by working out the analysis of propositions in which such terms as " Self," " State," or " Time " occur. The philosophical analysis will reveal the ultimate nature of things, which is not clearly apprehended in ordinary unanalysed knowledge.

[1] J. Wisdom : " Ostentation," in *Psyché*, vol. xiii.

Now it will hardly be disputed that many of the expressions which we normally utter or write, even in scientific discussions, are in the logical sense unclear. For instance, it may quite reasonably be asked, What *is* the State? But the question that arises is: *How* is greater clarity to be reached? *How* is "ultimate," or at all events more ultimate, knowledge to be arrived at?

The way to answer this question is, I think, in essentials, not very difficult. If we want more ultimate knowledge about a thing than what we already possess, the way to gain such more ultimate knowledge is to undertake scientific investigation.

Take, for instance, the kind of questions which Mr. Wisdom thought should be answered by philosophical analysis.

"What is the State?" was one of his questions. This question has been answered scientifically in the scientific materialist theory of the State, first worked out by Marx and Engels. That theory does analyse the State. It does substitute for a vague and general concept of "the State" a very exact picture of the kind of facts we are referring to when the State is in question. It does enable us to express propositions about the State far more clearly than they could be expressed before. It does give far more ultimate knowledge about the constituents of the State than was possessed before the scientific theory was formulated.

But when the State was studied scientifically by Marx and Engels, they studied the actual exemplifications of State power; they studied the history of the State; they studied the State in its motion, change and development; they studied it in its actual real historical relations—not as an abstract, isolated fixed "concept." Thus they arrived at conclusions which could be actually tested and verified in practice. On the other hand, to sit down and try to work out "a logical analysis of the State" in the abstract, simply out of one's head, could not possibly produce anything but baseless and abstract speculations.

Mr. Wisdom also wanted to know what is the nature of the facts we are referring to when we speak of the Self, or Time, and likewise of tables and chairs, electrons, vitamins, and all other things. To answer him, it is necessary only to say that, whether contemporary science has a complete answer to all such questions or not, there seems to be no reason to doubt, and every reason to affirm, that it is by the continuation of scientific methods of empirical investigation that we shall be able to answer such questions. Any *other* mode of investigation—a *philosophical* as opposed to an empirical *scientific* mode of investigation—would be quite superfluous and would get us nowhere.

To put the point in a nutshell: When we ask for "deeper," more "exact," more "ultimate" knowledge of the nature of the things to which our knowledge relates, how are we to get it? We answer:—By scientific investigation, by experiment, by putting forward hypotheses which we can *test* and *verify* and *use*, in a word, by a continuation of the well-tried methods of scientific research. In this way our knowledge does get more and more "exact" and "ultimate"—never *absolutely* exact and ultimate, it is true; that is a final limit which, so far as we can see, never can be reached, though we may more and more approximate to it.

Now, therefore, it is possible to begin to indicate the basic character of the mistake made in the formulation of the method of logico-analytic philosophy. This method supposes that the more precise, more clear, and more ultimate knowledge which we desire of the nature of things, can be obtained by a purely logical-philosophical analysis, *as distinct from* a continuation of scientific investigation—by passive contemplation as distinct from active investigation.

More ultimate knowledge, it thinks, is not to be obtained by a continuation of scientific investigation, but by going outside science altogether.

Here the place of logic in the system of scientific thought is altogether perverted. Logic is not regarded as an instrument in the hands of science itself, to aid in the criticism and formulation of scientific results. But it is regarded as an instrument for the extra-scientific criticism of science; that is, for the construction of a philosophic interpretation of the propositions of normal experience and of science, not based on empirical and scientific methods of analysis, but on some sort of philosophical method of analysis.

This postulate of a specialised logical-*philosophical* mode of analysis being needed in order to clarify and interpret the propositions not only of ordinary uncritical " common sense " but also of science, places the analytic philosophers, incidentally, in rather strange company.

It is not a new doctrine, nor one peculiar to logical analysis, that the empirical investigations of science need to be supplemented by some extra-scientific mode of knowledge, if the ultimate nature of things is to be revealed. This is the view, for instance, of all those theologians who hold that Faith provides some special mode of apprehension. It is also the view of all those idealists who, in the words of Russell, hold that " a-priori reasoning can reveal otherwise undiscoverable secrets about the universe."

The assumption that some purely philosophical investigation of the nature of things was needed, over and above the mode of investigation carried out by science, was criticised long ago by Engels, in connection with the German " naturphilosophie " or " philosophy of nature," which also based itself on this assumption.

The advance of natural science itself, Engels wrote, means that it " no longer needs any philosophy standing above the sciences."[1] And : " Today," he wrote, " when one needs to comprehend the results of natural scientific investigation only . . . in the sense of their own inter-connections in order to arrive at a ' system of nature ' sufficient for our own time . . . this natural philosophy is finally disposed of. Every attempt at resurrecting it would be not only superfluous but a step backwards."[2] That was written in 1888. But if it was true then, it is truer still now.

The logical-analytic philosophers, then, with their postulate of some extra-scientific non-empirical mode of logical-philosophical analysis, call on us to leave the path of science, where all hypotheses and analyses are founded on observation and verified by experience, and to embark on dubious philosophical adventures. Instead of investigating the real world, we are to " construct a world " out of supposedly logically ultimate elements. The " method of analysis " is, in fact, no method of analysis at all, but rather a method of speculation.

---

[1] Engels : *Anti-Dühring*, p. 32.

[2] Engels : *Feuerbach*, p. 57.

Indeed, this fact results from the very mathematical constructions in which the " method of analysis " had its first origins.

Russell's derivation of mathematics from logic made its start in the conception of the world as consisting of individuals, with their qualities and relations. Thence he defined " classes," thence " classes of classes," thence the natural numbers, thence the rational numbers, thence the real numbers, thence the imaginary or complex numbers, and so on. The whole of mathematics was represented as a logical construction, proceeding from definition to definition, a purely speculative enterprise, divorced from the real world, from real quantities and motions and relationships. In the same way, if Russell's projected philosophical analysis could be carried out, then starting from the ultimate simple data—whether these are sense-data or whatever they might be—then a world would be constructed by a series of definitions, by an enterprise of philosophical speculation, absolutely unrelated to investigation of the real world.

Such speculations are always barren ; and because they cannot be tested or verified, once embarked upon they always lead to endless empty arguments without conclusion.

This indeed is already the fate of Russell's mathematical speculation itself. Logical and mathematical criticism has led to the conclusion that a system of mathematics cannot be deduced from logic, in the way that Russell attempted. In attempting such a deduction, Russell was compelled to introduce into his " system " several " axioms " and " postulates " for which no justification whatever can be found. And moreover it has been shown that no such set of axioms can be proved to be free of contradiction, a consequence fatal for any " formal system " such as that attempted by Russell. So we are as far away as ever from possessing even a logical analysis of mathematical knowledge, let alone of the whole mass of empirical and scientific knowledge.

Thus in the sphere of mathematics also, it will not do to carry out a logical analysis, attempting to construct a system of pure mathematics by a chain of speculative definitions. To elucidate the foundations of mathematics it is rather necessary to show how mathematics is derived from the investigation of real quantities and figures and motions : thus alone can we arrive at a conception of what mathematics is truly about, and what is the subject matter it is studying.

The purely speculative character of logical analysis, its absolute inability to arrive at any verifiable conclusions, its whole tendency to lead away from the path of knowledge into the path of empty argument about words, can be further exemplified by the writings of other " analytic philosophers," who followed the lead of Russell, but tried to improve upon Russell's own conclusions.

6. " *Common Sense* " *gets into difficulties*

In an article entitled *A Defence of Common Sense*,[1] G. E. Moore remarked : " I am not at all sceptical as to the truth of . . . propositions which assert the existence of material things : on the contrary, I hold that we all know, with certainty, many such propositions to be true. But I am very sceptical as to what, in certain respects, the correct analysis of such propositions is."

He continued : " It seems to me a surprising thing that so few philosophers . . . have attempted to give a clear account as to what precisely they suppose themselves to know, or to judge . . . when they know or judge such things as ' This is a hand,' ' That is the sun,' ' This is a dog,' etc., etc."

This is the familiar preamble of logical analysis. But unlike Russell, who thought he could carry his analysis straight to the ultimate elements of our knowledge of the external world, Moore approached the analysis in a most cautious and careful way.

" Two things only," he said, " seem to me to be quite certain about the analysis of such propositions (and even with regard to these I am afraid some philosophers would differ from me), namely, that whenever I know, or judge, such a proposition to be true, (1) there is always some *sense-datum* about which the proposition in question is a proposition . . . and (2) that, nevertheless, *what* I am knowing or judging to be true about this sense-datum is not (in general) that it is *itself* a hand, or a dog, or the sun, etc., etc., as the case may be."

After some explanation of the term " sense-datum," Moore

[1] In *Contemporary British Philosophy*, Second Series.

raised the question of completing the analysis. And immediately he got into inextricable difficulties, in the midst of which Engels' words prove very relevant :—" But sound *common sense*, respectable fellow as he is within the homely precincts of his own four walls, has most wonderful adventures as soon as he ventures out into the wide world . . ."—as soon as he gets involved in analysis.

" There seem to me," said Moore, " to be three, and only three, alternative types of answer possible ; and to any answer yet suggested, of any of these types, there seem to me to be very grave objections."

Here are the three types of analysis :—

(1) " What I am knowing really is that the sense-datum *itself* is part of the surface of a human hand."

(2) The second type of analysis is far more complicated. " When I know ' This is part of the surface of a human hand,' what I am knowing with regard to the sense-datum which is *of* that surface is . . . something of the following kind. There is some relation, R, such that what I am knowing with regard to the sense-datum is either : ' There is one and only one thing, of which it is true both that it is a part of the surface of a human hand, and it has R to this sense-datum,' or else : ' There are a set of things, of which it is true both that that set, taken collectively, are part of the surface of a human hand, and also that each member of the set has *R* to this sense-datum, and that nothing which is not a member of the set has *R* to it.' "

(3) " What I am knowing with regard to the sense-datum which is the principal subject of the fact is . . . a whole set of hypothetical facts, each of which is a fact of the form : ' If *these* conditions had been fulfilled, I should have been perceiving a sense-datum intrinsically related to *this* sense-datum in *this* way,' ' If *these* (other) conditions had been fulfilled, I should have been perceiving a sense-datum intrinsically related to *this* sense-datum in *this* (other) way,' etc., etc."

If Moore's three types of analysis have been understood, it will be perceived that the third type roughly corresponds to the philosophy of Berkeley and Hume ; the second type roughly corresponds to the philosophy of Locke ; while the first, and simpler, type roughly corresponds to the philosophy of Mach.

This first and simplest type of analysis was the type of analysis worked out by Russell, which I examined in the first section of this chapter. Moore quite correctly pointed out that several other analyses were equally possible ; " but as to what is the correct analysis . . . there seems to me to be the *gravest doubt*." And there he leaves the matter. Nor has he resolved these doubts in other of his several published attempts at philosophical analysis.

The position is, therefore, that when the analytic philosopher sits down to do a philosophical analysis, all sorts of different analyses, each more complicated and far-fetched than the last, present themselves ; but the method gives no means whatever for deciding which of them, if any, is the right one, that is, the one which actually corresponds with the facts.

Mr. Wisdom, in fact, in one of his attempts to describe this method, went so far as to say : " We must put the philosophic stimulus in the form, not of a question, but of a prayer—Please give me clearer apprehension of the Arrangement of the Elements in the Fact finally located by the sentence, ' aRb.' "[1] According to Mr. Wisdom, therefore, those who feel " stimulated " to undertake philosophical analysis must seek for truth in prayer ; there is no other way, and the " armchair philosopher " finds himself resting on his knees, rather than on the more usual support of such philosophers. But it is to be feared that even God cannot give him " apprehension " of the " Elements."

Thus on the showing of the analytic philosophers themselves, the logical-analytic method contains no germ of a method for reaching philosophical truth. On the contrary, it is productive merely of baseless and endless speculations.

7. *The Philosophical-Social Tendency of Logical Analysis*

Some years ago Sir James Jeans and the late Sir Arthur Eddington wrote popular books on the interpretation of the results of physical science. But instead of showing to the public how modern science was succeeding in unravelling " the riddle of the universe " and was advancing our knowledge of the constitution of matter and its laws of motion, Jeans and

[1] J. Wisdom : " Ostentation," in *Psyche*, vol. xiii.

Eddington declared that the further the technique of physics advanced, the more mysterious and unknowable did the nature of the real world appear to be. Thus Jeans entitled his book, *The Mysterious Universe*, while Eddington wrote: "Something unknown is doing we don't know what—that is what our theory amounts to."[1]

Analytic philosophers have pointed out that these writings of Jeans and Eddington were extremely muddled and lacking in clear logical analysis. This was very true. And yet the philosophical activity of logical analysis is itself very closely related indeed to the philosophical activity of Jeans and Eddington. They are just two sides of the same process.

Logical-philosophical analysis does for the sophisticated and scientific elite what the crude idealism of Jeans and Eddington did for the unsophisticated general public; namely, it obscures for them the fact that scientific advance is steadily building up a clear materialistic picture of the world, and encourages instead a vague and baseless speculation about "what things are really like," what "lies behind" our empirical knowledge.

It is in this way that logical-analytic philosophy inherits and continues to play the very same philosophical-social role as was played by the philosophy of Berkeley and the others who followed after him.

In the present century, tremendous new advances have been won in all spheres of natural science, particularly in the basic science of physics. People have spoken of "a revolution in natural science." The old mechanistic physics has been superseded; there is a wider completer synthesis of our knowledge of the constitution and laws of motion of matter, and this increased knowledge is at the same time increased power to utilise natural forces for our own ends.

But the same tendency which arose in the 18th century in regard to science continues to operate today. A scientific view of the world cannot be accepted. It contradicts too harshly the traditional notions of a class society. It shows too plainly how, having gained ever wider objective knowledge, men could combine to utilise the mastery over nature which this gives in the interests of the whole of the people. While the uninformed millions remain in relative ignorance and

[1] Eddington: *The Nature of the Physical World*, p. 291.

continue to be doped by varied forms of superstition and irrational teachings, those who are versed in scientific knowledge draw back from the consequences of the advance of science. They begin to philosophise, to interpret, to analyse, to speculate. This is the social significance of the philosophical method of logical analysis.

Corresponding to the advancement of science, and to the generality of its basic theories and the wide extension of its development and applications, the philosophical interpretation of our knowledge by logical analysis takes on an extraordinarily abstract form, plunges into the most complicated speculations, and makes use of pseudo-scientific and pseudo-mathematical expressions in order to construct a world of metaphysical speculation.

In all essentials this speculation is simply a continuation under modern conditions of the old philosophy of Berkeley, Hume, Mach and the rest, which pretends to give an extra-scientific interpretation of the results of science. Whether science is interpreted in terms of "sensations and ideas," or of "elements," "sense-data," or any other of the philosophic concepts in use today, the upshot is the same: to *reject* the clear objective import of scientific knowledge, as an ever-developing and ever more accurate comprehensive picture of the objective world; to obscure the fact that we have gained and are gaining objective knowledge in relation to which we need, not a speculative interpretation, but an understanding of how to apply it fully to gain a mastery over nature and over our own destinies.

CHAPTER 8

LOGICAL ATOMISM

1. *Logical Form*

A SURVEY of the logical-analytic method needs to be supplemented by some examination of the conceptions of formal logic which provided its basis, and of which it made use in carrying out its attempted "analyses." "Logic," said Russell, "is the essence of philosophy."[1] The speculations and interpretations of knowledge worked out by analytic philosophers all make use of the Russellian system of logic, and the attempts to construct a world by methods of analysis are attempts to construct a world conforming to the postulates of that logic.

Fundamental for Russell's view of logic, and for the whole logic of the modern logical schools, is the idea of *logical form*.

"In every proposition and in every inference," Russell explained, "there is, besides the particular subject matter concerned, a certain *form*, a way in which the constituents of the proposition or inference are put together."[2]

He proceeded to explain by examples what he meant by *the form* of a proposition.

"If I say 'Socrates is mortal,' 'Jones is angry,' 'the sun is hot,' there is something in common in these three cases, something indicated by the word 'is.' What is in common is the *form* of the proposition, not an actual constituent. If I say a number of things about Socrates—that he was an Athenian, that he married Xantippe, that he drank the hemlock—there is a common constituent, namely Socrates, in all the propositions I enunciate, but they have diverse forms. If, on the other hand, I take any one of these propositions and replace its constituents, one at a time, by other constituents, the form remains constant, but no constituent remains. Take (say) the series of propositions, 'Socrates

[1] Russell: *Our Knowledge of the External World*, ch. 2.

[2] Ibid., p. 42.

drank the hemlock,' 'Coleridge drank the hemlock,' 'Coleridge drank opium,' 'Coleridge ate opium.' The form remains unchanged throughout this series, but all the constituents are altered. Thus form is not another constituent, but is the way the constituents are put together. It is forms, in this sense, that are the proper objects of philosophical logic."[1]

To this must be added, that the logical form of a proposition is not necessarily expressed adequately by the form of words in which the proposition is usually expressed in ordinary speech or writing.

Take, for instance, these three propositions :—

"Socrates is mortal."

"The philosopher who drank the hemlock is mortal."

"All men are mortal."

They all appear, linguistically, to have the same form, namely, the subject-predicate form. Linguistically, it would appear that these three propositions each assert the predicate "mortal" of the respective subjects, "Socrates," "the philosopher who drank the hemlock," and "all men."

Such was, indeed, the view of Aristotle, who thought all propositions were of a subject-predicate form. But Russell was at pains to point out that this is not the case.

Thus Russell would contend that, of the three propositions mentioned above, only the first is a simple subject-predicate proposition ; the third is a generalisation, and the second is another form of proposition involving a "description." All three propositions are of different logical forms, though this may not appear in their ordinary verbal expression.

Thus in the first proposition, "Socrates" *stands for* a certain individual, a man, and "mortal" *stands for* a certain property, which is predicated of that individual. It is a genuine subject-predicate proposition. But in the second proposition, the *description*, "the philosopher who drank the hemlock," does *not* stand for an individual, in the way that a *name*, such as "Socrates," stands for an individual. (This is shown by the fact that we can formulate descriptions of things which do not exist ; obviously such descriptions could "stand for"—nothing.) Thus, in point of logical form, the second

[1] Russell : *Our Knowledge of the External World*, pp. 42, 43.

proposition does *not* predicate any property of an individual subject. Its correct logical form will rather be revealed by re-wording it in an expanded form, thus: "There exists an individual, such that he is a philosopher, he drank hemlock, and that individual is mortal." So again with the third proposition. The phrase "All men" does *not* denote *an individual subject*, like the name "Socrates." The correct logical form of "All men are mortal" will only be revealed by re-wording it, thus: "For every individual, if he is a man, then he is mortal."

From this Russell drew the conclusion that normal linguistic expression often conceals and confuses, rather than reveals and makes manifest, the logical form of the propositions it is intended to express.

It follows that when we come to philosophise about our knowledge, this fact inevitably gives rise to many errors, unless we are aware of it. And most traditional philosophy, according to Russell, consisted of just such errors. On the other hand, such errors are corrected, and philosophy finds its true vocation, in the process of logical analysis—subjecting our knowledge to logical analysis which reveals the correct logical form of the propositions which we know. Such logical analysis needs to have as its main instrument a logical theory of the nature of propositions and of the different forms of propositions.

2. *Analysis of the Forms of Propositions*

In his works on formal logic, and notably in the *Principia Mathematica*, Russell worked out the main series of the logical forms of propositions. His work in this sphere was further perfected by Wittgenstein, in his *Tractatus Logico-Philosophicus*.

The three main forms of propositions (according to this analysis) are:—(1) Elementary Propositions, (2) Truth-Functions of Elementary Propositions, (3) Generalisations. The basic conception is that of an Elementary Proposition, and all the other forms of propositions are derivable from Elementary Propositions by a series of simple logical operations. I shall deal here only with so much of the Russell logic as is strictly necessary to understand the philosophical superstructure which has been erected on the basis of this analysis.

(1) *Elementary Propositions*

The simplest form of elementary proposition (according to this analysis) is the simple subject-predicate form, which we may express :—

s is p.

Here s stands for any simple subject, and p for any simple predicate that may belong to it. For instance :—

" This is red,"
" Socrates is mortal,"
" Churchill is mortal."

The simplest form of elementary proposition, then, asserts a characteristic of a single individual. The next form asserts a relation between two individuals. Thus we get a second form of elementary proposition :—

a R b

where a and b are individuals, and R is some relation between them. For instance :—

" This is redder than that,"
" Churchill conferred with Stalin."

But there can be relations between more than two individuals. This is immediately apparent in the example of Churchill. For instance :—

" Churchill conferred with Stalin,"
" Churchill conferred with Stalin and Roosevelt,"
" Churchill conferred with Stalin, Roosevelt and Chiang-Kai-Shek."

These are all elementary propositions, but the first expresses a relation between two terms, the second between three terms, and the third between four terms. There is in fact no limit to the number of terms that can enter into a relationship. To carry forward the same type of example : suppose an organisation holds a conference attended by 1,000 delegates ; here there are 1,000 people conferring together, in other words, a relationship between 1,000 terms.

It will now be convenient to introduce a different symbolism for expressing the forms of elementary propositions. Instead of writing as above " a R b," we shall adopt the familiar functional symbolism of mathematics, and use it in logic. Thus we shall write :—

$$R\ (x, y)$$
$$R\ (x, y, z)$$
$$R\ (x, y, z\ .\ .\ .)$$

for any number of terms. And similarly, instead of " s is p," we can just write the " function " :—

$$f\ (x).$$

Such expressions as these Russell called " Propositional Functions." Thus f (x), R (x, y), etc., do not assert anything, and are not themselves propositions ; but when values are given to the variable symbols contained in these functional expressions, then the result is an elementary proposition of a certain form, for instance : " Churchill is mortal," and " Churchill conferred with Stalin."

Thus the propositional function expresses the pure logical form of a proposition. And thus finally we may represent the series of elementary forms of propositions by means of the series of propositional functions :—

$$f\ (x),\ f\ (x_1, x_2),\ f\ (x_1, x_2, x_3),\ f\ (x_1, x_2, x_3\ .\ .\ .x_n),\ .\ .\ .$$

The invention of the propositional function was of great importance in Russell's development of logical theory.

(2) *Truth Functions*

Now comes another series of forms of propositions. Let us express elementary propositions, of whatever forms, by the variables " p," " q." Then at once we discover a new form of proposition, which is obtained by the simple and familiar operation of negation. This is the negative proposition, which is just simply the denial of an elementary proposition. For example : " Churchill is not mortal," " Churchill did not confer with Stalin," or " This is not red." The form of all such negative propositions is expressed in the simple functional expression :—

" not-p."

A proposition of the form " not-p " can obviously be

defined as a proposition which is true when " p " is false, and false when " p " is true.

Thus a proposition of the form " not-p " can be very aptly termed a " Truth Function." For it can be defined in terms of the truth or falsity of the elementary proposition from which it is constructed.

Thus we find the beginning of a new series of forms of propositions, which are not in form elementary propositions at all, but are of a higher form—truth functions of elementary propositions.

The negative form of proposition, " not-p," is, then, the simplest form of truth function. But the continuation of the same operation whereby " not-p " was derived from the elementary proposition, " p," will simply restore again the original proposition, " p." Thus " not-not-p " is exactly the same as " p." But if now, instead of operating with only the one elementary proposition, " p," we take two, " p " and " q," we can again obtain further forms of truth functions—for example, compound propositions of the forms:—

" p implies q,"

" either p or q,"

" not both p and q,"

" p and q."

Logicians have given many accounts of such compound propositions. But according to Russell they are simply truth functions. According to Russell, and this thesis was developed in detail by Wittgenstein, such forms of compound propositions can be defined exclusively in terms of the truth or falsity of the elementary propositions from which they are constructed.

Thus, just as " not-p " can be defined as the proposition which is true when " p " is false and false when " p " is true, so, for example, can " p implies q " be defined as the proposition which is false when " p " is true but " q " is false, but which otherwise is true. Thus " p implies q " says that, as a matter of fact, whenever " p " is true, " q " is true as well. All that it says can be defined in terms of the truth or falsity of the elementary propositions which are its constituents, or from which it is constructed. Again, " p and q " can be defined as the proposition which is true when " p " is true and " q " is true, but which otherwise is false. And so on.

There is no need to go into detail about all the truth functions which can now be constructed ; for quite clearly, we can now construct truth functions of any order of complexity.[1]

It is interesting to note, however, certain consequences which follow from this logical analysis of truth functions.

Thus in the first place, certain forms of expressions turn out to be exactly equivalent one with another. For example, " not both p and q " and " p implies not-q." If we work out the definition of these two expressions in terms of the truth or falsity of their constituents, " p " and " q," we will find that the result is the same in both cases—namely, both these compound expressions are defined as being false when " p " and " q " are both true, but otherwise as being true. They are therefore exactly equivalent. Hence there are many different ways of expressing exactly the same proposition. The equivalence of " not-not-p " with " p " is another example.

And further, this logical analysis claims to throw considerable light upon the logical nature of deductive inference.

For instance, if I know that " p implies q," and that " q implies r," I can infer deductively that " p implies r." If I have established the first two propositions, no further investigation is needed to establish the third. This is explained from the fact that, if I work out the logical conditions for the truth of " p implies q " and " q implies r," I will find that these conditions include the conditions for the truth of " p implies r." Therefore, if I have discovered from observation that " p implies q " and that " q implies r," it needs no further observation to discover that " p implies r," for this is contained in what I have discovered already.

(3) *Generalisations*

Thirdly, by further operations with either elementary propositional functions or with truth functions, we arrive at a further series of forms of propositions, which may be called " generalisations."

[1] In *Principia Mathematica* Russell includes truth functions as "elementary" propositions. He calls them "molecular" as distinct from "atomic."

There are two types of generalisations, or two operations by means of which generalisations may be constructed :—

(i) The assertion of something of *every* x.
(ii) The assertion of something of *some* x, or of at least one x.

Let us take a propositional function, f (x). Then we can obtain generalisations from it by asserting : (i) of every x, that f (x) ; (ii) of some x's, or of at least one x, that f (x). Let us express these generalisations :—

(i) (x). f (x)
(ii) (∃x). f (x)

Two examples of such generalisations are : " All men are mortal," and " Some men are philosophers." How these two propositions are examples of the general form of propositions can be seen by writing them :—

(x). x is a man implies x is mortal.
(∃x). x is a man and x is a philosopher.

Clearly, generalisations of any order of complexity can now be obtained from propositional functions by means of the two simple operations " for every x " and " there is an x," expressed by the operators (x) and (∃x.).

Such, then, is the catalogue or classification of the forms of propositions according to the Russell-Wittgenstein logic. It will be seen that all the forms are obtainable by means of a few simple logical operations from the elementary propositional function.

Before proceeding further, two remarks may be made on some consequences of this theory of generalisations.

First of all, the logical expansion, or re-writing, of " All men are mortal," as " For every x, x is a man implies x is mortal," provides a good example of the way Russell thought logical analysis cleared up philosophical confusions. Thus if a philosopher were to think—as many have thought—that " All men are mortal " was not a generalisation, but a proposition of a subject-predicate form, then he may be led to suppose that, besides particular men, there also exists a very mysterious sort of object, namely, " all men," or " the class " of men. Thus as well as Tom, Dick and Harry, he will postulate a transcendent reality, Mankind, or something of that sort, and will begin to spin out many strange and misleading theories about it. But if such a philosopher can only be brought to understand the correct logical analysis of " All men are mortal," then he will see that the only things it refers to are particular concrete individuals, with their characteristics and properties, and that his supposed " all men " or " the class of men " or " mankind " is a mere fiction, that disappears in analysis.

Secondly, if we ask : on what does the *truth* of a generalisation depend, the answer is that its truth depends entirely on the truth or falsity of the elementary propositions which are its *instances*.

Just as the truth of a truth function depended on the truth or falsity of the elementary propositions which were its constituents, so the truth of a generalisation depends on the truth or falsity of the elementary propositions which are its instances.

In general, then, the truth of every form of proposition depends on the truth of elementary propositions ; for the higher forms of propositions are only constructed by means of logical operations with elementary propositions.

For example, the truth of the generalisation " All men are mortal," depends on that of a whole series of elementary propositions, which can be called the instances of that generalisation ; thus, " Tom is mortal," " Dick is mortal," " Harry is mortal," " Churchill is mortal," " Stalin is mortal," and so on.

Thus if we want to establish the truth of any generalisation, we can only do so by, as it were, turning up all its instances, to find if they are true. Thus, to establish that all men are mortal, we must establish that Tom died, that Dick died, that Harry died, and so on for all men. But as there is very often no limit to the number of instances of a generalisation, and as a generalisation very often continually refers into the future, so that in however many instances we might verify it, fresh verification will always be required, it follows, that not only is it often practically impossible to establish the truth of a generalisation, but it is often logically impossible as well. Thus truth, in an absolute and unconditional sense, does not apply to generalisations, as it applies to elementary propositions.

This can be expressed by saying that generalisations are not strictly speaking propositions at all, as understood by those traditional logicians who define a proposition as " that which is either true or false " ; but they are rather of the nature of formulæ, or rules, or predictions, for saying which elementary propositions may be expected to be true.

This has an obvious application to the propositions of science. For instance, the law of gravitation is not an absolute truth, but it is rather of the nature of a useful rule for the construction of a number of elementary propositions, each one of which will tell us the particular gravitational attraction to be found operating in a particular system of bodies.

3. *What is a Proposition ?—The Pictorial Theory*

I have now attempted to demonstrate the elements of the logical apparatus by means of which Russell proposed to reform philosophy, and to solve philosophical problems, by the method of logical-philosophical analysis. But it will be found that this apparatus at once begins to produce some strange results.

Everyone familiar with logical theory must agree that the Russell system of formal logic represented a significant advance, as compared with the traditional Aristotelian logic. For Aristotle, all propositions were subject-predicate propositions, and all inference was syllogistic. Russell's analysis provided a far more comprehensive theory of the forms of propositions and of deductive inference.

In taking the subject-predicate form as the essential form of all propositions, Aristotle was regarding the main function of propositions as being the subsumption of individuals within a class. His logic corresponded to the level of development of the science of his time, which still moved to a great extent within the stage of classification. Russell, rather more than 2,000 years later, was concerned with the development of a system of formal logic which would embrace, not merely the classification of things within their appropriate classes, but the relations between things, and their dependence one on another. Hence his insistence on the " propositional function " " R (x, y . . .) " as being the typical form of elementary proposition, rather than the simple Aristotelian " S is P " ; his development of the theory of truth functions ; and his theory of generalisations, involving the use of the mathematical idea of variable terms.

But nevertheless, in carrying out this extension and elaboration of logical theory, Russell's logic remains within the Aristotelian tradition. For both, a proposition is essentially an arrangement of terms whose logical nature is defined by the Aristotelian laws of Identity, Non-Contradiction and Excluded Middle. That is to say, if A is the object denoted by any term, then A is just exactly A and not anything else, we cannot have both A and not-A, and we must have either A or not-A. For Aristotle, the world consisted of fixed individual things, each and all of which could be classified according to its definite properties. Russell, in carrying out his elaboration of logical theory, does not overcome this metaphysical standpoint. If Russell writes " R (x, y . . .) " then " x " and " y " stand for definite individual things, and " R " for a fixed relationship which does or does not hold between them.

Thus the Russell logic, like the Aristotelian, involves far-reaching " metaphysical " presuppositions and " metaphysical " implications.

For the logical theory is based on a certain view of the nature of a proposition, and its correspondence with what it signifies. A proposition is a definite arrangement of terms, and those terms stand for definite objects—for individuals, their characters and relations. If a term does not stand for an object, then it can be given no meaning in the proposition. The objects are combined in fact in a definite way : individuals are related by certain relations and not by others, an individual has a certain character and not another character. If the terms in the proposition are combined in a way corresponding to that in which the objects that they stand for are combined in fact, then the proposition is true ; and otherwise it is false.

The development of the theory, implicit in the Russell logic, of the nature of propositions and of their correspondence with facts (or of truth and falsity) has been most clearly and consistently developed by Wittgenstein, in his *Tractatus Logico-Philosophicus*.

Dealing particularly with the basic form of proposition, the elementary proposition, Wittgenstein said that *a proposition is a picture of a fact.*

"We make to ourselves pictures of facts," he said. "The elements in the picture stand, in the picture, for the objects. That the elements of the picture are combined with one another in a definite way, represents that the things are so combined with one another."[1]

He went on to explain that: "What every picture, of whatever form, must have in common with reality in order to be able to represent it at all—rightly or falsely—is the logical form, that is, the form of reality."[2]

Thus: "The picture agrees with reality or not; it is right or wrong, true or false."[3]

And: "In order to discover whether the picture is true or false we must compare it with reality. It cannot be discovered from the picture alone whether it is true or false."[4]

He went on to say that: "The logical picture of the fact is the thought." And: "The thought is the significant proposition."[5]

So the (elementary) proposition is a certain arrangement of terms; and that the terms are arranged in a certain way in the proposition, says that the objects which those terms signify are correspondingly arranged in the fact. If the objects are so arranged in fact, the proposition is true; otherwise it is false.

Such is the simple, and, to use a mathematical phrase, elegant, theory of the nature and signification, or truth and falsity, of propositions, which is implicit in and results from the formal logical analysis.

A proposition is a picture of a fact, and the relation between proposition and fact is a pictorial relation.

This seems to accord with the very strictest empiricism. Whether a proposition is true or false must be discovered by examining the facts. "There is no picture which is a-priori true."[6]

[1] Wittgenstein: *Tractatus Logico-Philosophicus*, 2.131.15.
[2] Ibid., 2.18.
[3] Ibid., 2.21.
[4] Ibid., 2.223.224.
[5] Ibid., 3, 4.
[6] Ibid., 2.225.

But for all that, the pictorial theory entails consequences respecting the nature of facts ; more exactly, consequences respecting the " logical structure " of facts, the " logical structure " of the world. Having begun with the forms of propositions, we find ourselves dealing with " the form " of the world. We began with logic, but it has led into metaphysics.

4. *Logical Atomism—a system of metaphysics*

From a logical analysis of propositions, Wittgenstein, in complete accordance with the Russell logic, arrived at a logical analysis of the form of the world. (In his *Tractatus* he started with the latter analysis, which is one of the things that makes this book unnecessarily hard to understand.)

" The world is everything that is the case," said Wittgenstein, and went on to explain what he meant by this. " The world is the totality of facts, not of things. The world divides into facts. Any one can either be the case, or not be the case, and everything else remain the same."[1]

Just as the elementary propositions are the basic sort of propositions, from which all other forms of propositions can be constructed, so, corresponding to the elementary propositions, and " pictured " by them, there are elementary—or " atomic " —facts. Each is logically independent of every other.

And so the logical-metaphysical analysis continues :

" What is the case, the fact, is the existence of atomic facts. The totality of existent atomic facts is the world. Atomic facts are independent of one another. From the existence or non-existence of an atomic fact we cannot infer the existence or non-existence of another."[2]

And just as elementary propositions are combinations of terms, so atomic facts are combinations of objects. And just as the terms by themselves have no meaning except in so far as they can be combined in propositions, so the objects have no existence apart from their combination in facts.

" An atomic fact is a combination of objects (entities, things). It is essential to a thing that it can be a constituent part of an atomic fact."[3]

---

[1] Wittgenstein : *Tractatus Logico-Philosophicus*, 1.1.2.21.
[2] Ibid., 2.04.061.062.
[3] Ibid., 2.01.011.

Further : " The object is simple. Objects form the substance of the world. Therefore they cannot be compound." And : " In the atomic facts objects hang one in another, like the members of a chain. In the atomic fact the objects are combined in a definite way. The way in which the objects hang together in the atomic fact is the structure of the atomic fact."[1]

Turning back now to Russell, the same view of " the nature of the world " is to be found expressed in more popular and easily comprehensible—if less " scientifically accurate "—language :

" The existing world consists of many things with many qualities and relations. A complete description of the existing world would require not only a catalogue of the things, but also a mention of all their qualities and relations. We should have to know, not only this, that and the other thing, but also which was red, which yellow, which was earlier than which, which was between which two others, and so on. When I speak of a ' fact,' I do not mean one of the simple things in the world ; I mean that a certain thing has a certain quality, or that certain things have a certain relation."[2]

It emerges, therefore, from the logical theory of the forms of propositions, which postulates the elementary proposition as the basic form of proposition, and as a picture of the fact, that the world itself is of a certain form. The world consists of " atomic facts," each of which is independent of every other. And the constituents of these " atomic facts " are " simple objects."

This general view of the basic logical structure of the world, derived from formal logic, has been aptly called " Logical Atomism."

But this remarkable result was not reached by any process of generalisation from the mass of empirically verified results of science. Indeed, it has, and can claim to have, no empirical foundation whatever. It is deduced from pure logic.

It turns out, therefore, that the logicians and analytic philosophers who differentiated themselves so carefully from " the classical tradition," and who overthrew that tradition by

[1] Wittgenstein : *Tractatus Logico-Philosophicus*, 2.02.03.031.032.

[2] Russell : *Our Knowledge of the External World*, p. 51.

a Galilean revolution, have not really departed from "the classical tradition" by a single inch. Their's too is a case in which "a-priori reasoning reveals otherwise undiscoverable secrets about the universe." For by no other method could they have discovered such a "secret" as that the universe consists of simple objects, arranged in atomic facts, each of which is absolutely independent of every other.

Whether the universe is really like this is, indeed, on merely empirical evidence, more than doubtful. Observation and experiment have never yet revealed any atomic fact or simple object.

The standpoint of logical atomism, a purely metaphysical standpoint, based on no evidence but resting on pure a-priori grounds, comes out into sharp relief, and is given a clear and uncompromising formulation, as a result of the development of the Russell logic. But at the same time it is not difficult to see that this standpoint only brings out and makes explicit assumptions that were already implicit in the philosophy of pure empiricists, long before logical analysis arrived on the scene, with its "clarifying" mission.

Already when Locke defined "an idea" as "whatsoever is the object of the understanding when a man thinks," and went on to distinguish elementary simple ideas, and to regard the whole of knowledge as a compounding of simple ideas, he was preparing the way for the standpoint of logical atomism. Hume's philosophy introduced the most complete and rigid atomism as regards the objects of knowledge. For Hume the only realities we were cognisant with were analysable into simple "impressions and ideas," each independent of every other. Thus the standpoint of logical atomism, based on Russell's system of formal logic, does no more than bring out and make explicit the logic already implicit in the philosophy of pure empiricism. In the same way, the logical-analytic method of philosophy itself was seen to be no more than a repetition in new terms of the pure empiricist interpretation of our knowledge.

5. *Critique of Logical Atomism*

The standpoint of logical atomism obviously stands or falls by the concept of the elementary proposition, and of the atomic fact which is signified by an elementary proposition.

All other forms of propositions (truth functions and generalisations) are derived from elementary propositions by simply defined logical operations ; and the unique importance, in this system, of the elementary proposition can be seen in the following way.

It is clear that (from the standpoint of logical atomism) *everything* that is the case, the *whole* truth about the world, is expressible in a set, or in a series, of elementary propositions. An enumeration of all true elementary propositions would be a complete picture of the world, of all facts, and would leave nothing else to be said. It would be found that the truth of all other true propositions—truth functions and generalisations—was already contained in that of the elementary propositions.

For instance, imagine a very simple " world," answering to the basic postulates of logical atomism, and having as its constituent " objects " just two individuals, called " a " and " b," two qualities, called " p " and " q," and one relation, called " R."

Suppose further that the following elementary propositions are true of this world :

" a is p,"
" b is q,"
" a is R to b,"
" b is R to a."

For instance : " a is red, b is green, a is unlike b and b is unlike a."

Then, having enunciated these elementary propositions, we have a complete picture of the world. Nothing further that may be said will add anything new to the picture.

For, having enunciated these elementary propositions, the truth of a number of truth functions and generalisations about the world can be immediately deduced : it can be deduced because all that these truth functions and generalisations have to say about the world is already contained in the elementary propositions. The same few atomic facts which make true the elementary propositions, also make true the truth functions and generalisations.

For example, here are some of these truth functions and generalisations :

> " a is not q,"
> " b is not p,"
> " a is p and b is q,"
> " a is p implies a is not q,"
> " for every x, x is p implies x is not q,"
> " there is an x, x is p and x is not q,"
> " for every x, y, xRy implies yRx."

Or : " a is not green ; b is not red ; a is red and b is green ; that a is red implies that a is not green ; if anything is red, then it is not green ; there exists at least one individual, such that it is red and not green ; for any two individuals, x and y, if x is unlike y then y is unlike x."

The example of this very simple " world," which just consists of four atomic facts, and the complete truth about which is accordingly expressible in four elementary propositions, can be generalised for the case of any world that consists of atomic facts, however many such facts may be the case in it. The complete truth about the world, according to logical atomism, is expressible in elementary propositions.

Such being the conclusion of logical atomism, which absolutely certainly and infallibly follows from the Russell-Wittgenstein system of formal logic, it is necessary to apply this conclusion in the domain of our actual knowledge, in order to see what progress can be made in expressing known facts in the form of elementary propositions. Having, so to speak, completed the process of construction in the shipyard of logical theory, it is necessary to launch the logical ship upon the ocean of actual experience. But when this launching is carried out, it is found that the ship is so constructed as to be unseaworthy and it immediately sinks and disappears.

The complete truth about the world is expressible in elementary propositions. If that is really so, then let us proceed to express it, or at least a part of it, in elementary propositions, bearing in mind that an elementary proposition is one which is (*a*) logically independent of any other proposition, and (*b*) is the statement of an atomic fact. Can this enterprise be carried out ? The answer is that it cannot.

Not much help is to be received from the actual exponents of logical atomism, for they have never thought it necessary to furnish even a single example of an elementary proposition. For my part, I have often searched, and searched in vain, both in my inner consciousness and in my consciousness of the outside world, for an elementary proposition. But I have never found one. And reflection shows that no one else is likely to be more fortunate.

Take for instance propositions about material objects—" This flower is red," " This stone is heavy," " This man is fat," etc. ; or : " This is a flower," " This is a stone," " This is a man." Such propositions are certainly expressed in the elementary form, " s is p " ; but they are not absolutely elementary propositions. They certainly do not state atomic facts ; they are not logically independent of any other propositions. For things like flowers and stones and men, and their qualities like being red and being heavy and being fat, are not simple and unanalysable things and qualities ; so facts involving such things and their qualities, and propositions stating such facts, are neither atomic nor elementary, in the logically absolute sense.

Is the case any better if we try to deal with propositions, not about things on the ordinary perceptual level, but about the ultimate constituents of the material world ? No, this line of research holds out no hopes for the seeker after elementary propositions. The most ultimate constituents of the material world that have been discovered up to the present consist of things like electrons ; but we cannot formulate elementary propositions about them. We cannot say, " this electron," and pin that name on to one particular simple and unanalysable individual ; and even if we could, we could not ascribe simple and unanalysable qualities and relations to such individuals.

One line of logical thought has tried to find, not in " things " but in " events " the ultimate logical or metaphysical constituents of the world. But here again, what is to be included in one single event is altogether arbitrary, nor can precise and simple qualities and relations be ascribed to events. There may be sense in a " logic of events "—but it could not be an atomistic logic. In the search for something logically-metaphysically simple and ultimate, " events " are sometimes whittled down to "point-events," or "point-instants"; and the ultimate elementary propositions would then be infinite in number, expressing the ultimate qualities and relations attached to every point-instant in the total system of space-time. But yet it is clear that point-instants, and the properties of matter at a point-instant, are not ultimate logical-metaphysical constituents of the world, but could only be defined by means of an elaborate process of mathematical analysis.[1] No elementary propositions about point-instants could possibly be formulated.

In general, then, the conclusion emerges that no proposition about the material world, and material objects, as ordinarily understood, can possibly be a logically elementary proposition, in the sense required by logical atomism.

But can we perhaps formulate elementary propositions which refer, not to the objective material world, but to the content of one's own immediate experience?

The hunt for elementary propositions is very like the Hunting of the Snark. We must seek them "in some place unfrequented by man"; since in general people do not formulate propositions exclusively about their own immediate experiences.

Suppose then I say, "I am seeing something red." Can a proposition such as this be a logically elementary proposition? Evidently not: for even if "something red" can be regarded as an ultimate constituent of the world of experience, the term "I" and the relation of "seeing" cannot possibly be regarded as ultimate, simple and unanalysable. An elementary proposition which refers to immediate experience would have rather to be sought in such expressions as: "Red here-now"; where "red" stands for the simple object, a colour, that I am immediately aware of, and "here-now" stands for another simple object, its position in my "visual field." Here at last, perhaps, is an absolutely elementary proposition; here at last, perhaps, the logical snark is entrapped in its lair in the regions of immediate experience.

But suppose someone really did say, "Red here-now." What would he be understood to mean? Clearly, he would be understood to mean that he was seeing something

---

[1] Cf. Whitehead: "The Method of Extensive Abstraction," explained in his two books, *The Concept of Nature* and *The Principles of Natural Knowledge*.

red ; what he would be understood to mean would be something rather indefinite, and certainly not a logically elementary proposition. So if a logical atomist were to make this remark, he would have to explain that what he would be understood to mean by it was something different from what he " really " meant ; for what he " really " meant would refer to alleged objects contained in his own immediate experience, which would be absolutely inaccessible to anyone else. So what *would* he " really " mean ? The answer is—nothing. What he would be trying to say would be something incommunicable, which is only to say that he would be saying nothing at all. Hence, just like the snark, the logically elementary proposition continues to be absolutely elusive.

I think it would be futile to hunt further for logically elementary propositions. It can be positively asserted that no one has ever produced an example of one, and any attempt to do so leads to such stupid discussions as to provide abundant proof that the whole conception is unreal and artificial. Elementary propositions, in the logically absolute sense required by logical atomism, have therefore no relevance at all to the analysis of actual processes of thought, or to the expression of actual facts about the world.

When the elementary proposition and the atomic fact turn out to be mythological creations, the bottom falls out of the system of logical atomism.

It may now be remarked that the theory of logical atomism, like all metaphysical theories, obviously takes a very simplified view of the nature of the world. It supposes that the world divides up into ultimate atomic facts. But no experience and no science has ever given us grounds for accepting such a simplified view of the world. On the contrary, it seems as if the most general characteristic of reality is change and movement, so that never, at any stage of analysis, can we claim to have reached some absolutely fixed " object " which constitutes the ultimate " substance " of the world, as Wittgenstein once expressed it. Wittgenstein said : " Objects form the substance of the world. Therefore they cannot be compound." But yet, every substance resolves into a complex of changes and motions.

Hence whenever, for some particular purpose, we can

legitimately express a certain fact in terms of a proposition which asserts that some object has a certain quality or stands in certain relations, exactly the same fact can also be expressed in other terms, in which the unity and simplicity of the object and its qualities and relations is resolved into multiplicity.

A quality can always be expressed as a relation ; relations can be expressed as qualities ; objects can be represented as complexes of processes ; processes can be represented as objects ; and so on.

None of these modes of representation is *the* truth about the world ; rather, that they are all possible, expresses the infinite multiplicity and changefulness of the world.

Further, in the changing world one event arises out of another, processes interpenetrate and modify one another, nothing exists in isolation, but everything is modified and changed by its relationships with other things. To all this the atomistic view of the world stands in strange contrast. It states in the most rigid way the original view of Hume, when he said : " All events seem entirely loose and separate. One event follows another, but we can never observe any tie between them. They seem conjoined, but never connected." The dynamic flow and interpenetration of processes which we find in the world is artificially disrupted into separate unconnected atomic events or facts, each of which is supposed to be capable of expression in a proposition logically independent of every other proposition.

Thus the thesis of logical atomism, that the whole truth about the world is expressible in elementary propositions, each expressing an atomic fact, each logically independent of every other, is completely untenable.

Further, I have already remarked above that the system of logical atomism does no more than bring out and make explicit the logic already contained in the philosophy of pure empiricism, in the philosophy of Hume in particular. It is indeed the proper logic of a philosophy of pure empiricism.

Thus for pure empiricism, the objects of our knowledge are confined to the contents of pure immediate experience. All knowledge, all truth, all scientific theories and scientific laws, are to be interpreted as referring to the order and connections of our subjective sensible experience. How is this expressed in terms of logical theory? Precisely that the totality of elementary propositions expresses the totality of the facts of pure experience; the whole superstructure of more general propositions, in the form of truth functions and generalisations, refers to no other facts.

I want to remark on one more curious consequence of this theory. Who is the knower, and the scientist, who, in the system of logical atomism, understands the elementary propositions, perceives their truth by comparing them with the atomic facts, and derives from them the general superstructure of truth functions and generalisations? Referring once again to the simple example of the "world" consisting of four atomic facts, it is very obvious in this model that the *subject* who cognises these facts does not exist *in* the world at all, but looks into the world, as it were, from *outside.* So in general, if we suppose the world to consist of atomic facts, and the whole of truth to be expressible in elementary propositions, what has been left out of the picture is the subject, the mind or ego, that formulates the picture and understands it. The knowing mind is outside the known world. The knower plays no part in the world.

Absolutely in accordance with this, Wittgenstein, in a curious passage in his *Tractatus*, says: "The thinking, presenting subject; there is no such thing. . . . The subject does not belong to the world but is a limit of the world. Where *in* the world is a metaphysical subject to be noted? You say that this case is altogether like that of the eye and the field of sight. But you do *not* really see the eye. And from nothing in the field of sight can it be concluded that it is seen from an eye. For the field of sight has not a form like this:

"[1]

I endeavoured to show in an earlier chapter how the general philosophy of pure empiricism takes a view wherein knowledge arises simply from the passive contemplation of given facts by

[1] Wittgenstein: *Tractatus Logico-Philosophicus*, 5.631.633.

the individual mind ; not from the interaction of the knowers and the known, those who gain knowledge being themselves a part of the world, and gaining knowledge through the practical activity of changing the world. In the same way the general theory of logical atomism, the logic of pure empiricism, constructs a logical model of the world which allows no place in the world for the knowing subject and his activity.

To summarise :

The whole standpoint of logical atomism (which derives all forms of propositions from the basic form of the logically elementary proposition, and which implies that the whole truth of the world is expressible in elementary propositions, each stating an atomic fact and each logically independent of every other) is untenable, because it is impossible to find any atomic fact in the world, or to formulate any elementary proposition satisfying the postulates of the logical theory.

This logic leads to and is based on a view of the known world which supposes it to divide into atomic facts—" entirely loose and separate . . . we can never observe any tie between them "—and a view of knowledge which bases it on passive contemplation and allows no place for the knower and his activity within the known world. Neither this view of the world nor this view of knowledge has any basis in actual experience. Both the one and the other are artificial abstract theoretical constructions.

CHAPTER 9

THE PHILOSOPHY OF WITTGENSTEIN

1. *Drawing a Limit to Thinking*

I HAVE already indicated something of the contribution made by Wittgenstein in the development of the logical standpoint of Russell; particularly his elaboration of the "pictorial" theory of propositions, elementary propositions being regarded as "pictures" of facts.

But if Wittgenstein, in his *Tractatus Logico-Philosophicus*, developed, sharpened and refined the basic logical conception of the proposition as employed in the Russell logic, he also thought that he could carry much further Russell's application of logical theory in the solution of the problems of philosophy.

Take, for instance, "the problem of the external world": *Is* there an external world, and if there is, of what does it consist, what are its ultimate elements? Russell thought that this problem could be answered by working out the logical analysis of propositions referring to external objects. But, as I have shown, neither he himself nor his colleagues and followers, ever succeeded in reaching agreement on any analysis which could be said to definitively answer the "problem."

In the light of his further analysis of the basic logical nature of propositions, Wittgenstein thought that such "problems" could be treated in quite another way. For instance, philosophers have argued continually as to whether propositions about material objects refer merely to the order of sensations or "sense-data," or whether they refer to independently existing objects external to consciousness or experience.

Russell would pose this as the question: Which is the right way of analysing propositions about material objects? Wittgenstein replies that if you understand the logical nature of propositions, you cannot ask such a question. A significant proposition is *a picture* of the facts, which can be *compared* with the facts to test whether it is true or false. So when one philosopher says : " This material object is a complex of sense-data," and another philosopher says : " This material object is not a complex of sense-data, but exists independent of all sense-data "—of what facts are these two assertions pictures, and how are they to be compared with facts to test which is the truth and which is falsehood ? Both assertions are revealed as pseudo-assertions, pseudo-propositions, which may appear to be significant to persons who do not understand logic, but which an understanding of logic reveals as insignificant.

The " problem of the external world," therefore, as presented by Russell and other philosophers, is not to be solved by working out either one or another " analysis " of propositions about external objects. But it is solved by showing that the whole way in which the problem is put is based on a misunderstanding of the basic logical nature of propositions ; or, as Wittgenstein expresses it, " of the logic of our language."

Thus in the Preface to his *Tractatus Logico-Philosophicus*, Wittgenstein summed up his philosophical aim as follows :—

" This book deals with the problems of philosophy and shows, as I believe, that the method of formulating these problems rests on the misunderstanding of the logic of our language. . . ."

For Wittgenstein, therefore, the task of philosophy is to analyse the logic of our language. And this means, to elucidate the logical principles which determine what forms of words are significant and what insignificant, and to elucidate the logical principles which determine what forms of questions can be significantly asked and answered, and what cannot be significantly asked, and cannot be answered.

It is in this way that he maintained that " the problems of philosophy " are " in essentials finally solved." But they are solved by showing that they are not real problems at all, because they " rest on the misunderstanding of the logic of our language." The formulation of the problems is nonsensical—and that is the answer to them.

At the end of his *Tractatus*, Wittgenstein remarked : " The right method of philosophy would be this. To say nothing except what can be said, i.e., the propositions of natural science, i.e., something that has nothing to do with philosophy.

And then always, when someone else wished to say something metaphysical, to demonstrate to him that he had given no meaning to certain signs in his propositions. This method would be unsatisfying to the other—he would not have the feeling that we were teaching him philosophy—but it would be the only strictly correct method."[1]

"What can be said," a significant proposition, is a picture of the facts, which can be compared with the facts, i.e., verified. By "something metaphysical," on the other hand, is meant a combination of words which gives no verifiable picture of the facts.

Wittgenstein says of his book, therefore, in the Preface: "The book will, therefore, *draw a limit to thinking*, or rather—not to thinking, but to the expression of thoughts. For in order to draw a limit to thinking we should have to be able to think both sides of this limit (we should therefore have to be able to think what cannot be thought). *The limit can, therefore, only be drawn in language, and what lies on the other side of the limit will be simply nonsense.*"

2. *Saying and Showing*

When Wittgenstein began to "draw a limit to thinking," however, that is to say, to "what can be said," he made a very important qualification. He drew a distinction between what can be "said," and what can be "shown."

"Propositions," he said, "can represent the whole reality, but they cannot represent what they must have in common with reality in order to be able to represent it—the logical form. . . . Propositions cannot represent the logical form: this mirrors itself in the propositions. That which mirrors itself in language, language cannot represent. That which expresses *itself* in language, *we* cannot express by language. The propositions *show* the logical form of reality. They exhibit it. . . . What *can* be shown *cannot* be said."[2]

This means that when (in philosophical mood) we may want to say "something metaphysical," although we cannot

[1] Wittgenstein: *Tractatus Logico-Philosophicus*, 6.53.
[2] Ibid., 4.12.

"say" it, nevertheless it can be "shown." We cannot "say" in significant propositions what is the "ultimate nature" of the "reality" which we picture in our thoughts. But nevertheless, if we understand "the logic of our language," and understand "the limits" of "what can be said," that which we seek vainly in speculative metaphysics will "show itself," although it cannot be "said." "The logical form of reality" cannot be "said," it is "inexpressible"; but it "shows itself."

This distinction between what is "said" by a proposition, and what is "shown," which is based on Wittgenstein's theory of propositions as pictures of reality, is of very great importance in his philosophy, as will appear more clearly in the sequel. And it is treated by him in a highly mystical fashion. Matter-of-fact and scientific as his philosophical outlook appears to be, it ends up with the claim to some mystical insight into the Real.

What can be "said" are only statements of fact, scientific statements. But: "We feel that even if all possible scientific questions be answered, the problems of life have still not been touched at all. Of course there is then no question left, and just this is the answer. The solution of the problem of life is seen in the vanishing of this problem. (Is not this the reason why men to whom after long doubting the sense of life became clear, could not then say wherein this sense consisted?) There is indeed the inexpressible. This *shows* itself; it is the mystical."[1]

I have now to examine Wittgenstein's method of determining what can and what cannot be said, and of drawing a limit to the expression of thoughts; and to examine also what it is that is shown thereby.

3. *The Principle of Verification*

In Wittgenstein's *Tractatus* the principle or criterion determining what can and what cannot be "said" is developed in two stages. First of all, a proposition to be significant must conform to the laws of logic. And this involves, secondly, that it must be verifiable. A proposition is a picture of the

---

[1] Wittgenstein: *Tractatus Logico-Philosophicus*, 6.54.

facts, and a picture implies some basis for comparison between the picture and that which it pictures. Therefore some method must be conceivable for comparing the picture with the facts.

The logical side is developed at the beginning of the *Tractatus*. "In logic," said Wittgenstein, "nothing is accidental. If a thing *can* occur in an atomic fact, the possibility of that atomic fact must already be prejudged in the thing. Just as we cannot think of spatial objects at all apart from space, or temporal objects apart from time, so we cannot think of *any* object apart from the possibility of its connection with other things. . . . A spatial object must lie in infinite space. A speck in a visual field need not be red, but it must have a colour; it has, so to speak, a colour-space around it. A tone must have a pitch, the object of the sense of touch a hardness."[1]

Thus certain terms *can* be combined, because their logical nature, or logical form, permits of the possibility of their combination; but on the other hand, certain terms *cannot* be combined. And of those that can be combined, while two particular terms may not be combined, they must exist in some combination.

The logical conception involved is a very simple one. For instance, I can significantly say, "This speck is red," and it must have a colour—if not red, then blue or green or yellow, etc. But I cannot significantly say, "This speck is loud," because specks cannot by their logical nature have sounds. Similarly, I can say, "This noise is loud," but not, "This noise is red." "This speck is loud" and "This noise is red," are not false propositions; they are not propositions at all, but merely insignificant combinations of words—nonsense.

Thus in the first place, the logical nature of the terms we employ is such that certain combinations of them are logically possible, while others are not. Language becomes insignificant when it starts combining terms in a way that contradicts their logical nature.

The logical nature of the terms is here of course *shown* by the laws of logic, or logical rules, which express how the terms may and may not be significantly combined. These laws of logic are *syntactical rules* for the significant use of language.

---

[1] Wittgenstein: *Tractatus Logico-Philosophicus*, 2.01.

But such rules are not arbitrary, because they *show* the logical form of the world.

Thus Wittgenstein would say that " a speck " exists in " a colour space." This means that a speck-word may be significantly combined with a colour-word, but not, for example, with a sound-word. This syntactical rule shows the logical nature of the speck.

Summing up, Wittgenstein stated : " What is thinkable is also possible. We cannot think anything illogical. . . . It used to be said that God could create everything, except what was contrary to the laws of logic. The truth is, we could not *say* of an ' unlogical ' world how it would look. To present in language anything which ' contradicts logic ' is as impossible as in geometry to present by its co-ordinates a figure which contradicts the laws of space, or to give the co-ordinates of a point which does not exist. We could present spatially an atomic fact which contradicted the laws of physics, but not one which contradicted the laws of geometry."[1]

The sense of the example here given will be understood by regarding geometry as " the logic of space," or as " the syntax of spatial language." To speak of a spatial object which contradicted the laws of geometry would then be, not to say something false, but to say something insignificant.

Here, then, is what I have called the first stage of the principle determining what can and what cannot be said. To be significant, a proposition must conform to the laws of logic. The second stage, which introduces the notion of verification, has most far-reaching consequences, but has nowhere been very systematically expounded by Wittgenstein, and must be gleaned from odd remarks scattered through his *Tractatus*.

After the laws of logic, Wittgenstein came to deal with what is necessary in order to *understand* a proposition. Naturally, whatever conforms to the laws of logic can be understood, and whatever can be understood must conform to the laws of logic. Nevertheless, the introduction of the subjective or personal conception of understanding does introduce new features into the criterion of significance.

---

[1] Wittgenstein : *Tractatus Logico-Philosophicus*, 3.03.

"To understand a proposition," said Wittgenstein, "means to know what is the case, if it is true."[1]

Elsewhere Wittgenstein had used the expression, "how it would look." Evidently, then, to understand a proposition means that we must be able to imagine "how it would look," "what it would be like," if that proposition were true.

Wittgenstein said further: "In order to discover whether the picture (i.e., the proposition) is true or false, we must compare it with reality."[2]

Piecing such remarks as these together, fairly definite conclusions begin to emerge.

First of all, to understand a proposition we must be able to imagine "how it would look if it were true." If we cannot imagine this, then we cannot understand the proposition. But further, we cannot imagine "how it would look if it were true" unless we can imagine some method to "compare it with reality." If we know "how it would look," then, even if physical limitations prevent us from actually being able to "compare it with reality," we must at all events be able to *imagine some method* to carry out that comparison. In other words, *some method of verification*; for to verify a proposition means just to "compare it with reality."

If no method of verification is given, then the proposition cannot be understood, that is, it is insignificant. Thus to be significant, a proposition must be verifiable; it must be capable of some method of verification.

It will now, I think, be seen that the whole of the principle determining what can and what cannot be said is contained in this principle of verification. To give significance to a proposition, we must be able to show how it would be verified. If we cannot show any method to verify what we say, then we are in fact saying nothing. We are putting words together in an insignificant way. We are talking nonsense. This principle of verification contains within itself the principle that what we say must conform to the laws of logic. For very clearly what does not conform to the laws of logic, cannot be verified. As Wittgenstein truly remarked, "We could not say of an 'unlogical' world, how it would look."

[1] Wittgenstein: *Tractatus Logico-Philosophicus*, 4.024.

[2] Ibid., 2.223.

Some examples may help to make clear the scope and application of the principle of verification :

" Parliament is now sitting in London." Method of verification : Travel up to the House of Commons and look in and see. Alternatively : Ring up and ask ; listen to the news on the B.B.C. ; read the parliamentary report in the newspaper.

" Water boils at 100° centigrade." Method of verification : put a thermometer in some water, heat the water, and note the temperature when it boils.

" The positions of the stars determines the course of human affairs." Method of verification : look up the astrological forecasts in back numbers of *The People*, *The News of the World*, *Old Moore's Almanac*, etc., and compare these forecasts with reports of what actually did take place.

" If unequal weights operate at equal distances, the larger weighs down the smaller." Method of verification : carry out experiments with unequal weights.

On the other hand, some " metaphysical " examples may be taken, for which no method of verification can be given.

" The final reason of things must be in a necessary substance . . . and this substance we call God " (Leibniz). There is no method of verification for this statement, we can imagine no method for determining how it would look if this were so, rather than not so. Therefore this statement is meaningless.

" The things perceived by sense have no existence distinct from being perceived " (Berkeley). There is no method of verification for this statement. No method is given for determining how things would " look " different if they existed unperceived from what they would " look " if they had no existence apart from being perceived. Therefore this statement is meaningless.

" Our consciousness is only an image of the external world, and the latter exists independently " (Lenin). There is no method of verification for this statement, which is therefore meaningless, for the same reason as Berkeley's contrary statement was meaningless.

These latter examples (which can be multiplied almost indefinitely by anyone who likes to go through the writings of philosophers with this end in view) show that, quite in accord with the object " to draw a limit to thinking," Wittgenstein's principle of verification can be used to demolish almost the whole of previous philosophy, whether idealism or materialism, as well as the whole of theology. Wittgenstein's principle of verification is an extraordinarily powerful weapon of criticism. It leaves nothing standing. It " draws a limit to thinking " with a vengeance, and represents practically the whole development of philosophy as nothing but a development of nonsense.

Meanwhile, those who feel drawn to this principle because it seems to uphold science and to demolish theology and idealism, should remember that it also demolishes materialism —and thereby leaves theology and idealism standing exactly where they were, by demolishing their only real opponent. I shall show in the sequel how Wittgenstein's principle leads straight to subjective idealism of the most extreme form, i.e., solipsism.

4. *The Meaning of Propositions and the Method of Verification*

It is now necessary to deal rather more fully with what is in general the method of verification of a proposition, and with some of the conclusions about the meaning of propositions which follow from the general concept of the method of verification.

What is involved in the method of verification ?

Here it is necessary to refer once again to Wittgenstein's logical theory of the nature of propositions and their " pictorial relationship " with facts. The proposition to be verified is " a configuration of signs " to which " corresponds the configuration of objects in the state of affairs." And " in order to discover whether the picture is true or false (i.e., to verify it) we must compare it with reality." Hence the process of verification is a process involving some comparison of a proposition with the facts, or of a configuration of signs with a configuration of objects signified. The method of verification proper to any proposition is the method whereby such a comparison can be made.

But how can such a comparison be made ? Such a comparison can be made when " the facts " or " the reality " of which the proposition is a picture, are *presented in experience*, in such a way that the correspondence or non-correspondence of the facts and the picture can be perceived. Unless the reality is presented in experience, no comparison can be made. I cannot compare a picture with something which I do not see. *I cannot verify a proposition except by reference to facts presented in my experience.*

To take an example. " The House of Commons is sitting today in London." I verify this proposition by going up to London and looking at them. With what do I compare the picture? I compare it with my experience, with what I see and hear and (if I am unusually sceptical) touch in my visit to Parliament.

If, while I am carrying out this verification, I hear the voice of some metaphysician—a Communist M.P. perhaps, who is a philosophical materialist—saying, " Of course this Parliament has objective material existence quite independent of experience," I should ignore his words as being altogether unverifiable and meaningless.

Because " experience " is necessarily something private and personal (in philosophical language, " subjective "), the conclusions that follow from this theory of verification would be best expressed in terms of " I " and " my," and not in the usual " we " and " our." For instance, it is clear already that when Wittgenstein said : " In order to discover whether the picture is true or false, *we* must compare it with *reality*," what he means would be better expressed : " In order to discover whether the picture is true or false, *I* must compare it with *my experience*."

Wittgenstein would, however, get out of this by saying that, since no mode of verification can be imagined whereby I should verify a proposition in any other way than in my own experience, and since I cannot imagine experience as anything other than " mine," therefore the expressions " I " and " my experience " used in this context are unnecessary expressions, therefore meaningless, and therefore they might as well be omitted.

In general, the subjectivism and solipsism of Wittgenstein's views is very hard to pin down in discussion, precisely because his theory insists that any philosophical statement of a subjectivist and solipsist position is as meaningless as any opposing statements of " realism " or materialism. But nevertheless, it " shows itself " even if it " cannot be said," as Wittgenstein himself admits.

Nevertheless, for the sake of clarity, even if at the cost of being accused of using unnecessary signs and of trying to " say " what can only be " shown," I shall continue here to use the words " I," " my " and " mine." The conclusion now reached, then, is that for me to be able to give any meaning to a proposition, I must be able to imagine some possible experience of mine which would verify it—that is, some possible experience of mine such that, if I had that experience, I could compare the proposition with the experience, and say either this experience verifies this proposition or it falsifies it.

Therefore, to understand the *meaning* of a proposition, and to know what possible experience of mine would verify it, are one and the same thing.

The meaning of a proposition is given by its method of verification in (my) experience. What a proposition means is what would be the case if it were true. And what would be the case if it were true is whatever would be the content of my experience if it were true.

What this involves can be roughly elucidated by some more examples.

Example : " Parliament is sitting in London."

Verification, i.e., meaning, of the proposition : Seeing and hearing the Parliamentary debate, following on the chain of experiences which would verify the proposition, " I travel to London and enter the Houses of Parliament."

Metaphysical misinterpretation of the meaning : That the House of Commons has real material existence external to experience, and that real material organisms called Members of Parliament, endowed (some of them) with consciousness and reason, are sitting in it.

Here the " metaphysical " expressions, " real material " and " external to experience " have no meaning. How can I compare the proposition with " real material " facts " external to experience " ?

But the consequences of Wittgenstein's principle of verification are illustrated more strikingly by examples of propositions (*a*) referring to the past, and (*b*) referring to the experiences of other people.

Example : " Dinosaurs used to live on the earth in the Mesozoic period."

Verification, i.e. meaning : Seeing and touching certain objects, of an appearance which would verify the proposition, " These are fossils " ; verifying that the form of these objects is such that they belong to the class of fossils which paleontologists agree to call fossil remains of dinosaurs ; verifying that the appearance of the strata in which these fossils are found to be embedded is such that they are strata of the sort that geologists agree to call strata deposited in the Mesozoic period.

Metaphysical misinterpretation : The earth had real material existence long before I myself, or any paleontologists or geologists, ever existed or had experiences ; and in the Mesozoic period of the earth's real material history it was inhabited by dinosaurs.

This is unverifiable metaphysical nonsense. For how can I compare the proposition with what took place millions of years ago " outside " my own or anyone else's experience ?

Example : " Mr. Drury has toothache."[1]

Verification, i.e. meaning : Seeing his swollen face ; hearing his groans and complaints ; looking in his mouth and seeing his decayed tooth ; etc.

Metaphysical misinterpretation : Another really existing person, Mr. Drury, has an experience of pain in his tooth, very similar to my own and other peoples' experiences of pain when we have decaying teeth.

This again is unverifiable metaphysical nonsense. For how can I compare the proposition with what takes place in someone else's experience, that is, with something absolutely inaccessible to me ? (It follows, incidentally, that if I say, " I have toothache," and " Mr. Drury has toothache," the verification, and therefore the meaning, of the two propositions is very different. My own toothache I verify by an experience of pain. But if I and Mr. Drury both have toothache, it is metaphysical nonsense to suggest that two similar experiences

---

[1] This was a popular example once in Wittgenstein's discussions which I attended in Cambridge. If Mr. Drury should read these words, I send him my best wishes and hope he has got over the toothache.

of pain exist : I cannot verify the existence of the second—Mr. Drury's—experience of pain, nor can I compare the two experiences to establish their similarity.)

These examples can be multiplied indefinitely by anyone who finds it instructive or amusing to do so. Their importance is that they " show " what is involved in Wittgenstein's logical principle of verification.

Thus Wittgenstein's criterion for determining the conditions for the significance of propositions, leads to a position of out and out solipsism. I cannot speak, or what is the same thing, think significantly about anything outside the limits of my own experience, my own subjective world. The whole world shrinks into " the narrow compass " of my own immediate present experience, which exists mysteriously on its own, and in the void.

But according to Wittgenstein's principles about " saying " and " showing," this solipsism cannot be *said ;* it is rather *shown* when we understand the principles of " the logic of our language." Hence his solipsism is expressed in a series of cryptic utterances :

" The world is my world."

" What solipsism means is quite correct, only it cannot be said."

" The world of the happy is quite another than that of the unhappy."

" In death the world does not change but ceases."[1]

Here indeed is " a limit " drawn " to thinking." Some might prefer to say that here " thinking " has reached the uttermost limit of absurdity.

5. *The Interpretation of Science*

While Wittgenstein's principle of verification reduces nearly all philosophy to nonsense, in the sense that most " philosophical questions " are nonsense-questions, and the answers given to such questions by philosophers are nonsense, the same principle apparently treats science with the greatest respect. The study of " the logic of our language " rules out of order all " metaphysical propositions," and allows only statements of fact, and scientific statements.

[1] Wittgenstein : *Tractatus Logico-Philosophicus,* 5.62, 6.43.431.

Unlike the statements of metaphysicians, scientific statements are verifiable. And therefore while rejecting the "metaphysical" theories of philosophy as meaningless, we are to accept science. Science, in fact, provides the one road towards constructing verifiable, and therefore significant, theories about the world.

But while the principle of verification thus elevates science to the privileged position of comprising the sum-total of human knowledge, it does not leave science alone. It can be applied with considerable rigour to the interpretation of science. Since the meaning of any proposition is given by its mode of verification, the meaning of any scientific generalisation is to be interpreted in terms of the set of experiences by which it is to be verified.

According to this, any scientific theory is to be regarded as simply a shorthand expression for saying that certain sorts of experiences may be expected under certain conditions.

For instance, the Copernican theory is a shorthand expression for saying what I may expect to observe about the position of the sun, moon and stars.

The Darwinian theory of evolution is a shorthand expression for saying what I may expect to observe about species of living organisms.

The modern atomic theory is a shorthand expression for saying what I may expect to observe when I take certain readings off electrical apparatus.

And so on.

The Copernican theory does not say anything about the existence of the sun, moon and stars, apart from what is observed, and outside my own experience. Nor does the theory of evolution say anything about the existence and history of living organisms apart from what is observed, and outside my own experience. Nor does the atomic theory say anything about the constitution of matter, existing objectively and outside anyone's experience.

All such scientific theories are based on the experiences of past observations, and are elaborated from these according to very complicated linguistic rules. Should future experiences not correspond with what a scientific theory says is to be expected, then the theory has to be altered.

From this analysis is deduced also the famous " Principle of Occam's Razor " or " Principle of Economy," which says : " Entities must not be multiplied beyond necessity."

A theory which deals with, say, two entities, a and b, thus :

f (a, b),

and a theory which deals with, say four, a, b, c and d :

f (a, b, c, d),

can both mean exactly the same thing, if each gives the same rules for the expectation of future experiences. But in that case, the first is preferable to the second, because it is the simpler mode of expression. And moreover, since the extra expressions, " c " and " d " are *unnecessary* in the symbolism expressing the rule, they are in fact *meaningless* symbols. For if " f (a, b, c, d) " has exactly the same verification as " f (a, b)," how can we verify that " c " and " d " exist, rather than do not exist ? Thus Wittgenstein states : " If a sign is not necessary, then it is meaningless. That is the meaning of Occam's Razor."[1]

For instance, take Maxwell's equations for the electromagnetic field. It was common in the 19th century to try to invent all manner of complicated " mechanical models " to explain the phenomena of electricity and magnetism. But the observed facts could be described just as well in terms of Maxwell's equations without the mechanical models ; all the mechanical hypotheses were unnecessary, and therefore meaningless.

Again, the Ptolomaic and Copernican theories, in so far as each expresses the observed facts, mean the same. But the Copernican theory is the simpler ; and all the epicycles and other complicated hypotheses of the Ptolomaic theory are meaningless, because unnecessary. It is not a matter at all of trying to find out the real motions of the heavenly bodies relative to one another—for that is metaphysics ; it is a matter of describing certain parts of our experience.

Again, in the 17th century Newton propounded a corpuscular theory of light, according to which light consisted of a stream of corpuscles, while Huygens maintained that light consisted of waves. Both theories described all the observed facts, and

[1] Wittgenstein : *Tractatus Logico-Philosophicus*, 3.328.

so there was nothing to choose between them ; the controversy as to whether light " really " consisted of corpuscles or waves was meaningless. Later on, when the interference phenomena of light were observed, these observations were described most simply by the wave theory ; and so that theory was preferred.

6. *Where has Wittgenstein led us ?*

In now examining the results of Wittgenstein's philosophy (as distinct from the peculiar method and premises that led to those results), one cannot but be struck by the fact that there is nothing new in them. The upshot of the whole of Wittgenstein's theorising is but to lead back again to the old subjectivism of Berkeley.

The parallel between Wittgenstein and Berkeley is indeed a very close one. In the intervening two hundred years, this type of philosophy has advanced no further than to find new-fangled ways of saying the same thing.

Berkeley said that the world I perceive has no existence apart from my own perceptions. Wittgenstein says that propositions have no meaning apart from their verification in my own experience, and that " the world is my world."

Berkeley said that to talk of material substance existing external to experience was to use words without attaching any meaning to them. Wittgenstein says the same.

In order to try to provide some why and wherefore for human experience detached from all material existence, Berkeley called in the aid of God. Wittgenstein, at the end of his *Tractatus*, has resort to " the mystical " for the same purpose.

Finally, both philosophies have much the same kind of internal inconsistency.

This inconsistency showed itself in Berkeley when, after insisting on the impossibility of non-empirical ideas, he began to introduce " notions " of God, the Soul, Causality, and whatever else suited him, and distinguished " notions," with non-empirical content, from empirical " ideas."

In the case of Wittgenstein, it is equally easy to see that nearly all the philosophical " propositions " of his *Tractatus Logico-Philosophicus* sin against his own principle of verifiability, and should therefore be, on his own showing, meaningless.

Like Berkeley with his "notions," Wittgenstein tries to get round this difficulty by maintaining that philosophical truths "show themselves," though they cannot be "said." But this does not alter the fact that he has said them.

"My propositions are elucidatory in this way," said Wittgenstein, at the end of his *Tractatus*. "He who understands me finally recognises them as senseless, when he has climbed out through them, on them, over them. He must so to speak throw away the ladder, after he has climbed up on it."[1]

This is only an admission of the complete internal inconsistency of the whole philosophy. (To look ahead for a moment, just as Hume tried to eliminate the inconsistency of Berkeley, so I shall presently show how Carnap has tried to eliminate the inconsistency of Wittgenstein. Thus does history repeat itself; and moreover, "on the second occasion, as farce.")

Wittgenstein's teachings are, then, only a repetition of the teachings of Berkeley. There are new words, a great many principles about "the logic of our language;" but what we conclude from it all is exactly the same.

It is in relation to the interpretation of science that this philosophy finds its point and importance, now as in the past. Does science provide knowledge of things outside us, of the objective material world existing prior to and independent of all experience or other spiritual or mental activity? This philosophy answers, no. Science refers only to the subjective contents of experience. This philosophy continues to interpret or to analyse scientific truth philosophically, as dealing merely with sequences of perceptions, not with the constitution and laws of the objective world.

In relation to the "new method" of logical analysis, the outcome of Wittgenstein's "logical analysis of language" was definitely to tie down the interpretation or analysis of propositions within the limits of Berkeleyan subjective idealism. There was after all something very faintly materialist about the efforts of Moore or Wisdom to find "the analysis" of propositions which would reveal the ultimate objects to which those propositions referred. Evidently they thought there

[1] Wittgenstein: *Tractatus Logico-Philosophicus*, 6.54.

might be an objective material world, even though they tried to find out about it by metaphysical speculation instead of by scientific investigation. But by means of the principle of verification, Wittgenstein has rigidly insisted that every " analysis " shall be in terms of the contents of sense experience. The meaning of a proposition is its mode of verification. Any proposition, whether it is a simple statement of fact or a proposition of science, means only something about experience. For no sense can be given to saying anything that refers to objects outside experience and external to consciousness.

Thus it is only a continuation still of the old story of the disarming of science, and the denial of scientific knowledge of the objective material world.

But evidently science is hard to disarm, for the method of disarming it has become, with Wittgenstein, extremely tricky and subtle. This trickiness and subtlety it is very important to understand. What Berkeley meant is very easy to understand—but what Wittgenstein means, very difficult. And so people can very easily be deceived. For they accept such a dogma as the principle of verification, without understanding what it means.

I referred above to the fact that, while the principle of verification very clearly means that the meaning of any proposition is given in the mode of verification in my own experience, yet Wittgenstein would not allow that such an expression as " in my own experience " should be used. Why not? Because—what else can a proposition mean? There is no sense in saying that I verify a proposition outside my experience, or in someone else's experience ; and so there is no sense in saying that I verify it *in my* experience. The expression " in my own experience " is not necessary, and therefore it is meaningless. For " if a sign is not necessary, then it is meaningless."

Thus while Wittgenstein's logical principles very clearly do limit the meaning or interpretation of all propositions to their mode of verification in my experience, and so will not allow it to be significant to refer in any way to objective material things external to consciousness, but restrict our knowledge within " the narrow compass " of a mysterious subjective world ; yet the same logical principles expressly forbid us to say that this is so. To say so is unnecessary, and therefore meaningless.

As Wittgenstein remarked : " He who understands me . . . must so to speak throw away the ladder after he has climbed up on it." I think a more apt injunction would be, that he must cover up all traces of the crime after he has committed it. For objective truth has been foully murdered, and subjectivism installed in its place ; but the murder and the substitution must be covered up. This is done by erasing all statements which point to them.

But this procedure, while it sometimes completely takes in people who have adopted a standpoint, so to speak, inside the circle of Wittgenstein's ideas, cannot deceive those who stand outside that circle. And as evidence there is always Wittgenstein's own statement at the end of the *Tractatus* : " What solipsism (and subjectivism) means is correct, only it cannot be said." While his subjective idealism " cannot be said," it nevertheless does very clearly " show itself."

7. *A Philosophy divorced from life*

The most obvious, but at the same time most profound and most complete, criticism of the philosophy of Wittgenstein, is, that it leads to consequences which are manifestly absurd.

This absurdity is summed up in one word—solipsism.

It is clearest in relation to the account given of propositions about the past, and propositions about other people.

In the realm of the interpretation of science, the absurdity may not appear so manifest. For example, we read about photons and electrons, etc., and we suppose that this applies to the constitution of the material world outside our own consciousness. But Wittgenstein says, no—these terms are rather ways of describing certain aspects of our own experience, and to try to apply them to a " real " " external " material world leads to metaphysical nonsense. This may seem arguable so long as the precise meaning of such terms as " photon " or " electron " is left obscure.

But now let us speak in more familiar terms, about the feelings and experiences of other people with whom we come in contact, and about events that took place in the past. Again we are told that these terms too are only ways of describing our own experience, and that to think they apply to really existing other people with consciousness and feelings like our own, or to a past that really took place, is likewise metaphysical nonsense. But this can be recognised by anyone as an absurdity.

"The world is my world." "What solipsism means is correct." These statements are absurd.

To say that Wittgenstein's philosophy and its consequences are absurd, is less a criticism of pure theory, than a practical social criticism.

It is not an argument of "*reductio ad absurdum*," as understood in the logical text-books. Such an argument consists in showing that a certain proposition is false, because it implies conclusions which contradict other propositions which are either axiomatic or have already been proved. No such logical criticism is here made of Wittgenstein's philosophy.

To put forward and expound a philosophy is an activity, a social activity. And to put forward a solipsist philosophy is an absurd activity. That is the point. It is absurd, just as it would be absurd to walk about naked and say you were living in the Garden of Eden, or to sit down all day in your allotment and say you were a cabbage. The point of view of the latter persons may be perfectly self-consistent; but it is not consistent with the facts of their social life. Similarly, a solipsist philosophy may be perfectly self-consistent; but it is not consistent with the conditions of the social life of mankind. We live in society, we take part in affairs, we are born, grow up, reach maturity, and die—for anyone to invent a solipsist philosophy is absurd.

Thus this solipsist philosophy is characterised by the fact that it is completely divorced from life. Our conditions of social life and our relationships with the world about us, set us many problems, some of which are being solved and others await solution; a solipsist philosophy merely separates itself entirely from the problems of life.

Wittgenstein too spoke about "the problem of life." In fact, he claimed to solve it. "The solution of the problem of life," he wrote, "is seen in the vanishing of this problem."[1] Of course it will "vanish," if you shut your eyes and dream;

[1] Wittgenstein: *Tractatus Logico-Philosophicus*, 6.521.

but it is there just the same, only you have cut yourself off from it.

However, what of Wittgenstein's arguments about Verification? Is he not simply saying that we should say nothing that cannot be verified, and that what is unverifiable is meaningless? What is there absurd about that?

There is nothing absurd in saying that what we say should be verifiable. But the way in which Wittgenstein approaches the question of verification illustrates the way in which his whole theoretical outlook is divorced from life. His account of verification is obviously an incorrect account, because the consequences to which it leads are absurd.

Let us then set on one side the theory that a proposition is a picture of the facts, and that we verify it by comparing it with the facts which it pictures—and make a different approach, not from the basis of a logical theory, but in the light of the plain facts of everyday and scientific experience.

What is verification?

Without going into any detail about the theory of scientific method, it may be said, in the first place, that verification is *a practical activity*; that is, it involves some interaction between a person and his environment, in which he consciously alters his environment in some way. When any proposition is verified, and is put to the test of experience, the method of verification always involves that the person who is verifying the proposition performs some action, or series of actions, in which he arranges and alters things, in a manner to test the truth or falsity of the proposition he is interested in.

We verify our ideas about the world—i.e., propositions—not by contemplation, but by action. We verify whether our ideas about the world are right or wrong by changing the world in accordance with our ideas of it.

A proposition is not, then, verified through a sequence of events in "pure experience," but by a sequence of actions; and action, of course, leads to experience.

For instance—"There is coal in the coal-scuttle": how do I verify this? I verify it first of all by looking, but further by picking up whatever is in the scuttle, breaking some of it up, putting it on the fire, etc., in order to tell whether it really answers to the description of coal.

Verification is, then, in the first place a practical activity.

In the second place, the method of verification is usually, and always in the case of scientific verification, *a co-operative social activity*, involving the practical co-operation of a number of people.

Very often an individual person can verify his own ideas for himself. This is in general the case with ideas about very familiar objects—for instance : that there is coal in the coal scuttle, that Mrs. Brown lives at No. 32, that it's raining today, and so on. But that is only because we each have at our command a great deal of socially accumulated experience and knowledge, which makes us immediately able to recognise familiar objects and their properties when we see them. In certain cases we might well desire the collaboration of others in verifying our ideas.

The social character of the method of verification is most evident in science. The verification of a proposition of science is always social, and must be—partly because the observations of one observer will never be accepted unless they are checked by the observations of others ; and also because the verification of many propositions of science is such that one observer could not possibly verify them, and the method of verification must necessarily be a social method, carried out co-operatively by several observers.

For example, one consequence of Einstein's theory about gravitation is that a ray of light passing at a distance, r, from the centre of the sun will be deflected by an amount $\frac{4m}{r}$, where m is the gravitational mass of the sun. According to the previously accepted Newtonian theory, the deflection would be $\frac{2m}{r}$. What is the method of verification to tell which theory is right, Einstein's or Newton's ?[1]

The method is to take photographs of a star so situated in relation to the earth and the sun that light coming from it passes very close to the sun on its way to the camera. Such photographs can only be taken during a solar eclipse, and the position of the point of light on the photograph will enable the amount of the deflection to be calculated.

[1] See Eddington : *Space, Time and Gravitation*, chs. 6 and 7.

This method of verification was undertaken by six astronomers during the solar eclipse in May, 1919. Three of them went with two telescopes to Brazil, and three went with another to the Gulf of Guinea; and their apparatus was prepared and tested before they set out by a Joint Committee of the Royal Society and the Royal Astronomical Society. The process of taking the photographs was a difficult and elaborate one, and each of the three observers at each observation point was busy with a different job during the making of the observations. When they got home, measurements were made of all the photographs which had been taken—and the result was that Einstein's prediction was verified.

This is an example of the social character of scientific method, and that the method of verification is a co-operative social activity. In this case it involved a Joint Committee plus six astronomers, two journeys half across the world and back, the setting up of elaborate telescopes, the taking of photographs, the development of the plates, the measurement of the position of points of light appearing on the plates, and so on.

Verification is, then, a practical activity, usually carried on by a number of people in co-operation; and in that case verification is not carried out by any one of them, but is the social result of their joint activity.

Taking into account, therefore, that verification is a practical activity, carried out co-operatively by socially organised people—what conclusion is presented? The conclusion is presented that verification is concerned with testing our knowledge of the objects and properties of the objective material world; objective and material in the sense that all people live in and know the same world, to which their particular experiences relate and in which their activities are carried on.

In any case, what is there in the method of verification to suggest the conclusions that Wittgenstein draws, namely, that the meaning of a proposition is its mode of verification in experience, and that "the world is my world"? The principle of verification—that all propositions must be verifiable—gives in fact no support to Wittgenstein's views.

On the contrary, far from the principle of verification giving support to Wittgenstein, the nature of the process of verification seems altogether incompatible with his views.

For if verification is a practical activity, carried out co-operatively by several different people, how can verification be the work of one person in a solipsistic world of his own? It is the social work of many people, who live in a common world.

If verification is an activity in which we bring about changes in the world in order to test the correspondence of our ideas with the world, how can verification be a process confined to one person's subjective experience? Verification is not "a comparison" of a proposition with "facts" which turn up in my experience. It is a testing of the correspondence of the proposition with objective facts, a testing which can only be carried out in the practical activity of changing the world.

If I say Parliament is sitting in London, I mean it is sitting in London whether I go there to listen or not.

If I say dinosaurs used to walk the earth, I mean that they used to exist, whether I dig up their fossils or not.

If I say my friend has toothache, I mean he suffers pain, even though I cannot feel it myself.

If I say that light is deflected by gravitational attraction according to the formula $\frac{4m}{r}$, I mean that that is how it travels through space, not merely that certain dots on a photographic plate will occupy certain positions rather than others.

It is now not very hard to see how Wittgenstein has twisted and falsified the principle of verification.

He has been guilty of exactly the same muddle as all other pure empiricists—the muddle which was analysed in Chapter 6. They all regard knowledge as built up by some hypothetical atomic individual, on the basis of his own sensations; whereas in fact knowledge is the social product of the co-operative social practice of many individuals, who act upon and are acted upon by material objects which are independent of their own existence and consciousness.

Wittgenstein seems to regard verification as a process carried on by some hypothetical atomic individual consciousness, which has its own "world," which "ceases" with its death; and in verification propositions are simply "compared" with "facts" which turn up in the private "world" of pure experience.

But this is a completely false account of the process of verification. It leaves out the two most essential features of verification—that it is practical and that it is social. When we reflect upon the practical and social character of the method of verification, then we see that to use verification as an argument for subjectivism and solipsism is indeed utterly absurd.

What is the importance of verification in the system of human thought?

Its importance is not that by showing how a proposition can be verified we show what it *means*. Its importance is that by showing how a proposition can be verified we show how it can be *known*. Verification is not a test or definition of meaning, but is a far more important test, namely, a test of knowledge. Verification is the test whereby we can tell that our thoughts are not mere idle speculations, but constitute, if only partially and approximately, knowledge of the objective world.

It is only an introspective and contemplative philosophy which concerns itself primarily with the criticism of the meaning of thoughts. For the advancement of human life, what is important is that the system of our ideas should be based on knowledge. And for the advancement of knowledge, what cannot be verified is of no use or value whatever. A proposition or a theory for which no method of verification is put forward is at best only a guess or speculation. The great value of science is that it is a method for formulating theories which can be verified, that is, for constructing a body of knowledge. For as Bacon said, "Knowledge of nature is the same thing as power over nature."

It may be thought perhaps that Wittgenstein's insistence on the principle of verification bears a close relationship to some of the fundamental ideas of materialism. Did not Bacon, the founder of modern materialism, start from the standpoint that whatever we can claim to know must be capable of verification?

But Wittgenstein's approach is a different one. Bacon started with the object of seeking for the indefinite expansion of our knowledge of the objective world; and pointed out that the criterion of such knowledge is that it is verifiable, as distinct from the unverifiable dogmas of narrow scholastic philosophy. But Wittgenstein started with an entirely different object. His object was to "draw a limit to thinking." He did not take as his starting point the objective world and our expanding knowledge about it and power to change it; but he took as his starting point an introspective criticism of the process of thinking, with a view to "limiting" that process. Thus these philosophies are poles asunder.

It may perhaps be said that Wittgenstein's philosophy has at all events the outstanding merit of insisting on our giving a method of verification for all propositions. But where is the merit? This standpoint has been insisted upon and developed by materialist philosophy for the past three hundred years. Wittgenstein's alleged merit consists only in his having introduced confusions into the conception of the method of verification, and having systematised these confusions into a rigid system of "logical philosophy." But this is a merit only from the point of view of those who are interested in introducing confusions into our conception of the sciences; but such a point of view has its roots deep in the character of class society today, as in days gone by.

The outstanding characteristic of Wittgenstein's philosophy is, first, that it represents a system of introspective scholastic theorising, altogether divorced from life and from the realities of our practical social existence. Second, the aim of this philosophy, "to draw a limit to thinking," can correspond only with the aims of those who are interested "to draw a limit" to thinking out the implications of scientific knowledge—as knowledge of the objective world, and therefore as power over nature, pointing to the need for a social organisation to enable that power to be used for the purposes of social progress. Third, this philosophy, divorced from life as it is, is nevertheless a part of life—a social force, but one serving in the main the purposes of the reactionary classes in their struggle against materialist enlightenment.

CHAPTER 10

LOGICAL POSITIVISM (1)

1. *Philosophy as the Logical Syntax of the Language of Science*

I NOW come to the latest and, it is to be hoped, last stage in the development of modern empirical philosophy—the special and peculiar doctrines of Carnap and his " circle."

This " circle " was closely organised before the war, though the impact of the war broke it up, temporarily at all events. Their real fountain-head and progenitor was Wittgenstein; but Carnap had several (to them) very important differences from Wittgenstein, and indeed from all other empirical philosophers.

The main difference was that Carnap insisted on excluding from philosophy all references to *meanings*, and to *the relations of thoughts with things*. Such references, he thought, led straight to confusion and nonsense, and philosophy should confine itself absolutely exclusively to a programme of the logical analysis *of language*.

Such a programme had already been enunciated by Wittgenstein. But Wittgenstein, by allowing himself to become entangled in meanings, had not carried out the programme with full consistency. The downfall of Wittgenstein's philosophy was its solipsism. Carnap thought that this solipsism could be avoided by rigidly excluding from philosophical discussion any reference to the meaning of statements, and confining philosophy to the study, not of meaning, but of syntax.

Carnap speaks of " the problems of applied logic, of the logic of science, i.e., the logical analysis of the terms, statements, theories proper to the various departments of science. . . ."[1] " In this fashion," he explains, " we use logical analysis to investigate statements of the various kinds proper to the various departments of science."[2]

[1] Carnap: *Unity of Science*.

[2] Ibid.

Thus the basis of Carnap's position is that science is accepted as the vehicle of knowledge about the world, its constitution and laws; and the task of philosophy is to subject science to logical analysis. This is nothing new. But Carnap goes on to rigidly insist:

"A philosophical, i.e., a logical, investigation must be *an analysis of language*."[1]

And again: "Philosophy is to be replaced by the logic of science—that is to say, by the logical analysis of the concepts and sentences of the sciences; for the logic of science is nothing else than *the logical syntax of the language of science*."[2]

Thus Carnap maintains that logical analysis, and the logical analysis of science in particular, is not concerned, as his predecessors thought, with analysing the *meaning* of terms and exhibiting the ultimate logical nature of the facts and laws established by science (e.g., that they are facts and laws concerning the order of events in experience); but is concerned with analysing *the language* of science, and exhibiting what he calls "the logical syntax" of that language.

This is the standpoint, so Carnap thinks, which finally purges philosophy, that is, logical analysis, from all confusion, speculation and "metaphysics."

2. *Object-questions and Logical-questions: Formal Theories and the Principle of Tolerance*

"The questions dealt with in any theoretical field," says Carnap, ". . . can be roughly divided into *object-questions* and *logical-questions*. . . . By object-questions are to be understood those which have to do with the objects of the domain under consideration, such as inquiries regarding their properties and relations. The logical questions, on the other hand, do not refer directly to the objects, but to sentences, terms, theories, and so on, which themselves refer to objects."[3]

Thus science deals with objects. But philosophy, that is the logical analysis of science, does not deal with objects at all, but with "sentences, terms, theories, and so on"—in a word, with *language*.

---

[1] Carnap: *Unity of Science.*
[2] Carnap: *Logical Syntax,* p. xiii.
[3] Ibid., p. 277.

Thus it appears that Russell and Wittgenstein should not have spoken of objects and facts, of the meaning of propositions, and of the comparison of propositions with reality. All that led them into " metaphysics." It is wrong to try to say anything of the relations of propositions and *facts*, of thought and *reality*. Scientific philosophy must confine its discourse to the relations of propositions with *propositions*, of thoughts with *thoughts*, and will deal exclusively with " the logic of language." (Thus incidentally, the materialist criticism of Wittgenstein's ideas about verification which I gave in the last chapter, would appear to be entirely the wrong criticism : the right criticism would be to criticise Wittgenstein for attempting to say anything at all about the comparison of propositions with facts, for nothing should be said upon such a subject.)

It is clear that this standpoint means that Carnap and his " circle " takes a rather different view of logic from that expounded by Russell and Wittgenstein. And since the account given of pure formal logic must stand at the base of the " applied logic " or " logic of science," I must briefly direct attention to it before proceeding any further.

According to Carnap, " logic is syntax."[1] And he explains : " By the logical syntax of a language, we mean the formal theory of the linguistic forms of that language—the systematic statement of the formal rules which govern it, together with the development of the consequences which follow from these rules."[2]

He goes on to explain what he means by a " formal theory." " A theory, a rule, a definition, or the like is to be called formal when no reference is made in it either to the meaning of the symbols (for example, the words) or to the sense of the expressions (e.g., the sentences), but simply and solely to the kinds and order of the symbols from which the expressions are constructed."[3]

Formal logic, or " logical syntax," is, then, concerned " simply and solely " with symbols, or with language, without regard to meaning.

This means that " logical syntax " is " the system which

[1] Carnap : *Logical Syntax*, p. 259.

[2] Ibid., p. 1.

[3] Ibid., p. 1.

comprises the rules of formation and transformation " of a language.

Every language, considered formally (in the above sense of " formal," that is, without regard to its meaning), is based on " rules of formation and transformation."

The rules of formation show how symbols may be combined together to form sentences. The rules of transformation show how sentences may be obtained from other sentences.

Thus if we know the rules of formation, then that corresponds to knowing which sentences are significant and which insignificant : and from a formal point of view, significant just means allowed in that language, and insignificant means not allowed. And if we know the rules of transformation, then that corresponds to knowing which sentences can be validly deduced or follow from which other sentences, and which do not follow from or are contradictory to which other sentences. From a formal point of view, that " p " follows from " q " means that if you say " q " you are allowed by the rules of the language to say " p," but not to say " not-p."

Hence whether a sentence is significant or insignificant, and whether a sentence follows from another or does not follow from it or is contradictory to it, does not depend at all on the *meaning* of the sentences, but can be seen solely from their syntactical form, given a knowledge of the rules of formation and transformation of the language.

This " corrects " the usually accepted opinions of logicians. " The prevalent opinion," says Carnap, " is that syntax and logic, in spite of some points of contact between them, are fundamentally theories of a very different type. The syntax of a language is supposed to lay down rules according to which the linguistic structures (e.g., the sentences) are to be built up from the elements (such as words or parts of words). The chief task of logic, on the other hand, is supposed to be that of formulating rules according to which judgments may be inferred from other judgments ; in other words, according to which conclusions may be drawn from premises." And he continues : " Even those modern logicians who agree with us in our opinion that logic is concerned with sentences, are yet for the most part convinced that logic is equally concerned with the relations of meaning between sentences. They consider that, in contrast with the rules of syntax, the rules of logic are non-formal,"[1] that is, have reference to meanings.

But all this is wrong. The principles of logic can be, and should be, formulated without any reference at all to the meaning of words. They should be formulated simply as syntactical rules of formation and transformation.

But, it will be objected, how do we know which are the *right* rules of formation and transformation? Only by knowing the meaning of the sentences.

Carnap answers this objection. It arises, he explains, from the prejudice that the principles of logic must " constitute a faithful rendering of the 'true logic.' "[2] But the idea that there exists " the true logic "—the eternally valid principles of logic—which any system of logic must contrive to mirror (or to " show," in Wittgenstein's expression), is a mere " metaphysical " illusion.

" We have in every respect," Carnap writes, " complete liberty with regard to the forms of language ; both the rules for construction of sentences and the rules of transformation (the latter are usually designated as ' postulates ' and ' rules of inference ') may be chosen quite arbitrarily. Up to now, in constructing a language, the procedure has usually been, first to assign a meaning to the fundamental mathematico-logical symbols, and then to consider what sentences and inferences are seen to be logically correct in accordance with this meaning. Since the assignment of the meaning is expressed in words and is, in consequence, inexact, no conclusion arrived at in this way can very well be otherwise than inexact and ambiguous. The connection will only become clear when approached from the opposite direction : let any postulates and any rules of inference be chosen arbitrarily ; then this choice, whatever it may be, will determine what meaning is to be assigned to the fundamental logical symbols."[3]

This standpoint is called by Carnap " the principle of tolerance."[4]

" The first attempts to cast the ship of logic off from the

[1] Carnap : *Logical Syntax*, p. 1.

[2] Ibid.

[3] Ibid., p. xv.

[4] Ibid. pp. xv and 51.

terra firma of the classical forms were certainly bold ones," writes Carnap, referring to the various modern systems of symbolic logic. "But they were hampered by the striving after correctness," that is, by the prejudice that they must "constitute a faithful rendering of 'the true logic.'" "Now, however, that impediment has been overcome, and before us lies the boundless ocean of unlimited possibilities."[1] —"Unlimited possibilities" of "arbitrarily" inventing all sorts of "languages."

Explaining his own method of developing the principles of logical syntax, Carnap writes: "In consequence of the unsystematic and logically imperfect structure of the natural word-languages (such as German or Latin), the statement of their formal rules of formation and transformation would be so complicated that it would be hardly feasible in practice." And so: "Owing to the deficiencies of the word-languages, the logical syntax of a language of this kind will not be developed, but, instead we shall consider the syntax of two artificially constructed symbolic languages (that is to say, such languages as employ formal symbols instead of words)."[2] On this basis he is then able to formulate certain principles of "general syntax," applicable to any language whatsoever.

Such is the programme and standpoint of Carnap and his "circle" in the domain of logic.

Referring back to the logical theories of Russell and Wittgenstein, it will be seen that Carnap's standpoint makes short work of the system of "metaphysics" which they erected on the basis of logic.

Believing that logic must refer to the meaning of words and sentences, and that there must be certain absolute and ultimate logical forms of propositions which mirror the ultimate and absolute logical form of reality, Russell and Wittgenstein were led to consider the relations of propositions and facts, and to speak of "atomic facts," "simple objects," "elements," and the like.

Carnap will have none of this. For him, it is all "metaphysics" and quite inadmissible.

---

[1] Carnap: *Logical Syntax*, p. xv.

[2] Ibid., pp. 2, 3.

Logical analysis is not concerned with meanings, and with exhibiting the logical form of reality. It is concerned with the syntax of language. So the logical analysis of science likewise is not concerned with making clear the ultimate meaning and justification of science, but with making clear the syntactical principles according to which scientific statements are constructed, and the relations of such statements one to another.

The next step is the application of these logical principles to the problems of philosophy, that is, to " the problems of applied logic, the logic of science."

3. *The Formal and Material Modes of Speech*

In dealing with the logical analysis of science, Carnap distinguishes two " modes of speech " in which the results of this analysis may be expressed. The first he calls " the material mode of speech," the second, " the formal mode of speech."

" The first speaks of objects, states of affairs, of the sense, content and meaning of words ; while the second refers only to linguistic forms."

Clearly, the material mode is " the more usual mode of speech." But the formal mode is nevertheless " the correct mode of speaking."[1]

In his book, *Logical Syntax*, Carnap gives some examples of the material and formal modes of speech in philosophy. In these examples the same philosophical proposition is expressed in both modes of speech :

" *Material Mode*	*Formal Mode*
A thing is a complex of sense data.	Every sentence in which a thing-designation occurs is equipollent to a class of sentences in which no thing-designations but sense-data designations occur.

[1] Carnap : *Unity of Science*.

" *Material Mode*	*Formal Mode*
A thing is a complex of atoms.	Every sentence in which a thing-designation occurs is equipollent to a sentence in which space-time co-ordinates and certain descriptive functors (of physics) occur.
The world is the totality of facts, not of things.	Science is a system of sentences, not of names.
A fact is a combination of objects (entities, things).	A sentence is a series of symbols.
Time is infinite in both directions, forwards and backwards.	Every positive and negative real number expression can be used as a time co-ordinate."[1]

These examples are evidently intended to show how philosophical sentences in the material mode can be translated into the formal mode; and how moreover the material mode is apt to be misleading, whereas the formal mode is clear and "correct."

For the above sentences in the material mode sound as if they were asserting some property of the objective world—namely, important philosophical properties of things, the world, facts, and time. But when translated into the formal mode, it is clear that they are really only syntactical assertions, that is, not assertions about objects but about words.

Thus philosophical propositions are not really concerned, as philosophers usually believe, with making clear "the nature" or properties of things, the world, facts, time, etc., etc.; but they are syntactical propositions, about words, not about objects. And that this is so will be made clear by using "the correct formal mode of speech."

"Accordingly," says Carnap, "we distinguish three kinds of sentences: 1. Object-sentences. 2. Pseudo-object sentences. 3. Syntactical sentences."[2]

---

[1] Carnap: *Logical Syntax,* pp. 301–307.

[2] Ibid., p. 286.

The sentences of science are object-sentences. To use the material mode, they are about the properties of objects : but as we should not use the material mode at all, we must not say so. On the other hand, philosophical sentences of the analysis of science are pseudo-object sentences, when they are expressed in the material mode. Thus they seem to be " about objects " ; but if they are significant at all, then they are " equipollent " to syntactical sentences, that is, sentences in the formal mode.

" The use of the material mode," Carnap explains, " leads to questions whose discussion ends in contradiction and insoluble difficulties. The contradictions however disappear immediately we restrict ourselves to the correct formal mode of speech. The questions of the kinds of facts and objects referred to by the various languages are revealed as pseudo-questions."[1]

Carnap gives various examples of the difficulties and misleading controversies which arise from the unwise use of the material mode of speech. For instance, arising out of the first two assertions given in the list quoted above :

" Suppose that a positivist maintains the thesis, ' A thing is a complex of sense-data,' and a realist the thesis, ' A thing is a complex of atoms.' Then an endless dispute will arise over the pseudo-question of what a thing actually is. If we transfer to the formal mode of speech it is in this case possible to reconcile the two theses. . . . For the various possibilities of translating a thing-sentence into an equipollent syntactical sentence are obviously not incompatible with one another. The controversy between positivism and realism is an idle dispute about pseudo-theses, which owes its origin entirely to the use of the material mode of speech."[2]

" For complete safety," Carnap concludes, meaning safety from " idle disputes about pseudo-theses," " it would be better to avoid the use of the material mode entirely. . . . If this mode is still to be used, particular care must be taken that the statements expressed are such as might also be expressed in the formal mode. That is the criterion which distinguishes statements from pseudo-statements in philosophy."[3]

---

[1] Carnap : *Unity of Science*.

[2] Carnap : *Logical Syntax*, p. 301.

[3] Ibid.

4. *The Logic of Science*

Having established this distinction between the material and formal mode of speech, the next business is "the logic of science," in which care must be taken to speak in "the correct formal mode" throughout, or, if we do use the material mode, to make sure that what is said in the material mode can be translated into the formal mode.

Speaking of science in general, Carnap says: "Science is a system of statements based on direct experience and controlled by experimental verification. . . . Verification is based on protocol statements."[1]

This generalisation must be interpreted carefully, because the references to "direct experience" and "experimental verification" savour strongly of the material mode of speech. In formal strictness and purity, Carnap does not analyse science as "based on experience," but investigates science as "a scientific language," or set of "scientific languages" (corresponding to the different sciences). He is concerned with science as "a system of statements"; and the important feature of science, he alleges, is that its statements are based on "protocol statements."

What then are protocol statements? Carnap proceeds to explain:

"The simplest statements in the protocol language refer to the given, and describe directly given experiences or phenomena, i.e., the simplest states of which knowledge can be had."[2]

This, however, is expressed in the material mode. Here is the same explanation in the formal mode:

"The simplest statements in the protocol language are protocol statements, i.e., statements needing no justification and serving as foundations for all the remaining statements of science."[3]

The programme of the logical analysis of science is, then, of a strictly formal syntactical nature. It aims to show how

---

[1] Carnap: *Unity of Science*.

[2] Ibid.

[3] Ibid.

science, the whole system of scientific statements, is derived from protocol statements according to certain formal rules.

Obviously these rules must in actual scientific practice be enormously complicated. However, the sort of thing meant can be made clear by an elementary example :

Suppose we are concerned with two pointer-readings, x and y, and our aim is to formulate a scientific generalisation showing how y depends on x. The readings will then be our protocol. Suppose, then, that we have the following protocol statements :

$$x=1 \qquad y=2$$
$$x=2 \qquad y=4$$
$$x=3 \qquad y=6$$
$$x=4 \qquad y=8$$

Then from this protocol we may derive the following generalisation, or scientific statement :

$$y = 2\ (x).$$

This part of the procedure corresponds to that aspect of science described by Carnap in saying that its statements are " based on direct experience." That is, it shows how scientific statements are first derived from protocols. But the scientific statements are further " controlled by experimental verification." That is, having been derived from the protocol, they have further to be controlled, tested, revised, in relation to the protocol.

Let us therefore take some more readings. If the generalisation continues to fit the protocols, well and good, the generalisation stands. But suppose we now find that it no longer fits the protocols ? Then in that case the generalisation has to be revised, and another made which does fit the protocols.

For instance, suppose that on taking the readings a second time we have the protocols :

$$x=1 \qquad y=4$$
$$x=2 \qquad y=8$$
$$x=3 \qquad y=12$$
$$x=4 \qquad y=16$$

Then our former generalisation must be scrapped. But a new simple generalisation, namely : $y = 4\ (x)$, will not do, since the first protocol still stands, and this generalisation, which would fit the second, would not fit the first. The best course now will be to look for some third factor, z, whose variations will enable us to arrive at a generalisation which will fit both the protocols. So we now arrive at a third protocol :

z=1	x=1	y=2	z=2	x=1	y= 4
z=1	x=2	y=4	z=2	x=2	y= 8
z=1	x=3	y=6	z=2	x=3	y=12
z=1	x=4	y=8	z=2	x=4	y=16

Then we derive the revised and corrected generalisation :

$$y = 2\ (zx).$$

The "logical analysis of science," then, shows how the whole system of scientific statements is founded on protocol statements. It further shows how a scientific statement is of the nature of a generalisation or rule which sums up a set of protocol statements, and forecasts further statements of the same set.

For instance, the generalisation, $y = 2\ (zx)$, sums up the set of protocol statements on which it was based, and forecasts further statements of the same set—as for example, if we have : $z=5$ and $x=3$, then we shall have $y=30$.

Thus the whole logic of science is expressed in a purely formal syntactical way. We deal with nothing but statements and the formal relations of statements—not with the meaning of statements, nor with objective reality and the relation of statements to objective reality.

Thus science is based on given protocol statements ; and science progresses and is tested and verified by the comparison of scientific statements—not with reality—but with further relevant protocol statements.

This result is summed up by a follower of Carnap, Neurath, as follows :—

"Sentences are to be compared with sentences, not with 'experiences,' not with a 'world,' nor with anything else. All these senseless duplications belong to a more or less refined metaphysics, and are therefore to be rejected. Every new sentence is confronted with the totality of sentences which are present and which have been brought into agreement. *Then a sentence is called correct if it can be brought into the system.* Whatever we cannot systematise is rejected as incorrect. Instead of rejecting the new sentences we can also, wherever we find it generally difficult to make a decision, alter the whole system of sentences until the new sentence can be included. . . . In the present theory we always remain within the realm of speech-thinking."[1]

Carnap makes some interesting applications of this general "logical analysis of science" to particular sciences. Each science is distinguished by its own "language," and he speaks of the "various languages" which "can be distinguished in science."

Now although science, as distinct from philosophy or "the logical analysis of science," speaks in an "object-language" (that is, in the material mode, is about objects), nevertheless "the questions of the kinds of facts and objects referred to by the various sciences are revealed as pseudo-questions." Thus to give an account of any science, nothing should be said of "the kinds of facts and objects" which that science studies, how it studies them, or what it finds out about them. On the contrary, the science should be regarded simply as a system for producing statements in its own peculiar language.

Thus Carnap says of Economics: "Let us for example consider the language of economics, which can be characterised in somewhat the following fashion, i.e., by the fact that its sentences can be constructed from expressions 'supply and demand,' 'wage,' 'price,' etc., put together in such and such a way."[2]

Thus it appears that neither economics nor the logical analysis of economics is in the least concerned with "the kinds of facts" which underlie, say, the wages system. Economics is a "language" based on protocols in which words like "wages" occur.

5. *Physicalism*

Having given this general "logical analysis of science," and having shown that the different sciences are distinguished by their "various languages," Carnap proceeds to make a sweeping generalisation which must be regarded as the crowning point in his particular "system."

---

[1] Neurath: *Sociology in Physicalism*, quoted by Weinberg: *An Examination of Logical Positivism*, p. 277.

[2] Carnap: *The Unity of Science*.

The aim of this generalisation is to show that there can be one universal language of science, into which all statements in all the different languages of the different sciences can be translated. Thus instead of being a mere assembly of different languages, science is revealed as a unity—" the unity of science" is established by showing that there is a universal language of science into which all scientific statements can be translated.

This language is called " the physical language " ; and this theory of " the unity of science " is called " physicalism."

To slip for one sentence into the material mode of speech, this " physicalist " theory of the unity of science is supposed to show that all science is about one world, and to indicate the fundamental physical nature of that world. But since to say this is vulgar " metaphysics," I shall return forthwith to " the correct formal mode of speech."

The theory of physicalism is capable of very simple expression. There is a language, called the physical language, into which all scientific statements can be translated ; in other words, there is a statement in the physical language equipollent to any scientific statement.

Carnap proceeds to define the physical language in both the formal and material modes of speech :—

" The physical language is characterised by the fact that statements of the simplest form :—

" *Formal Mode*	*Material Mode*
attach to a specific set of co-ordinates (three space and one time co-ordinate) a definite value or range of values of physical state.	express a quantitatively determined property of a definite position at a definite time."[1]

And he thus sums up the theory of physicalism :

" Our investigations of the various departments of science therefore lead to the conclusion :—

Formal Mode	*Material Mode*
that every scientific statement can be translated into physical language.	that every fact contained in the subject matter of science can be described in physical language."[2]

[1] Carnap : *The Unity of Science*.
[2] Ibid.

Carnap also explains that not only scientific generalisations but the protocols on which those generalisations are based, and by which they are tested, can all be translated into physical language. Thus :—

" *Formal Mode*	*Material Mode*
Statements in protocol language can be translated into physical language.	Given direct experiences are physical, i.e., spatio-temporal events."[1]

" The physical language," Carnap concludes, " is a universal language, and, since no other is known, the language of all science. . . .

" It is convenient of course for each department of science to have a special terminology adapted to its distinct subject matter." (Question : Isn't this " metaphysics ? ") " All our thesis asserts is that immediately these terminologies are arranged in the form of a system of definitions, they must ultimately refer back to physical determinations. . . . If we have a single language for the whole of science, the cleavage between different departments disappears. Hence the thesis of physicalism leads to the thesis of the unity of science."[2]

6. *Materialism—Methodical and Purified*

Lastly, on the basis of this " thesis," it turns out that Carnap is a materialist—a " methodical " materialist.

" Our view that protocols constitute the basis of the entire scientific edifice might be termed Methodical Positivism," Carnap writes. " Similarly the thesis that the physical language is the universal language might be denoted as Methodical Materialism. . . . Our approach has often been termed positivist ; it might equally well be termed materialist. No objection can be made to such a title, provided that the distinction between the older form of Materialism, and Methodical Materialism—the same theory in a purified form —is not neglected. Nevertheless for the sake of clarity we would prefer the name Physicalism. For our theory is that the physical language is the universal language and can therefore serve as the basic language of science."[3]

---

[1] Carnap : *The Unity of Science.*

[2] Ibid.

[3] Ibid.

Thus it would appear that pure empiricism, logical analysis, logical positivism, on the one hand, and materialism on the other hand, which throughout the years, and in the pages of this book in particular, have been at loggerheads, are at last reconciled by the physicalist theory of Carnap.

Hegel once likened " The Absolute," in which all different or conflicting things were supposed to be reconciled and to become identical, to " the night in which all cows are black."[1] Maybe the theory of physicalism is the same.

But it must be insisted that the " Methodical Materialism " of Carnap is a theory which moves in the realm of " logical syntax " or " speech-thinking " exclusively. It is a theory about the syntax of the language of science, and forbids us to think about the " kinds of facts and objects " referred to by any science.

Thus Carnap states : " All statements belonging to metaphysics, regulative ethics, and metaphysical epistemology . . . are in fact unverifiable and therefore unscientific. We are accustomed to describe such statements as nonsense. . . . We make no assertions as to whether the given is real and the physical world appearance, or vice versa ; for logical analysis shows that such assertions belong to the class of unverifiable pseudo-statements."[2]

Such is in general outline the philosophy of Carnap, and of the logical positivists and physicalists.

---

[1] Hegel : *The Phenomenology of Mind*, Preface.

[2] Carnap : *The Unity of Science*.

CHAPTER II

LOGICAL POSITIVISM (2)

1. *The " Analysis " of Science*

The logical (or " methodical ") positivists claim that their " logical analysis of science " is entirely free from the dubious subjectivism and solipsism which characterised the theories of Mach, Russell or Wittgenstein. These " methodical materialists " claim indeed that their analysis is entirely free from " metaphysics " of any sort, whether the " metaphysics " of the Berkeley-Hume tradition or that of the Bacon-Hobbes tradition.

Perhaps it is. But it is only free from such influences because it refuses to say anything about the *content* of science or the *meaning* of science, and its relations to human life and the real world in which that life is led ; because it deals only with *words* and not with the meaning and justification of those words ; and because in fact it does not regard science as *knowledge* at all, not even as knowledge relating to " my own experience."

A whole chain of philosophers, from Berkeley to Wittgenstein, have " interpreted " or " analysed " science, in order to make out that its subject matter is restricted to the order and arrangement of the " impressions," " elements " or " sense-data " found in sense-experience. And by means of such an " interpretation " or " analysis " they have obscured and covered up the *objective reference* of science, as scientific *knowledge* of the objective material world.

Carnap's " analysis " of science, although he studiously tries to avoid subjectivist conclusions, and calls himself a materialist, is in effect exactly the same. For this analysis *also* obscures and covers up the objective reference of science, as scientific knowledge of the objective material world. It does this by refusing to allow anything to be said of the content or meaning of science, and virtually saying that science has no reference at all, either to the objective world, or to the world of experience, or to anything else.

It has always been an essential argument of the pure empiricists, from Berkeley to Wittgenstein, that any talk of the objective material world, or of matter, is senseless " metaphysics." Carnap repeats this argument. Only he adds that the same applies to Berkeley's and Wittgenstein's talk of experience. For : " We make no assertions as to whether the given (i.e., given experience) is real and the physical world appearance, or vice versa ; for logical analysis shows that such assertions belong to the class of unverifiable pseudo-statements."

In other words, " we make no assertions " as to what science is about, and " we " will not allow anyone else to make such assertions, for they have no meaning. Science is to be regarded as a set of statements, founded on certain given primitive protocol statements, and tested and verified also by reference to such protocol statements ; and science does not compare its statements " with experience, nor with a world, nor with anything else."

Very clearly, therefore, this is to confound and cover up the objective reference of science, as effectively as it was confounded by the most dogmatic subjectivism.

Those who, after long puzzling about the meaning of science and the extent or limitation of possible scientific knowledge, at length embrace the principles of " logical positivism " and " the logical analysis of science," are in the same happy position as the crew described by Lewis Carroll in *The Hunting of the Snark :*

> " Other maps are such shapes, with their islands and capes,
> But we have our brave Captain to thank,
> (So the crew would protest) that he's bought us the best—
> A perfect and absolute blank ! "

It is important not to be misled by Carnap's distinction between " object sentences " and " syntactical sentences." The " logical analysis of science " consists of syntactical sentences, but science itself does not consist of syntactical sentences but of object sentences. Expressed in the material mode, it is about objects.

Very well then, it will be said, science is about objects.

So why complain that this analysis confounds the objective reference of science ?

However, " science is about objects " is equivalent to saying, and would be more correctly expressed by saying, that " science consists of object sentences " ; that is, that it consists of sentences in which terms like " supply and demand," " wages," " vitamins," " atoms," " electrons," etc., etc., occur. No one will dispute this obvious truth—it is only a statement about the language of science, and is quite trivial. But when it is asked, Do the terms employed by science stand for anything in the objective world ?—then Carnap replies that we must not ask such " pseudo-questions."

Hence, while it may be agreed that science is expressed in an object language, this statement does not advance us a step further towards understanding the objective reference of science.

For when we speak of the objective reference of science, we are not thinking so much of the syntax of the language of science, as of the relations between scientific thought and material reality. Carnap says, however, that we must not think of the relations between statements and their objects, or of thought and reality, but only of the relations between statements and other statements, and of thoughts with thoughts.

Hence his assertion that scientific statements are " object sentences " does not remove the confusion introduced into the question of the objective reference of science, but only makes that confusion a little more confounded.

Carnap here shows the same trickiness with regard to the formulation of his conclusions as I remarked in the case of Wittgenstein. What his conclusions plainly mean—namely, that we do not have knowledge of the objective material world—is not allowed to be said. Carnap says, of course, that he does not deny the objectivity of our knowledge—he merely makes no assertions about it, one way or the other. But if you do not deny the objectivity of our knowledge, why go to such elaborate lengths to try to prevent it from being asserted ? What is the purpose of this ? What is its meaning ? Simply to obscure and to cover up the objectivity of our knowledge.

Thus Carnap's " logical analysis," however novel some of

its features may be, is essentially a continuation of the Berkeley-Wittgenstein tradition.

I shall now proceed to examine it in more detail.

2. *Protocol Statements*

The conception of the protocol, of " protocol statements " and of the " protocol language," is clearly of key importance in Carnap's " logic of science." Protocols not only form the ultimate basis of the whole system of scientific statements, but scientific statements are ultimately tested and verified, accepted, rejected or revised, by comparing them with the protocols.

Hence it is of some importance to investigate exactly what these protocols are supposed to be.

The type of " analysis " undertaken by Russell and Wittgenstein purported to show how all scientific propositions, and indeed all propositions whatever, were derived from absolutely elementary propositions. Thus the ultimate data on which science was alleged to be founded were expressed in absolutely elementary propositions, and scientific generalisations were alleged in the last analysis to have absolutely elementary propositions as their instances.

Carnap would claim to have purged logical analysis of the "metaphysical" conception of the absolutely elementary proposition. Nevertheless, in his logical syntax of the language of science, protocol statements play exactly the same part as did the absolutely elementary propositions in the less " pure " and " formalised " analysis of Russell and Wittgenstein.

The conception of the protocol is only a new version of the conception of the absolutely elementary proposition. Thus protocol statements are the ultimate data—the " simplest " statements, which " need no justification " ; and scientific statements are tested by reference to protocol statements, in the way that generalisations were tested by reference to the absolutely elementary propositions which were their instances.

And now it turns out that there is exactly the same difficulty in actually locating the ultimate protocols as there was in locating the ultimate elementary propositions.

Thus having given the general definition of a protocol statement, Carnap goes on to ask, in his double-barrelled way :

" *Formal Mode*	*Material Mode*
Question : What kinds of words occur in protocol statements ?	Question : What objects are the elements of given direct experience ? "

And after this question there follows, in his *Unity of Science*, a longish discussion (which it would be tedious to quote, as I have quoted one such discussion already when dealing with an earlier stage of " analysis "), the upshot of which is, that various answers can be given to this question, but it is hard to determine which answer is the right one.

It does not seem to occur to Carnap that the existence of such difficulties suggests that the question which gave rise to them must be a " pseudo-question," and that the whole method of analysis which gave rise to such a " pseudo-question " must be a " pseudo-" method.

The difficulty is much the same if we begin to ask, not only what the protocols are like, but how we arrive at them. The protocols are the ultimate basis of science ; but we must have some method whereby we may select and arrive at the statements which constitute this ultimate basis. Carnap, however, does not suggest such a method. He tells us, in the formal mode, that protocols are " statements needing no justification " ; and in the material mode, that they " describe directly given experience or phenomena." But how we may arrive at such ultimate and absolutely elementary statements, and what they are like when we do arrive at them, he does not tell us.

Hence it is only too clear that " the logical analysis of science," while formally it is very precise, begins to fail the moment it is applied to any actual body of scientific knowledge. For it says at the outset that science is founded on protocols, and then fails to say how the protocols may be recognised.

Precision in form may, and in this case does, mask the greatest confusion and lack of precision in content.

The difficulty here indicated has been tackled in what may appear a most bold and radical way by Carnap's follower, Neurath. But Neurath's philosophising only makes the inadequacy and confusing character of the " analysis " still more obvious.

It will be remembered that according to Carnap's logical "Principle of Tolerance," the syntax of a language may be chosen quite arbitrarily. Neurath applies this "principle" to science. According to him, it is only "a more or less refined metaphysics" to suppose that protocols are "the simplest statements," "needing no justification," "describing directly given experience," and so on. Scientists may therefore quite arbitrarily select whatever sentences they like to serve as their protocols—and if they get into any difficulties, they may reject these protocols and use others instead.

So the question as to which sentences are protocols and which are not, is decided from time to time by agreement between scientists. How they make that decision is their own business, and has nothing to do with logic or philosophy. And the study of the principles according to which such decisions are made is simply a matter of "sociology"—namely, a new branch of sociology which studies the peculiar social behaviour of scientists.[1]

I cannot but regard this very "radical" treatment of science as the *reductio ad absurdum* of the method of "analysis" which gave rise to it. It just dodges the issue of the logical foundations of science. It presents the method of science as merely a method of arbitrarily juggling with statements. And the principles which determine which statements are to be accepted by science, and which rejected, it dismisses by means of the formula: "sociology."

Thus the conception of the ultimate protocol, like its parent the absolutely elementary proposition, gives rise to nothing but difficulties and absurdities.

Two further remarks may be made under this heading.

First, whatever the protocol may or may not be, the "analysis" of science as based on protocols is an analysis which denies that science constitutes objective knowledge; that is to say, a system of propositions which are verifiable, and whose verification shows that they correspond with objective reality.

For according to this analysis, scientific statements are based on protocols and are verified by comparing them with the protocol. Hence their truth does not consist in any sort

[1] See Weinberg: *An Examination of Logical Positivism*, p. 276.

of correspondence with the objective world, but in correspondence with the protocol. As for the protocol itself, it is just "given," or arbitrarily selected. Hence nowhere is there any test which shows correspondence with the objective world. The "truth" of science does not consist in correspondence with the objective world—that is "a more or less refined metaphysics"; it consists in a certain internal coherence amongst the statements made by scientists.

Neurath says that how and why scientists arrive at their results may be explained by sociology. But even that will not get him far—for sociology, after all, is itself only a science like the rest, based, presumably, on arbitrarily selected statements. Why a body of "scientific" philosophers should go to such lengths to cover up the fact that science constitutes objective knowledge, is very hard to explain on purely philosophical grounds. But I suspect that, although sociology will not go all the way in explaining why scientists reach the results they do—it will explain why they tackle one problem rather than another, but not the particular solution of the problem which they reach; yet it will go a long way further in explaining the conclusions reached by some philosophers. For there is evidently a very strong and well-grounded sociological urge to conceal the fact that science constitutes objective truth.

Secondly, what is the real basis for all this theorising about protocols? For just as the theory of the absolutely elementary proposition had its basis in the fact that we do formulate propositions which are elementary in form, so also the theory of the protocols of science has its basis in the fact that there *are* scientific statements which record observations, as distinct from other statements which formulate theories based on those observations.

All scientific theories arise from observations, and are checked through observations. Hence it is of very great importance in developing the body of scientific knowledge, that the observations should be accurately recorded; and the more "exact" the science, the more important does this recording of the observations become.

It is this fact that Carnap and the logical positivists are evidently trying to express in their theory about protocols. But they have not expressed it correctly.

If " protocols " are to be defined as " the records of observations," well and good. But in that case:

(1) It cannot be said that they absolutely " require no justification "—for the records of observations do require justification, need to be very carefully checked and verified, and in actual practice not only require justification but receive the justification that they require.

(2) It cannot be said that they " describe directly given experience or phenomena," because what they describe are objective material facts. For instance, if a scientist records readings from a galvanometer, he is not recording his own subjective experience, but he is recording the objective effects of certain physical processes upon a certain physical object, namely, the galvanometer.

(3) Once it has been decided what observations are to be made, there is nothing in the least arbitrary about which records of observations are to be accepted or which rejected.

Where Carnap and his followers have gone astray, and have been led " into insoluble difficulties," is in their arbitrary and dogmatic insistence that the philosophy of science must not move out of the realm of logical syntax, or of " speech-thinking," and must not deal with the meaning of propositions or their relationship with facts. Thus observing that science is based on the records of observations, they try to give a syntactical or formal definition of the records of observations. There can be no such definition. What makes the record of an observation what it is, and gives it its place in the system of science, is the fact that it records an observation—which is a non-formal definition, referring to its meaning. There are no special words, or ways of putting words together, which can be shown to be equivalent to the recording of an observation. The self-imposed search for such a formal definition has led the logical positivists into a number of absurdities. Namely:

(1) They have postulated ultimately simple and non-justifiable statements, which lie at the logical basis of all other statements—corresponding to the absurdity of the absolutely elementary proposition.

(2) In trying to find out how these statements can be recognised, they have committed what they themselves admit

is the unforgivable sin in philosophy—asking questions to which there is no answer.

(3) In then giving up the attempt to answer this question, they have then fallen into an even greater absurdity, namely, supposing that the basic data for science are chosen quite arbitrarily, and that the choice of one scientific theory rather than another is only a matter of " sociology."

And finally (4) having been guilty of these absurdities, they accuse those who hold that science constitutes knowledge of the objective material world of being " metaphysicians " who engage in " idle dispute about pseudo-theses."

3. *The Physical Language*

I now pass on to some considerations about Carnap's theory of " physicalism," which he arrived at on the basis of his " logic of science."

Carnap's " logic of science " lays down a-priori what the logical form of science (or the general " logical syntax " of " the language of science ") must be. The theory of physicalism is derived from a-priori considerations.

The body of science, it is argued, consists in a number of different sciences, each with its own peculiar language and based on its own protocols—but somehow there must be a unity of science. This unity of science cannot be derived from examination of the actual way in which all the different branches of science deal with the same subject matter, namely, the objective material world, because we are forbidden to talk of the objective reference of science, other than simply by saying that science uses an " object-language." Consequently, the argument goes, if there is a unity of science, then this must mean that there is one universal language of science, into which all the statements of all the sciences can be translated.

Thus " the universal language of science " is produced as a means of helping the logical theory out of a difficulty. The necessity of such a language is based on its necessity in the logical theory of Carnap. It is not based at all on an examination of science and the subject matter of science. If we consider, not logical theories, but the actual sciences, as studies of various aspects of the real material world, then we can perceive no necessity whatever why all those different aspects of the objective material world should all be expressible in the same set of terms. The fact that Carnap's theory demands such a language indicates rather that there is something wrong with Carnap's theory, than that such a language necessarily exists.

Hence the very postulate of the universal language of science is an arbitrary postulate. Still more arbitrary is the characterisation of that language, namely, the assertion that the universal language is " the physical language."

Every statement of every science, it is asserted, " can be translated into physical language " ; that is, into a language " characterised by the fact that statements of the simplest form attach to a specific set of co-ordinates (three space and one time co-ordinate) a definite value or range of values of physical state."

Where is the justification of this sweeping generalisation? It may be sought, but sought in vain. All that Carnap supplies in *The Unity of Science* are some very general assertions, with regard to each science, that its principles *can* be so translated into the language of physics. In proceeding from generalities to the investigation of particular cases, then very considerable difficulty is encountered in the application of the theory of physicalism.

Take, for instance, the science of economics. Carnap has defined " the economic language " as a language in which " expressions ' supply and demand,' ' wage,' ' price,' etc." occur. Presumably " statements of the simplest form " in " the economic language " would be exemplified in such a statement as : " Hodge (a farm worker) receives £3 10s. (wages)." Can this statement be " translated " into physical language?

Now to me two things appear evident in this example.

(1) Whenever it is true that Hodge receives £3 10s. wages for his week's work on the farm, then a certain physical event takes place, which, as Carnap says, could be expressed by a statement which " attaches to a specific set of co-ordinates . . . a definite value or range of values of physical state." For Hodge and the Treasury notes which he receives as remuneration for his toil are all physical objects.

(2) But nevertheless, if that physical statement were made,

it would *not* be a translation of the statement that Hodge receives wages. For what is meant by being *a worker*, by *wages*, and by £3 10s. considered as a sum of *money*, cannot possibly be expressed in physical terms. The worker and the money have physical existence: but the relations which constitute their being as wage-worker and as money are not physical relations: and not Carnap nor anyone else can ever express them as physical relations.

Many other examples could be taken; but one example is sufficient to prove a negative. In general it may be confidently asserted that: (1) whatever may be stated, if it is true, then some physical statement is true; but (2) it is not the case that whatever may be stated, may be equally well stated in physical terms. The fact that some physical statement can theoretically be found to correspond to every statement, does not imply in any way that the language of physics is a universal language in which everything may be stated.

There exists a " unity of science." But this unity consists in the fact that the different sciences all study different, though related, aspects of one material world; not that all the statements of all the sciences can be expressed in the same set of terms, namely, physical terms.

Hence the theory of physicalism is not only a theory put forward on purely arbitrary and a-priori grounds, but it is certainly false into the bargain. And the fact that Carnap's method of " analysis " has need of such a theory, only shows that Carnap's rule that we must not study the content of science but only its syntactical form, is a rule which makes any correct analysis of science impossible.

The theory of physicalism is " correctly " expressed in the formal mode, as it has been expressed above. But Carnap also expresses it in the material mode. Expressed in the material mode, physicalism makes assertions about the nature of facts, as follows: " Every fact contained in the subject matter of science can be described in physical language," that is, in statements which " express a quantitatively determined property of a definite position at a definite time." In other words, all facts consist in the existence of " a quantitatively determined property of a definite position at a definite time."

Here, as was the case with Russell and Wittgenstein and their "atomic facts," Carnap's analysis leads at last to an a-priori presentation of the ultimate nature of the world.

Carnap calls this "Methodical Materialism," which is "a purified form" of "the older materialism." But where the "purification" comes in, it is hard to see. The theory of physicalism, expressed in its material mode, is merely a dogmatic statement of the very crudest form of "the older" mechanical materialism, which "reduces" everything to physical motions and says that qualitative differences are illusory. The advance of science itself has abundantly shown that this old cramped mechanical view of the nature of the material world is quite inadequate to explain the varied phenomena which we meet with in actual practice.

Nevertheless, there is a certain universality about physics. Considering the different forms of motion in the world, then every form of motion contains a physical motion.[1]

Matter enters into various forms of organisation. Under certain conditions, only physical motions take place. Under other conditions, the physical changes give rise to the organisation of chemical atoms and molecules, and chemical processes occur on the basis of physical processes. Under higher conditions of organisation, chemical processes give rise to organic processes, and organic processes to human thought and social life. At each stage of organisation, relations and corresponding laws of motion arise, which are not physical relations or laws, qualities come into being which are not physical qualities—but they have a physical basis. Physical phenomena, in this sense, are basic and universal.

But Carnap's theory of physicalism appears to distort the real nature of the universality of physics, that is, of the universality and basic character of physical motion. So long, indeed, as we have to deal purely with "the language of science," and are not allowed to deal with the content of science, and the kind of facts science is expressing, the real nature of the universality of physics and of "the unity of science" cannot be grasped.

Could we write a complete history of the evolution of the world, then the successive development of higher levels of the

[1] Cf. Engels: *Dialectics of Nature*, p. 36.

organisation of matter would be dealt with in that history. The first chapter would deal simply with physical motions. But it would be shown how those physical motions give rise to tendencies towards forming organisations of a more complex kind, and at a certain stage such tendencies are able to express themselves in the formation of molecules. Once this has come about, then there appear in the world new processes, chemical processes, the processes of chemical change and combination. Then come those particular chemical combinations which give rise to the phenomena of life. The evolution of living organisation gives rise to such an organisation as the brain, leading to conscious and purposive modes of life, social life, social history, and so on. Could then this history be written entirely in physical terms? No, it could not. Such a physical history of the world would not be able to describe all the new relationships, qualities and laws of motion which were successively appearing in the world in the course of the total world development.

To suppose that the history of the world would be only physical history is in fact a purely " metaphysical " supposition. This supposition is the supposition that physical events are in some absolute sense " the ultimate reality," so that a complete physical account of the world would say what the world ultimately is. But the truth is, that to approximate to a complete picture of the world, it would be necessary to describe the events at all levels. For instance, to deal in any completeness with the life of a human being, it would be necessary to study him socially, economically, psychologically, physiologically, chemically, etc., as well as physically: and the complex of motions that constitutes his life could not be " reduced " to physical motions.

4. *Methodical Materialism and Unmethodical Subjectivism*

On the basis of his theory of " physicalism," Carnap declared himself " a methodical materialist." I have shown how this " materialism " is in fact crude, dogmatic and untenable, and is in fact not materialism at all, for it is in truth only a theory about words. But it can also be shown how this " pseudo " materialism implies the very opposite of materialism, namely, the same subjectivism and solipsism as characterised all Carnap's philosophical ancestors—Berkeley, Hume, Mach, Russell, Wittgenstein.

Consider, for example, Carnap's statement, already quoted: " Suppose that a positivist maintains the thesis, ' A thing is a complex of sense-data,' and a realist the thesis, ' A thing is a complex of atoms.' . . . If we transfer to the formal mode of speech, it is in this case possible to reconcile the two theses."

Here Carnap proposes to " reconcile " materialism and subjectivism—the view that things have objective material being independent of all consciousness, and the view that things are complexes of sense-data. He effects this " reconciliation " by saying that to describe things in terms of sense-data and to describe them in material terms are not contradictory descriptions, but simply two alternative uses of language.

But if it is true *both* that things are complexes of atoms *and* that things are complexes of sense-data, this means that atoms are constructions from sense-data; for if atoms have objective material existence independent of consciousness, then if things *are* complexes of atoms they certainly are *not* complexes of sense-data.

Thus the " reconciliation " of materialism and subjectivism (or as Carnap says, of " realism " and " positivism "), means in fact the rejection of materialism and the acceptance of subjectivism. For if things can equally well be described in terms of sense-data as in material terms, then subjectivism is true, and materialism false. The " transference to the formal mode of speech " may obscure this fact, but cannot escape it.

Thus, disguised as it may be, there is the same subjectivism in Carnap as permeated the ideas of all his predecessors, from Berkeley to Wittgenstein.

Carnap insists as strongly as Berkeley or Mach or Wittgenstein, that the materialist " thesis " of the existence of the objective material world, and the correspondence of our perceptions and thoughts with this world, is nonsense and mere " metaphysics." He also insists that the opposite doctrine, as put forward by Berkeley or Mach, that what exists consists of our own sensations, ideas, experiences, is equally nonsense and " metaphysics." " We make no assertions as to whether the given is real and the physical world appearance, or vice versa;

for . . . such assertions belong to the class of unverifiable pseudo-statements."

But this method of settling a philosophical controversy by refusing to recognise its existence will not work. Whoever denies the existence of the material world—whether by saying straight out that it does not exist, or by saying that talk of it is nonsense—cannot escape the opposite position, the position of subjectivism and ultimately of solipsism, which says that nothing exists but sensations, ideas, experiences.

Consider again some of Carnap's statements, already quoted, respecting protocols. " The simplest statements in the protocol language . . . describe directly given experience or phenomena. . . . Question : What objects are the elements of given direct experience ? . . . Our investigations of the various departments of science lead to the conclusion that . . . given direct experiences are physical, i.e., spatio-temporal events."

Here the protocols are clearly supposed to deal with " the elements of direct experience." And since scientific knowledge can hardly deal with data beyond what is given in the protocols, scientific knowledge must deal with " given experience." Since " given experience " is " my experience," this means it would be hard to avoid solipsistic conclusions regarding knowledge, if it were not that " the correct formal mode of speech " comes to the rescue and prevents the obvious meaning and implication of the theory from being definitely stated. Since it is further stated that " given direct experiences are physical, i.e., spatio-temporal events," the form of subjectivism suggested here is similar to that popularised by Mach, according to which physical events are constructions out of elements of immediate or direct experience.[1]

[1] Mr. A. J. Ayer, in a book entitled *Foundations of Empirical Knowledge* (which foundations he selects from the materials provided by a number of different philosophers, but particularly from Carnap), very definitely states the subjectivist conclusion of logical positivism on his last page : " The most we can do is to elaborate a technique for predicting the course of our sensory experience."

CHAPTER 12

LOGICAL POSITIVISM (3)

1. *The " True Logic "*

In this chapter I shall examine some of the basic philosophical and logical presuppositions from whence Carnap's " analysis " of science was engendered.

Carnap says that it is an error to suppose that logical and philosophical principles " must constitute a faithful rendering of ' the true logic.' "

This statement has most obvious reference to the principles of logic in the narrow sense, that is, to what are sometimes called " the laws of thought " or " the principles of deductive inference," the type of principles that are worked out in systems of formal logic—such as: " p, and p implies q, implies q," or " if p implies q, and q implies r, then p implies r." Such principles, says Carnap, are merely syntactical rules. More precisely, they are syntactical rules of " formation and transformation." In no sense do they constitute a " rendering of the true logic." There is no objective standard determining their validity.

If by " the true logic " is here meant some transcendent system of timeless eternal truth, which has being independent of all thought and all existence, then doubtless Carnap is right. If we set up the platonic " ideal world " as the eternal truth, which must be mirrored in our logic, then we are demanding that logic must conform to something which is merely a figment of the philosophical imagination.

Russell, for instance, however unplatonic may have been his views on other subjects, did hold such platonic views about the subject of logic. " We shall find it convenient only to speak of things *existing* when they are in time," he wrote. " But universals do not exist in this sense ; we shall say that they *subsist* or *have being*, where ' being ' is opposed to ' existence ' as being timeless. The world of universals, therefore, may also be described as the world of being. The world of being is unchangeable, rigid, exact, delightful to the mathematician, the logician, the builder of metaphysical systems, and all who love perfection more than life."[1]

No doubt Carnap is quite right when he says that the principles of logic do not "constitute a faithful rendering of 'the true logic'" in this sense. But that is not to say that they are merely principles of syntax, which do not in any way conform to the world of being, and to the "logic" of that world, in the sense which would be understood by any ordinary person, who does not retire into the realms of platonic imagination in search of perfection.

There really is a world, in which we live, and which contains objects, events, facts, the passage of time, the transformation of one state of affairs into another. And we in the world perceive, think and act, and formulate the results of our perceptions, thoughts and actions in communicable propositions.

There exist, therefore, relations of correspondence between perceptions, thoughts and propositions, on the one hand, and objective things, events and facts on the other hand. These relations are tested in actual experience, in the practice of life. And in virtue of such relations, propositions represent things more or less correctly or incorrectly, adequately or inadequately; and moreover, in virtue of such relations, one method of thinking leads to results conformable with realities, while another method of thinking does not.

It follows from this that there must be a sense in which the principles of logic (or laws of thought) do have an objective validity, and represent something more than just syntactical "rules of formation and transformation" as defined by Carnap. It is quite another question, of course, whether "the laws of thought" as formulated in the usual logical text-books are correctly and adequately formulated.

The essential issue here involved is that Carnap deliberately ignores the fact that propositions have a meaning. But yet, if you abstract from the meaning of propositions, that is, their relation with facts, or with the world, then you have ceased to deal with propositions.

To construct a theory of logic on the basis of ignoring that propositions refer to facts, is on a par with constructing a theory of, for instance, money, on the basis of ignoring that

[1] Russell: *Problems of Philosophy*, p. 155.

money is a means of exchange. Some " formal " theory of economics might be constructed on such a basis, but it would not be a theory of money. And that propositions are a means of communicating information, true or false, about the world, can no more be ignored, than that money is a means of promoting the exchange of commodities.

While, then, it remains perfectly true that the principles of logic do have a syntactical aspect—syntactically they certainly do serve as " rules of formation and transformation "—there nevertheless remains more to be said on the matter.

Propositions communicate information. And the principles of logic, or laws of thought, do accordingly possess an objective validity, or if you like " constitute a faithful rendering of the true logic," in the sense that they show that, given certain information, what further is involved in or follows from it.

The validity of logical principles results from this, that the information expressed in the conclusion is involved in or contained in the information expressed in the premises. Understanding this, one is entitled to say that a principle is *valid* ; which is more than just saying that it represents a rule of transformation employed in the syntax of a particular language.

Thus the idea that the principles of logic are just rules of syntax, which in no sense " constitute a rendering of the true logic," arises from Carnap's insistence that we may deal only with the relations between propositions, but not with the relations between propositions and facts. But since the very essence of a proposition lies in that relation, this insistence is an insistence on a false abstraction which falsifies the significance of the principles of logic.

2. *Philosophical Principles as " Syntactical Rules." Some Remarks about Time*

Having asserted that the principles of logic, in the strict and narrow sense, are syntactical rules which in no way " constitute a rendering of the true logic," Carnap goes much further, and extends this assertion to the wider sphere of philosophy.

He clearly asserts that all general " philosophical theses "—such as " Time is infinite," " A fact is a combination of objects," or " Matter is prior to mind," or " Motion is the mode of existence of matter "—can be correctly stated only " in the formal mode." They are not statements about the world, but about the way in which we use language. Such statements do not mirror "the true logic" of the world, but are simply statements of syntax.

Carnap further maintains that the reason why it is so necessary to interpret all such statements strictly as statements of syntax is, that if we attempt to use or interpret such theses as statements about the world, then this must lead to "questions whose discussion ends in contradictions and insoluble difficulties."

Moreover, because they are only statements of syntax, it follows that the choice of one such thesis rather than its opposite, is quite arbitrary. For instance, we can use "a time-language" which postulates an infinite or a finite past; the choice is one of convenience, not one of giving an account of time which corresponds to its objectively infinite or finite nature. In other words, if we say: "Time has a beginning," or if we say: "The world was created" or: "The world was never created," it is not time or the world we are referring to, but we are merely laying down rules for the use of language. And this will be made clear only if we express such statements strictly "in the formal mode."

It further follows, as Carnap has pointed out, that what have been taken to be contradictions between opposite philosophical standpoints (for example, between idealism and materialism, or between the theistic notion of creation and the atheistic notion that matter is eternal) are in reality not such contradictions, but simply differences between the syntactical rules of language which different groups of people choose to employ. They are mere differences of language, and so the controversies between such groups are only "pseudo-" controversies.

The best and clearest way of examining these assertions would be to take an example. Here then is an example from "Logical Syntax" of a general philosophical thesis, which is correctly to be formulated "in the formal mode":

Material Mode	*Formal Mode*
Time is infinite in both directions, forwards and backwards.	Every positive and negative real number expression can be used as a time-co-ordinate.

It must be noted that, according to Carnap, the discussion of such a thesis in " the material mode " must give rise to " insoluble difficulties and contradictions."

I am going to test this assertion by trying the experiment of a brief discussion.

In this example it may at once be remarked that the " difficulties and contradictions " referred to had already been encountered by Kant in his discussion of this very question about the infinity or otherwise of time.

In what he called *The First Antinomy of Pure Reason*, Kant discussed whether time has a beginning or not ; and he came to the conclusion that it could be proved equally conclusively both that time has a beginning and that it has none. This can certainly be recognised as both a difficulty and a contradiction.

As is well known, Kant proposed to remove this difficulty and to solve this contradiction by maintaining that time does not apply to " things in themselves " at all, but is merely a phenomenal appearance arising from the peculiar way in which we apprehend things.

It appears to me that Carnap's way of avoiding the alleged difficulties is not essentially different from Kant's. Kant hoped to avoid the alleged difficulties by transferring time from the sphere of " things in themselves " to the sphere of " phenomena." Carnap proposes to avoid the alleged difficulties by translating theses about time into theses " in the formal mode," dealing not with the world but with the use of words.

Thus according to Carnap, to assert the infinity of time—or on the other hand to assert that time has a beginning or an end—is not to assert anything about the world. It is simply a statement of a verbal convention which we propose to employ. And if it is asked why we should adopt this convention rather than some other—rather than the convention, for instance, which fixes a beginning or an end to time—then the answer is that this is the convention customarily employed in the science of physics ; but if for some reason physicists find it convenient to use another convention instead, they are at liberty to do so. It must not be supposed that the permission accorded in this convention to use any real number as a time-coordinate is " justified " because it corresponds to the really infinite nature of time. We must not suppose this, because it is a prejudice to suppose that such propositions should " constitute a faithful rendering of the true logic " of the world. On the contrary, " we have in every respect complete liberty with regard to the forms of language."

But is this account of the significance of the thesis of the infinity of time a correct account? I do not think it is. Forgetting, then, all about the formulation " in the formal mode," I shall proceed with the experiment of discussing the infinity of time " in the material mode," in order to test whether such discussion does so inevitably lead to difficulties and contradictions.

But to begin with, there is one point to make about words. For " time " is a somewhat obscure and confusing word. It must be understood, then, that if we make assertions about time, those assertions generally refer to nothing other than the events which take place in a time-order, and are about the time-order of those events. For time (and space) are not like a box, in which events are placed, but which could just as well exist empty without any events inside. Time is moreover a measurable quantity, though periods of time can be measured in many different ways.

It results from this that there can be a certain ambiguity associated with the word " time "; and so, in discussing time and wishing to avoid difficulties, we must try to make clear what it is we do mean by " time."

" Time " can have a double meaning. On the one hand it can be used to refer to some definite sequence of events the periods of which can be measured on some definite time-scale. But on the other hand it *can* be used in a wider sense, as referring not to any definite measurable time-order, but in a general way to any motion or sequence of events. Clearly, if we are to use real numbers as time-coordinates, it is to a definite time-order in the first sense that we must be referring; for unless there exists some definite scale of measurement there is no possibility of using real numbers as time-coordinates.

Let us take it, then, that in speaking about time we are referring to a definite sequence of events, the periods of which can be measured on the scale of the motions of the heavenly bodies, or of radiation, or of the periodicity of atomic processes.

In that case, it seems perfectly in order to ask, " in the material mode" ; Did time have a beginning?—meaning : Did this physical time-order of events, to which we ourselves belong, and the periods of which can be measured in terms of our clocks or other scales of time-measurement, have a beginning ? We can even ask, not merely did it have a beginning, but *when* did it begin ?

As proof of this it may be mentioned that according to the cosmology being worked out by E. A. Milne, the change in time of the physical properties of events is such that the time-order must have had a beginning, which took place approximately two thousand million years ago. This hypothesis is obviously of extraordinary philosophical interest. But whether it is to be accepted or not is not to be decided by philosophical arguments a-priori (of the sort that lead to "insoluble difficulties and contradictions "), but is to be decided in the way that a decision is reached about all scientific hypotheses, that is, by reference to its explanatory power and the extent to which it can be verified.

For instance, the fact that, on the basis of Milne's theory, J. B. S. Haldane was able to give a simultaneous and simple explanation of the origin of the solar system, of double stars, and of the irregularities of the motions of double stars, is decidedly an argument in favour of Milne's theory ; which was already able to explain another and quite different phenomenon, the apparent recession of the spiral nebulae.[1]

Thus it can be noted that the statement that the time-order did have a beginning, may be positively asserted, if we find evidence from the behaviour of things which points to the conclusion that the whole sequence of events to which they belong must have had an origin. But the case appears to be different with the opposite assertion, that the time-order did not have any beginning. For to say that it did not have any beginning could only rest on the negative assurance that so far no evidence pointing to a beginning had been found.

But what follows about time in the wider sense, as referring not to any definite measurable time-order, but in a general way to any motion or sequence of events ?

---

[1] See Haldane : *Marxist Philosophy and the Sciences*, Ch. 2. Also *Nature*, vol. 155, p. 133 ff, and *American Scientist*, vol. 33, No. 3.

In this wider sense, it would be quite in order to assert that there was a time before time began ; that is to say, before our particular time-order, containing the types of periodic events whereby *we* can measure time, began. Indeed, unless we are going to postulate creation, with all the difficulties which that particular conception does undoubtedly involve, we must suppose that in this wider sense time is infinite, even if in the narrower sense, which allows of our particular form of measurement of time, it had a beginning.

Thus if we are called upon (as in philosophy we are called upon) to try to answer the question : Is time finite or infinite ? then it would be in order to attempt to find an answer along the lines of saying : Both. Any sequence of events of a particular type, such that the period of their development can be measured by a particular time-scale, may be finite ; but there need nevertheless be no creation and no ultimate end.[1]

Now these statements, expressed " in the material mode " as they are, appear not to involve the " difficulties and contradictions " which, according to Carnap, are inevitably produced by such discussions " in the material mode," and which were so ably expounded by Kant for the particular example of time.

This can be shown briefly by quoting from Kant's *First Antinomy*.

The first side of the antinomy proves that time could not have had a beginning, by the argument that to postulate a beginning leads to an impossibility.

" Let us assume," said Kant, " that the world has a beginning. Since the beginning is an existence which is preceded by a time in which the thing is not, there must have been a preceding time in which the world was not, i.e., an empty time. . . ." But " an empty time " is an impossibility. Therefore time cannot have had any beginning.[2]

This difficulty does not arise in the " philosophy of time " which I am suggesting. The argument is not valid, if we are speaking about time in the first sense, that is, as applying to a sequence of events measured on a definite time-scale. For in assuming that " the world " has a beginning, that is, that the

[1] Cf. Haldane : " Time and Eternity," in *Rationalist Review*, 1945.

[2] Kant: *Critique of Pure Reason, Transcendental Dialectic*, II, 2.

physical world of which we are part and which contains the types of periodic events with which we are familiar and by which we define the time-order, has a beginning, we need not assume that that beginning was preceded by " an empty time," in the second wider sense of time. We need not assume any ultimate creation. For the world could have arisen out of something else : the first event in the series of events which constitute our time-order could have been preceded by other events of another type.

The second side of Kant's antinomy proves that time must have had a beginning, by the argument that to suppose it to have been going on for ever leads to an impossibility.

If we do not assume some beginning of time, argued Kant, " then up to every given moment an eternity has elapsed, and there has passed away in the world an infinite series of successive states of things. Now the infinity of a series consists in the fact that it can never be completed. . . . It thus follows that it is impossible for an infinite world-series to have passed away . . ." (i.e., to have been completed). Therefore time must have had a beginning.[1]

The " point " of this argument can also be expressed in a story, which I remember having once heard from Wittgenstein, I forget in what context. It is the story of a very old man, who was heard to gasp out the number " 3." " Thank God, I have finished ! " he exclaimed. " What have you finished ? " he was asked. " I have just finished repeating all the numbers in π backwards," was his reply. It can be recognised that this story says something utterly impossible and inconceivable. Kant's argument is that, if time had no beginning, then the attainment of every moment of time that passes repeats just this same impossibility of the completion of an infinite series.

But the argument is not valid, the difficulty is not involved, if we are speaking of time in the second wider sense. For in assuming that there is no beginning to time in this sense, that is, that there is no ultimate creation, we need not assume that any " infinite world-series " has " passed away." On the contrary, we need assume no " world series " that has not both a beginning and an end. In particular, we need not assume that any *date* in the system of the physical world-series

[1] Kant : *Critique of Pure Reason, Transcendental Dialectic*, II, 2.

in which we live is the last and latest of any *infinite* series of dates, nor that any *period of time* is the last of any *infinite* series of such periods. For we need not assume that the series of periods and dates in question has been going on for ever. On the contrary, we can assume that it had a beginning and is finite, even though that beginning was not an absolute creation.

Incidentally, if we are to speak in this way about " the time before time," then it would appear that we must admit that its content and character is unknown to us. Our knowledge would be limited within our own time-system, to the physical world-order from which we arise and of which we are part. For knowledge itself and the possibility of knowledge must essentially arise from the conditions of the interaction between the conscious human organism and the external world. When therefore we encountered the limits of those conditions and of that world, we would come up against the limits of our knowledge—though within these limits knowledge might be capable of an indefinite development. This thought bears a relation to Spinoza's idea of the " infinite attributes " of " substance." Spinoza said that besides its physical and mental attributes, substance had an infinity of other attributes. Maybe he was right, but not quite in the sense that he intended. Reality could have developed and could develop many forms unknown to us, beyond the physical space-time-system in which we have our being, and which contains the phenomena of our consciousness. If, then, the thought suggested of the finitude and also the eventual complete disappearance of our world, of human consciousness and all its works, seems perhaps pessimistic, this is balanced by the thought of other possibilities, to us unknown but capable of infinite development.

It is now my contention that this example proves the following : That Carnap's statement, which is absolutely basic in his whole philosophy, that it is incorrect to formulate " in the material mode " such a thesis as that of the infinity or finitude of time, because such formulation must lead to " insoluble difficulties and contradictions," is itself incorrect. On the contrary, taking the thesis " in the material mode," as a statement about the world, it can be made reasonably comprehensible, in a way that leads to neither " contradictions " nor " insoluble difficulties."

Hence there seems to be no good reason why such theses should be regarded as merely " formal " theses about words, and not as " material " statements about the world. Little is gained by such a translation. But what is lost is the whole possibility of explaining the meaning of the questions, and of trying to find at least provisional answers about the subjects with which they deal. In other words, what is lost is the whole possibility of a scientific philosophy.

It may be added briefly, that the same sort of considerations apply to other examples.

For instance, Carnap takes the statement of Wittgenstein : "A fact is a combination of objects (entities, things)." This he translates into " the formal mode " as follows : "A sentence is a series of symbols." This "formal" statement is certainly quite unexceptionable, but it belongs to grammar rather than to philosophy. Turning, however, to "the material mode," it is possible, and indeed desirable, to engage in philosophical discussion about the questions dealt with in this statement of Wittgenstein.

When Wittgenstein says, speaking of the world and not of words, that " the world divides into facts," and that " a fact is a combination of objects," he is making a clear statement of a certain metaphysical theory, which does admittedly lead to considerable difficulties, some of which I have commented on in previous chapters.

But what is the source of these difficulties ?

Their source is not that Wittgenstein should not have attempted to say anything " philosophical " about the world, but that he lays down a-priori a metaphysical theory of the world—that it consists of " atomic facts "—into which the world as we know it obstinately refuses to fit.

And so Wittgenstein's statement should be " corrected," not by translating it into a trivial statement about grammar (which in any case does clearly *not* represent what Wittgenstein meant), but by the more difficult though more interesting procedure of trying to find a more adequate formulation " in the material mode."

And I would suggest that if, instead of taking " facts " and " objects " as ultimate fixed constituents of the world, we tried to present them rather as derivative from the many-sided and changing *processes* going on in the world, then we could arrive at a much more satisfactory account of things, dealing with the world as it appears to us, and not just with words without consideration of their meaning.

" The world is not to be comprehended as a complex of ready-made *things*, but as a complex of processes, in which apparently stable things, and also their mind-images in our heads, go through an uninterrupted change of coming into being and passing away. . . ."[1]

This, I submit, is an example of a reasonably comprehensible philosophical statement " in the material mode," suggesting a line of philosophical thought which may lead to difficulties, but not difficulties which there is any reason to think " insoluble." And to translate this statement into " the formal mode " would not only not be helpful, but would destroy its whole meaning.

3. *Some Questions of Language*

I have tried to show that it is not true that all philosophical questions can be reduced to questions of language. But having said this, it is further necessary to point out that some questions which (when expressed in the usual " material mode ") seem to be questions about the nature of the world, *are* nevertheless in a sense questions of language.

It is this fact which gives the basis and apparent justification for Carnap's insistence on the necessity of translation " into the formal mode."

Hence it is not enough, in criticism of Carnap, to say simply that not all philosophical questions are questions of language. It is further necessary to sort out which questions are questions of language and which are not.

I must preface that in what follows I am putting forward some brief considerations and proposals rather than attempting to work out here the whole theory of this subject. It is a subject which raises some complicated problems of the logic of science, the full discussion of which would need a great deal more work.

[1] Engels : *Feuerbach*, Ch. 4.

Let us consider a simple example.

It is very generally believed that the nature of the world is such that any two sides of a triangle are greater than the third. Thus if I am standing at one corner of a triangular field, ABC, then if I measure the distance from A to B, it will always be less than from A to C and C to B. And this will be verified by measuring the three sides.

Nevertheless, if I choose to use a different method of measuring lengths from the usual method—for instance, not by a " rigid " scale or by such units as steps, but with an elastic tape—then I can find instances in which two sides of a triangle would not be greater than the third.[1]

Thus two sides of a triangle are or are not greater than the third according to the method of measurement we adopt. The difference, therefore, between someone who asserts that any two sides of a triangle are greater than the third, and someone who asserts the contrary, is not a difference between people making contradictory assertions about real triangles, one of which is true and the other false—for all real triangles will remain exactly the same in either case. It is only a difference between one who uses one mode of measuring the sides of triangles, and " a geometrical language " corresponding thereto, and one who uses another mode of measurement. Thus whether any two sides of a triangle are always greater than the third, is not a question whose answer depends simply on the nature of the world (the objective properties of real triangles), but it is a question of measure and language.

In general, there are many instances in which we can be presented with a choice between different methods of measurement, and different " languages " arising therefrom. According to which method of measurement and which language we use, we may seem to be formulating contradictory statements about the world. But the differences between those statements, correctly understood, are reduced to differences arising from different methods of measurement.

Thus cases in which contradictory statements about the world can be reduced to differences in language sometimes arise from the choice which exists, in describing the world, between different possible methods of measurement. Our

[1] Cp. Eddington : *Space, Time and Gravitation*, p. 3 ff.

description of the material world is often formulated in terms derived from measurements, and according as we use one or another possible method of measurement, our description of the world turns out very differently. Such differences are, then, differences in alternative "languages," not differences between rival world-theories.

The principle here involved can, however, be generalised further.

When we measure anything (for instance, the distance between A and B), what we are doing is to carry out a certain definite operation (such as stretching a tape from A to B), and we then express the distance in terms of the results of that operation.

A measurement is an operation the results of which can be expressed in a quantity. But in general whether we are measuring things or giving non-quantitative descriptions of them, the same principle applies. In formulating propositions about any kind of property or relationship occurring in the world, we do it by carrying out some operation, and then we express what we want to say in terms of the results of that operation. We cannot say or know anything about the world otherwise.

Therefore in so far as there may exist any choice in the mode of operation to be carried out, then a different mode of expression, a different language, will result corresponding to the different mode of operation used. And such expressions may in certain cases be contradictory.

Hence in the most general form the following may be stated. That cases in which contradictory statements about the world can be correctly traced to differences of language, arise from the choice which may exist, in describing the world, between different possible modes of operation for obtaining an expression of the properties of things. According as we use one method or another, our description of the world may turn out very different.

Here it must be insisted that this is already something very different from the contentions of Carnap. Carnap presents a somewhat simplified picture of the free choice which is alleged to exist between different languages with different syntaxes. But the fact is that the choice between different languages is *derivative* from the choice between different modes of operation for obtaining the expression of facts. And the syntax of the language is derivative from the character of the method of operation and from what follows if we are to express the facts in terms of that method.

We gain knowledge of the world by carrying out operational activities in the world. And the formulation of our conclusions about the same facts will be different, and may even be contradictory, according as they are based on one or another method.

There also arises this point, that an operation has a purpose. And hence it is certainly not the case that any choice of method which exists is an absolutely free and arbitrary choice. For a given purpose a given method will probably be better than any other.

To take an example from methods of measurement. It is certainly better for most purposes to measure lengths in the way in which we do measure them, so that two sides of a triangle are always greater than the third, than to measure them with an elastic tape ; for people who used elastic tapes would not find themselves in possession of much useful information for the guidance of their normal affairs.

In what follows I shall, for the sake of simplicity, confine my remarks in the first place to examples of measurement. How do different methods of measurement give rise to different languages ?

Every method of measurement depends upon the selection of a unit of measurement. The method of measurement, or rather the expression of the results of the measurement, entails the convention that all the units are the same. But that all the units are the same, is not a statement of fact. It is the statement of a convention which is adopted in the expression of facts in accordance with the given method of measurement. (In Carnap's phraseology, it is a statement of the syntax of the language which we choose to employ.)

For example, suppose we measure lengths with a foot rule. We then express all distances all over the world in terms of feet. But is it a fact that one foot is the same length in Timbuctoo as in London ? This is not a question of fact. For that one foot is always the same length is a convention. If we liked, we could say that feet got longer (or shorter) the greater the distance from London. We do not say this, because it would introduce unnecessary complications into our description of the world. But if we did decide to speak in this way, then the geography taught at schools would be rather different from that taught at present, and also we would not be taught euclidian geometry.

To take another example. Do similar atomic processes always continue at the same speed? Again, there is a convention involved in the question. It depends on your system of measuring and calculating times. Thus according to E. A. Milne we can measure time either on the "kinematic" scale or on the "dynamic" scale. "We can make our calculations using either kinematical or dynamical time, and every verifiable result will be just the same. Nevertheless it is roughly true to say that radiation keeps kinematical time and matter dynamical time."[1] Does radiation keep the right time and matter get fast or slow, or vice versa? This is not a question of fact, but of language, depending on your method of measuring and calculating time. Which is the right time is simply conventional.

It can be seen from these examples that many questions raised in contemporary physical theories of "the expanding universe," which appear to be extremely puzzling if understood "in the material mode," are in reality measurement and language questions. Is the whole universe expanding or not? That depends on how you look at it. At the present stage of physical science, the problem of sorting out questions which are matters of convention from those which are matters of fact, is a problem which essentially has to be tackled if a coherent picture of the material world is to emerge.

The reason why such questions of language, and of "the logical analysis of our language," have come forward rather prominently in the recent developments of the philosophy of science, arises from the development of science itself, and in the first place from the theory of relativity.

Let us say that there is Space, infinitely extended in three dimensions, and that euclidian geometry is true of it; that

[1] Haldane: "New Theory of the Past," *American Scientist*, vol. 33, No. 3, p. 131.

there is also Time, which flows evenly without beginning or end ; and that there is also Matter, bits of which are scattered all over space and act on each other in time with forces proportional to their distances. In that case everything must have an absolute measure. And the question of whether two sides of a triangle are greater than the third, of whether a foot always stays the same length, of whether atomic processes are speeding up or slowing down or going on at the same rate, of whether everything in the universe is expanding or contracting or staying the same size—are all questions of fact. But the fact that we are never able to establish such absolute measures is what has led to the rejection of this whole metaphysical theory.

We reject, then, the metaphysical theory that the world consists of (*a*) space, (*b*) time and (*c*) matter, which for a long time was uncritically accepted by science (because science had not yet advanced to a point where it made any difference whether you accepted this theory or not). This involves at once the realisation that many questions which on the old view were regarded as questions of fact are correctly to be understood as questions of language. It involves the realisation that in formulating a description of the world we must often be careful to specify that this is the description according to a particular set of observers using particular methods, and that other observers using other methods could describe the same facts in a different way.

But does this involve that we should say that there is no material world at all ? Or alternatively, that we must say that whether there is a material world or not is just another question of language ?

Of course not.

There is a world. There is an objective order of events in space and time. There are objective processes. We ourselves are a part of the world and know about it by living in it. And different aspects of the truth about the world are variously expressed in different ways according to the methods which we use for discovering and formulating that truth, and the different conventions which we accordingly employ for its expression.

Thus : " Space is real as a system of relationships between

material objects or events. But it has no absolute existence apart from matter, and a belief in its existence apart from matter is a step away from materialism towards metaphysics. The order of events in time within a given material system is an objective fact. The scale on which they are to be measured is a matter of convenience."[1]

Next arises the consideration (already referred to) that the choice between different possible methods of measurement and different conventions, is not a purely arbitrary choice, but that one convention is *better* than another for a given purpose.

Here the meaning, or at least an important part of the meaning, of "better" appears to be as follows. That one convention is better than another if it enables us to express the existence of certain uniformities in nature in which we are interested.

For example, the ancient Egyptians were interested in surveying their land and in predicting the date of the flooding of the Nile. Hence they needed to adopt a method of measuring time and space according to which the year would always take roughly the same time, and Egypt would always stay roughly the same size. Had they measured their lands with elastic tapes, and the time of events by the speed of their high priest's pulse, then they could not have carried out the surveys and predictions which they wanted. Their fields would have changed size and events would have speeded up or slowed down in a very confusing manner. Much the same considerations continue to apply for us today, and will go on applying until the order of events and the laws of nature become very different from the present.

It should be carefully noted that the statement that a certain method of measurement is better for certain purposes is clearly not a syntactical statement in Carnap's sense. It is not a statement about language, but about the relationship of language with what is expressed by language.

That uniformities exist in nature such that they can be best expressed in terms of certain conventions corresponding to certain methods of measurement, states a truth about nature.

For example, if we take the year as always lasting the same period, and Egypt as always staying the same size, then we

[1] Haldane: *Marxist Philosophy and the Sciences*, p. 67.

shall find regularities in the flooding of the Nile, in the movement of heavenly bodies, and also, when we investigate them, in the movements of atoms and electric charges—obviously this expresses an important truth about nature, namely, about the character of the processes involved in such events as the flooding of rivers, the movement of the heavenly bodies, and the movements of atoms.

When *new* discoveries are made and *new* fields of investigation opened out, this may often lead to the rejection, or at least the important modification, of former accepted conventions, because these fail in some way in the expression of the new material. And this change in language may in turn raise new questions, and suggest various clues leading to more new discoveries and more new fields of investigation.

Hence at no time can any method, or any language or mode of expression based on it, be regarded as final and perfect, as " the right expression " of " final truth." Thus the continual change and modification in the character of scientific theory as science advances, involving at certain stages what are called " crises " of science, when a whole philosophy, as it were, breaks down, and something new and different has to emerge from the catastrophe.

But it can happen that at one and the same time one convention can be better for one purpose and another for another. If one sort of uniformity is best expressed by one convention, a different sort of uniformity may be such that it is best expressed by quite a different convention. In that case we will appear to have two sets of contradictory results.

An example has already been given in Milne's use of the kinematical and dynamical time-scales.

According to Milne, radiation keeps kinematical time and matter keeps dynamical time, so that it is better to use kinematical time for some purposes and dynamical time for others. On the kinematic time-scale, the whole universe is expanding and the day and year are getting longer, whereas this is not so on the dynamical scale.

If it is the case, then, that two such time-scales can be used, what is the problem raised ? The problem raised is not the " metaphysical " and " insoluble " one of whether the universe is " really " expanding or not. The real problem arises from the fact that there exists a lack of uniformity between matter and radiation, and therefore the implications and consequences of such a lack of uniformity have to be worked out.

Thus Milne remarks : " It is not a fanciful speculation to see in the interplay of radiation keeping kinematical time with matter obeying the classical laws of mechanics on dynamical time a phenomenon giving rise to the possibility of a change in the universe in time, and so an origin for the action of evolution in both the inorganic and organic universe."[1]

Here, then, the fact (if it is a fact) that kinematical time is better for one purpose and dynamical time for another, and the resulting contradiction between statements based on the one time-scale and those based on the other, reflects the existence of a form of opposition between interacting processes in nature—an opposition that takes the form of matter and radiation " not keeping time."

The existence of forms of opposition between interacting processes in nature is something which inevitably must in the long run result in changes in the whole character of the total process within which the opposition exists.

Thus if it is the case that matter and radiation do not, over long periods of time, keep pace uniformly with one another, then as Milne points out, the resulting " interplay " over long periods would mean that not merely was there an evolution of different types of objects in the universe, but an evolution of the universe itself—a change in the fundamental laws of nature. Such an opposition between matter and radiation would in time bring about a change in the laws of nature, so that the laws of nature themselves could not be regarded as being fixed and eternal but must be subject to change like everything else.

Hence if one convention is better for one purpose and another for another, the resulting " contradictions " need not be dismissed as " mere differences in language." That one convention is better for one purpose and another for another may express the existence of an opposition between different processes in nature ; and the occurrence of the contradiction arising from the use of the rival conventions should therefore provide a clue for the deeper understanding of nature, and suggest the search for a mode of expression which will

[1] See *Nature*, February 3rd, 1945, p. 140.

adequately express the underlying opposition and its consequences, and so get rid of the employment of contradictory formulations for different purposes.

Here is another much simpler example. If the continents on the earth's surface are moving, then location by latitude and longitude and by reference to fixed material objects (for instance, some recognised landmark) must contradict one another over long periods. This contradiction would reflect the existence of the opposition and stress on the earth's surface due to the movement of the continents, and the resulting change in the configuration of the earth's surface.

A very suggestive example can be taken from a sphere other than the use of methods of measurement.

It is possible to describe observed facts in terms of our own sensations—to use, as some philosophers would say, a sense-datum language. This then involves an alternative and contradictory mode of expression to that employed in exact science. For instance, according to one way of speaking we describe the table as "solid," in terms of our sensation when we bump up against it. But in another context the table is anything but solid, but consists mainly of empty space. Again, I can describe the room as containing a number of coloured objects; or I can describe it in a way that does not allow of the occurrence of such "secondary qualities" as colour. Hence a contradiction.

Some philosophers say that the one language does not describe the real world at all, and that therefore one language is right and the other wrong. Thus certain mechanical materialists have said that it is wrong to say that things are really coloured, and certain subjective idealists have said that it is wrong to think that anything except our sensations of solidity, colour, etc., really exist in the world. Other philosophers, the logical positivists, then appear on the scene and say that the whole controversy is about pseudo-questions, and that all that is involved is alternative uses of language.

But none of these philosophers is correct. The existence of such contradictory formulations expresses the interaction of fundamental opposites in nature, matter and mind, being and consciousness. The content of consciousness reflects reality, but reflects it in its own way, according to its own laws, and not with an exact correspondence. Hence the contradiction reflects an "interplay" between the external world and its reflection in the human mind, and this interplay is fundamental for understanding the laws of the development of human thought and of human life.

Thus in general, the existence of different alternative methods of operation for arriving at results about the world, and of different languages involving contradictory formulations based on those different methods, is something which can provide important clues for the discovery of oppositional processes at work in nature, and so for the attainment of a deeper understanding of the laws of development.

To sum up.

Firstly. It is true that some questions, which may easily be taken to be questions of fact, are correctly to be understood as questions of language. Such questions can be recognised as arising from the different modes of operation possible for arriving at results expressing the truth. And in what way they are questions of language can be distinguished by analysis of the type of operation in question.

If we fail to recognise that such questions exist, but take them to be questions of fact, then it is quite true that we shall be led into many philosophical difficulties and con,usions. Thus far Carnap is in the right, that it is certainly important in philosophy to be on the look out for such questions arising from the use of language, and to know how to recognise them and to distinguish them.

Secondly. But in opposition to logical positivism, it must be insisted that these questions must be sorted out on the basis that the objective spatial-temporal world does exist external to all consciousness and thought. We ourselves, moreover, exist as part of the world, and gain our knowledge by interaction with the world around us. Our conclusions about the world are therefore to be understood as a representation of the world. But the character of that representation is determined by that of the methods which we adopt in arriving at it. And it can be a representation only of some partial aspect of the whole concrete reality, in terms expressing our own method and point of view.

Hence also it results that when the conclusions formulated

in any particular terms lead to contradictions, then it is not enough to say that such contradictions arise merely from the use of different languages, but the use of those different languages leading to different results can itself express the opposition between different aspects of reality; and from reflection on this can therefore emerge a fuller and more adequate conception of that reality.

Thirdly. Hence it does not follow by any means that philosophical questions are to be regarded as questions of language. The very contrary follows. Philosophical questions are basically not questions of language, but questions of the nature of the world and of our place in it. But in answering them it is certainly very important to understand the uses of language, and not to be misled into unjustifiable or even meaningless conclusions from misunderstanding the use of language.

Carnap is not wrong in drawing attention to the existence of questions of language. Where he goes wrong is in misinterpreting the significance of those questions. Like many other philosophers, he has got hold of one aspect of the truth, and distorted it into an error.

4. *The Formal Mode as Criterion of Sense and Nonsense*

I now proceed to some other questions arising from Carnap's conception of the essential " correctness " of " the formal mode of speech."

Carnap claims that the simple distinction between the " formal " and " material " modes of speech, and the consistent use of " the formal mode," enables him to avoid those " pseudo-theses " which are, he says, so common in philosophy and philosophical analysis.

" For complete safety," he says, " it would be better to avoid the use of the material mode entirely. . . . If this mode is still to be used, particular care must be taken that the statements expressed are such as might also be expressed in the formal mode. *This is the criterion which distinguishes statements from pseudo-statements in philosophy.*"

This statement is worth examining. Here is a claim that the distinction of the formal from the material mode of speech gives " the criterion which distinguishes statements from pseudo-statements in philosophy." Can the statements be translated into the formal mode? That is the test.

This test is itself worth testing.

I have several times maintained the materialist thesis that material things exist independent of consciousness. Expressed in the formal mode, this would presumably read something as follows: " Sentences occur containing material-object designations which are not implied by other sentences containing consciousness designations." So evidently the materialist thesis will pass the test, though it gets reduced to a mere statement about language in the process.

But I shall next select a very different type of thesis.

The *Monadology* of Leibniz surely provides a classic example of a philosophical work which abounds in " pseudo-theses," and which is one mass of " metaphysics " from beginning to end. So I shall submit the first proposition of this work to the test.

" The monad . . . is a simple substance."

But this thesis also, this typical metaphysical utterance, will pass the test. It can easily be formalised, something as follows: " Monad designations can occur only as subjects in sentences, and no sentence in which one monad designation occurs implies or is implied by any other sentence in which some other monad designation occurs." And going through the *Monadology*, the whole of it, from the infinity of monads to the pre-established harmony in the best of all possible worlds, can *all* be expressed in the formal mode.[1]

Thus the criterion seems a bit too wide. It lets through even the most notorious " pseudo-thesis."

And there is good reason for this. The expression in the formal mode asserts nothing of the meaning of language or of the truth or falsity of propositions; it simply asserts syntactical rules about sentences and terms in the particular " language " referred to. And bearing this in mind, it can easily be perceived that the translation of every thesis into the formal mode is really a completely trivial operation. Whatever thesis may be asserted, however wildly " metaphysical " it may be, that thesis involves the use of certain terms and of certain

[1] Cf. Russell, *The Philosophy of Leibniz*, where he makes some tentative beginning at the formalising of Leibniz.

syntactical rules governing the use of those terms. *Every* thesis, therefore, can be translated into the formal mode. And therefore the possibility of translation into the formal mode is certainly not, as Carnap claims it is, " the criterion " for distinguishing " statements from pseudo-statements."

What it *does* test is the logical consistency of a thesis. Thus if a theory is self-contradictory, so that it breaks its own " rules," then this will be shown up immediately the theory is formalised. Or again, if terms are used which are not defined, or if terms are used ambiguously, this also may be shown up by the use of the formal mode of speech. In this respect, translation into the formal mode may have on occasion a certain philosophic and scientific utility. But it is far from evident that by " a pseudo-thesis " Carnap means merely a thesis which is self-contradictory. In fact, exactly what he does mean by such derogatory terms as " pseudo-thesis " and " metaphysics " now begins to become very obscure indeed.

In the case of the formalising of such a typical " metaphysical " thesis as Leibniz's one about " monads," someone may object that there is no sense in " monad designations." But this objection is irrelevant. The reply is that we are not concerned with the sense of terms and sentences, but solely with the syntactical rules of the language in which they occur ; and, by the Principle of Tolerance, we can make a language with any syntactical rules we like, and therefore have a perfect right to make a " monad language " for which Leibniz's philosophy expresses the syntactical rules.

Thus far from having provided " the criterion " for distinguishing " statements from pseudo-statements," Carnap's distinction of the formal from the material mode of speech tells us that we can say whatever we like ; it is all one, so long as we invent rules of language and stick to them consistently. Far from finding an infallible " criterion " for distinguishing sense from nonsense in philosophy, we find ourselves utterly unable to determine which theses are sense, which nonsense, which true, which untrue—and utterly unable to understand the meaning of anything. All that is required is to stick to the formal mode of speech, and there is no limit to the flights of metaphysical fancy we may indulge in.

As Carnap says, " Before us lies the boundless ocean of unlimited possibilities."

Carnap's principle, then, that philosophical theses should be translated into the formal mode, and that " a philosophical, i.e., a logical investigation must be an analysis of language," leads to a position where philosophical and logical theses all become merely conventions for the use of language, which throw no light upon the nature of the world and the problems of life, and for which no sort of objective justification can be or ought to be sought. But on the contrary, what is necessary is that we should give a meaning to our terms, that is, be able to formulate our theses in the material mode, and then be able to test, in relation to life and the objective world, whether, or how far, our theses are justified.

But, Carnap warns us, if we think that philosophy deals with the nature of the world—and not with words and empty thoughts but with the relations of thinking and being—then we shall become lost, as many (according to him, all) philosophers have been, in a maze of " pseudo-questions," " difficulties " and " contradictions."

But it is not hard to answer this objection.

The " difficulties," " contradictions," " pseudo-questions," etc., which beset the path of philosophers arise when they try to deduce the ultimate constituents of reality a-priori, and invent terms for these constituents which have no foundations in experience, practice and science. Such methods necessarily lead to illusions and to illusory difficulties, because we can gain knowledge of things only by experiencing and acting upon them, not by withdrawing into our own minds. As examples of such " pseudo-theses " might be cited : the " thinking substance " of the Cartesians, the " monads " of Leibniz, the " neutral elements " of Mach, and the " sense-data," " atomic facts " and " simple objects " of some of our " scientific " and " logical " contemporaries.

The way to avoid such " pseudo-theses " in philosophy is not, therefore, to reject all philosophical statements whatsoever, and to confine our attention to the analysis of language ; but it is to investigate the logical and philosophical foundations of our statements. Is this statement founded in science, experience, practice, or is it founded in some a-priori speculation? That is the criterion for testing the value of philosophical statements.

And a-priori speculation being the source of "pseudo-theses" in philosophy, it follows that we shall seek to avoid such errors by refusing to embark upon a-priori speculations. It does not follow that we can only avoid such errors by refusing to think about the world at all, and about the real foundations (if any) of our statements, instead confining our thoughts to language and our language to "the formal mode." The latter expedient is like the course said to have been adopted by Origen, who, observing the incontinence rife among men, proceeded to castrate himself. Carnap, observing that to think about the world and our place in it often leads to nonsense, proceeds to perform a mental operation on himself which prevents him from ever thinking about the world at all.

5. *Conclusion*

Let it be admitted that there really is a world in which we live; and that we do not use a language in order to have a game with words, but in order to communicate our thoughts and to communicate information about the world.

Then in thinking and speaking about objects, facts and events, we find that the material we are dealing with comes under various main categories or headings—such as matter, mind, time, space, motion, quantity, quality, object, property, and so on.

Therefore as well as dealing with questions arising from the properties of particular objects and groups of objects or processes, we find also that questions arise in connection with the basic categories.

These, then, are the sort of questions which we may call philosophical questions, as distinct from scientific questions—though in practice the distinction is not a sharp one, and we find that philosophical questions involve scientific ones and vice versa.

Such questions, says Carnap, ought to be formulated strictly "in the formal mode," as questions not about the nature of the world but about language.

What I am maintaining, then, in opposition to Carnap, is that such basic philosophical questions do not refer to language merely, though confusions may be introduced into them by misuse of language and an understanding of the use of language is relevant to their solution. They do refer to the objective world. And if there is an objective world—as there certainly is—then philosophical statements need to conform to the nature of the world—to " the logic " of the world, if you like to use that expression—and are not mere syntactical rules, which can be postulated arbitrarily since there is no standard to which they should conform.

To this may be added a point very pertinent to Carnap's objection that the discussion of philosophical questions " in the material mode " leads to contradictions and difficulties.

It is a very marked characteristic of the progress of human knowledge that the truth about any subject, or at least a higher approximation to the truth, is often reached as a result of the difficulties and contradictions arising from some partial and one-sided theory, or from the conflict between two or more such alternative theories. Progress is then achieved as a result of a new synthesis which overcomes the onesidedness which gave rise to the difficulties.

For example, I believe that reflection upon the contradiction between the rival theories that time is infinite and that time is finite can enable us to formulate philosophical views about time which solve that contradiction; although further difficulties then very likely present themselves, which call for further work on the subject. Again, reflection upon the difficulties involved in the metaphysical view that the world is " a complex of ready-made things " can lead to a solution of those difficulties along the lines of regarding the world as a complex of processes. And so on. Examples of this dialectical mode of development of knowledge abound in the history of science. For example, there was a contradiction between classical mechanics and new discoveries about radio-activity; and this contradiction was solved in quantum mechanics, which includes classical mechanics as a limiting case. But again, new contradictions and difficulties continue to appear, calling for fresh efforts for their solution. There is at the present time a contradiction in the discovery that the same things behave sometimes like waves and sometimes like particles, and the solution of this contradiction is not yet fully developed, though no doubt it will be worked out in due course.

It is, then, in reality no objection at all to formulations " in the material mode " that they may give rise to contradictions and difficulties. On the contrary, it is precisely by tackling those contradictions and difficulties that philosophical progress can be achieved. But it will not be achieved by characterising such difficulties as " insoluble," and taking refuge from them in " the formal mode of speech," giving up the endeavour to formulate truth about the world.

In conclusion.

Logical positivism and physicalism, despite its " scientific " and even " materialist " pretentions, is only a variant and repetition of the old Berkeleyan pure empiricism, the essence of which is to " analyse " and " interpret " scientific knowledge in a way to deprive it of all objective materialistic content. Logical positivism represents the final stage of this false and misleading philosophy, wherein science is deprived of any meaning whatever, and is represented as a mere system-building with words.

Logical positivism rejects the historical controversy between idealism and materialism in philosophy, asserting that they are just two languages, and that both depend on the making of pseudo-statements " in the material mode." In this, logical positivism represents the last refuge of idealism.

Throughout, the dogma is advanced that we must not think of the relations of thought and reality, about the objective meaning of our knowledge or about the nature of the world. Instead we must limit our thought to " speech-thinking," referring " only to linguistic forms." But no justification is found for this dogma, which leads only to theoretical helplessness.

The " method " of logical positivism is therefore only a method to kill philosophy, which has always regarded the nature of the world and the relations between thought and reality as its main problems. In place of philosophy it puts word spinning, decked up as " logical analysis."

Logical positivism thus deprives philosophical and scientific thought of its whole content, and is a programme for the impoverishment of thought.

CHAPTER 13

THE INTERPRETATION OF SCIENCE

1. *The Problems of Science*

In this concluding chapter I want to introduce some considerations about the foundations, methods and meaning of science, in contrast to " the logic of science " which has been presented by the philosophers of " logical analysis " and " logical positivism."

The interpretation of science is the most crucial question facing the schools of philosophy which have been reviewed. There are two main alternatives. Either we regard scientific theory as knowledge of the objective material world, or else we regard it merely as a set of useful rules summing up the orders in which data of various sorts are presented to us in experience.

But the interpretation of science must be based upon the actual methods and procedure of the sciences, and upon the real part played by science in social progress ; not upon a-priori considerations, whether those of Berkeley's and Hume's theory of ideas, or the logical theories of contemporary schools. A comparison between science and " the logic of science " will reveal some of the ways in which " the logic of science," which denies the objectivity of scientific knowledge, has misinterpreted the actual character of the sciences.

Carnap set out to expound " the logical analysis of the concepts and sentences of the sciences." But one thing that is in the first place remarkable about his " analysis " is, that it is based on treating science as a self-contained theoretical system. I will ask in the first place whether such a treatment of science is legitimate, or whether it is not on the contrary very misleading ?

According to Carnap, science has its basic " protocol," and erects a system of propositions on that " protocol." True he does not present science as a static system, but as constantly developing, growing and changing—never complete, but always advancing. But he does present it as a system of propositions whose mode of development and construction requires no reference to anything outside itself. The foundation consists in the protocol, and the development of science consists in the elaboration of propositions which accord with the protocol according to certain complicated syntactical rules. Any other considerations are mere "sociology," which has nothing to do with the logical analysis of science.

According to other theories, the foundations of science consist in various facts that turn up in experience; for example, that the pointer indicates such and such a mark on the scale, that specks of light appear in such and such positions on the photographic plate, and so on. And the task of scientific theory is to work out generalisations which will accord with these experiences and predict other experiences of the same sort.

Thus the task of science is presented as the task of working out a theory which will accord with certain data, whether the data are represented as facts of experience or as protocol statements.

But yet in actual fact, science, which is a social product, does not arise so much from our desire to formulate a consistent theory to accord with certain experiences or certain statements, as from our efforts to control natural and social forces for our own practical ends. No doubt the motive of pure disinterested curiosity, and the desire to bring some theoretical order into apparently unordered data, quite apart from any practical aims, has played a part in the psychology of individual scientists. But this is only the way in which a much more fundamental social need becomes manifested through the activity of certain individual people. For in fact, at every stage, the direction of scientific investigation, the problems tackled, the theories propounded to solve those problems, are connected with practical problems of social production, and have been tested in the solution of those problems. And this is proved by the whole history of science.

In his philosophical *Autobiography*, Professor R. G. Collingwood remarked very truly, that to understand a theory involves understanding what questions it answers. If you represent a theory as answering the wrong question, you misrepresent it—your analysis will be faulty. For every theoretical activity arises from the attempt to solve some problem, or set of problems. So if you think that the problems which a theory is attempting to solve are quite different from the problems which in fact it is attempting to solve, then you misrepresent and misunderstand the theory.[1]

" The logical analysis of science " is guilty of just such a misrepresentation of scientific theory.

The type of problem which scientific theory is attempting to solve, is put like this : Given data, $P_1, _2, _3, _4, \ldots$ to construct a generalisation, G, which gives a rule predicting such data.

But in fact the basic type of problem which science is solving is not a problem of " pure theory," to produce a generalisation summing up certain experiences or protocols, but is a very different type of problem, namely, the problem of how to control natural and social forces.

A recent writer on science, Dr. S. Lilley, goes so far as to define science like this : " Science is a method of solving the problems we encounter in our lives ; problems of producing more houses or clothes or food with less labour, problems of preventing diseases, and so on. And science is also the search for the background of knowledge which is required to solve these problems. To do these things science has developed a whole series of special methods—experiment, carefully arranged to give information as exact as possible about what is happening and what are its causes ; theory, which brings together the results of many experiments in one comparatively simple explanation ; and the use of such theories to forecast what will happen under certain conditions in the future, and so to solve the practical problems that lie ahead. All these things constitute science."[2]

The logical positivists would say that this is all " sociology," which makes no difference at all to logic. For they like to keep all ideas in watertight compartments, and to keep theory strictly aloof from real life. Logic is simply concerned with statements and the relations between statements ; why people should formulate those particular statements, and what their use is, is simply a matter of sociology. Nevertheless it must

[1] See R. G. Collingwood : *Autobiography*, Ch. V.

[2] S. Lilley : *Science and Progress*, p. 6.

be insisted that even a " logical " analysis should pay some attention to whatever it is analysing. If the development of the body of scientific knowledge, that is, of the propositions of science, is conditioned at every stage by connections with social practice, then it cannot for any purpose be correctly represented as if it were a purely theoretical development. If the basic problems of science are problems of social practice, then it cannot be correct to interpret science as if it were concerned with the solution of purely theoretical problems.

For example.

There is an interesting theory being worked out about the elasticity of certain carbon compounds, of the sort that provide the basis for rubbers. The theory shows that carbon atoms have a way of linking up with one another in a chain, to form very long molecules, consisting of many thousands of atoms. It can be shown that such molecules must tend to curl up with one another and to intertwine ; but under certain conditions they can be pulled out, so that a substance composed of such molecules will have the property of very great extensibility.

This theory can be represented as based upon certain protocols or data, provided by experiments with carbon compounds, and as being a system of propositions which has been constructed in accordance with such data.

But it is also true that such a theory came to be formulated because of the development and practical importance of the rubber industry, which required an understanding of the constitution and properties of rubbers ; and that the theory is of basic importance for the manufacture of synthetic rubbers and allied substances.

Thus to regard the theory of the elasticity of rubbers simply as a theory based on certain protocols or data provided by experiments with carbon compounds, would be wrong. The question the theory answers, the problem it solves, or attempts to solve, is not the question of pure theory : Given such and such records of experiments, formulate a rule, etc. ; but it is the problem of finding out what are those peculiarities of rubber which account for its elasticity. And by answering the question, the theory advances the technique of the manufacture of synthetic rubbers. The theory arises from problems of social practice, not just from pure theoretical curiosity.

To take another example.

Part of the great scientific work of Galileo was that he formulated laws governing the motions of falling bodies, pendulums and projectiles. The significance of the formulation of these laws by Galileo could be represented simply in the following manner—that given such and such data about the motions of falling bodies, pendulums and projectiles, Galileo succeeded in formulating rules summing up those data. But yet Galileo's problem was not the purely academic one of formulating rules to fit certain data, but of finding out the laws manifested in the motions of falling bodies and projectiles. The need to find out such laws arose from contemporary developments of social production—for example, the development of mining, and of artillery ; and consequently the work of Galileo had the most important practical applications.

Thus in this example again, the scientific theories of Galileo arose from the need to solve problems of social practice.

If it is only grasped that the problems of science arise from the need to solve problems of social practice—not just from a need to formulate rules to bring order into experience, but from the need to gain power and control over natural forces—then it can be seen that what science is doing is to treat of the objective material world and our place in it.

The aim and task of science is not to give rules predicting experiences or rules according with given protocols, but is to advance our power and control over nature, by advancing knowledge of the constitution, properties and laws of the objective world.

2. *Experiment, Apparatus and Instruments*

I have attempted to show, in the first place, that in interpreting scientific theory in terms of the formulation of rules based on given experimental data or protocols, " the logic of science " has failed to take into account the real character of the problems which scientific theories seek to solve ; which basically are always problems of social practice, arising from our efforts to control nature. But in the second place, with regard to the data of science themselves—for in order to solve the problems, science must always establish certain facts and then seek to erect a theory on that basis—" the logic of science " has failed to take into account the character of those data and the way they are arrived at.

Carnap seeks for the foundations of scientific theory in protocols ; but he cannot or will not say how the protocols are arrived at. In general, " the logic of science " sees the foundations of science in given data ; but it neglects to take into account how those data are obtained.

When science is " analysed " in terms of the formulation of rules based on given data, the data usually turn out to be recordings off instruments—pointer readings, flashes on screens, etc. This at all events is the case with modern physics, which usually receives the main, or even the exclusive, attention of those engaged in " logical analysis."

And thus we find the most extraordinary and confusing conclusions presented, to the effect that scientific theory consists in the main in the formulation of rules about pointer readings and flashes on screens. For example, the science of physics—what is it all about ? It is not about the constitution of the physical world, but it consists of statements about pointer readings and flashes on screens.

It is well known that A. S. Eddington, in his philosophical book on *The Nature of the Physical World*, produced a complete mystification of physics along these lines. And to all intents and purposes exactly the same sort of mystification is produced by the " logical analysis " of such philosophers as Wittgenstein or Carnap.

What is the answer to this mystification ? The answer is to understand that such data as pointer readings and flashes on screens are not things which just happen in the experience of physicists, presenting them with the task of formulating rules governing the order of such strange events, but that these types of events are produced by the scientists themselves, and produced with a definite purpose.

It is true that from the point of view of a " pure " mathematical physicist, the data may be regarded as just " given." For there is often a division of labour, where the experimenter produces the data and the mathematician interprets them. But yet he cannot interpret them rightly if he just accepts them as given—for the point is, they were produced, and he needs to know how they were produced. The " data " of science are produced, by scientific investigation and experiment, with the end in view of extending knowledge of the world.

For instance, there are various different sorts of pointer readings—those taken, for example, off scales, clocks, galvanometers, etc. The pointer is, of course, a part of a physical object, namely, a scientific instrument, which was very carefully constructed and tested according to certain established principles in order to register certain changes by measurement on a scale.

Eddington said, and he seemed to be in full agreement with Russell, Wittgenstein and Carnap: "The whole subject matter of exact science consists of pointer readings and similar indications."[1] From this he concluded that what the pointer signified was "inscrutable," "something we know not what"—whereas the only difference of Wittgenstein or Carnap is that they say that they signify nothing, and that to ask what they signify is senseless.

But yet, if we consider how the pointer is constructed; and regard the reading, not as an ultimate given datum, but as something obtained by definite means for a definite purpose; then there is no puzzle. The subject matter is seen to be, not pointer readings in themselves at all, but various aspects of the world, which we record by the pointer readings.

In general, science is not founded on the given—given protocols, given experiences, given readings, etc. Science is not merely empirical, but experimental.

For example. Galileo wanted to obtain laws of acceleration of falling bodies. So he devised experiments. These consisted in rolling a polished ball down a smooth inclined plane; he laid a scale against the plane, so that he could mark off the distances travelled by the ball on different occasions; and he constructed a clock to tell how long the ball took to travel the distance on each occasion. (It was a very crude clock in this case, as our present more accurate clocks were only invented as a result of the work of Galileo.) From the results of these experiments he was able to formulate the law that the distance covered by a falling body, starting from rest, varies with the square of the time of the fall.

This law, as is clear from the experiments from which it

[1] Eddington: *Nature of the Physical World*, p. 252.

was derived, does not have the pointer readings (on the scale and the clock) as its "whole subject matter," but it relates to the motions of falling bodies.

To generalise further. An experiment takes place when a scientist or scientists bring about certain changes under pre-arranged conditions, to observe the results. An experiment is an activity, a real material event, in which people (the experimenters) consciously and with purpose handle and alter the objects around them.

Thus, in so far as science is based upon experiments, scientific knowledge is not obtained merely by recording the given—pointer readings, etc., as in Galileo's case—and working out rules based on the given readings ; but it is obtained on the basis of the activity of changing the world.

We interrogate nature. We interrogate nature by interfering with it, changing it.

So scientific knowledge is founded on the activity of changing the world. We ask a question about certain things—what is their composition, what are their laws of motion, etc.? And we find the answer by changing those things and noting the results of the changes.

For instance, physicists have now won considerable knowledge about atomic structures. This knowledge was obtained—not just by looking at flashes and pointer readings and formulating rules about them—but by causing atomic changes, bringing atoms under conditions in which they got knocked about. They found something out about what was inside the atom by knocking bits out of it, and examining what happened when those bits were knocked out.

Now it is obvious that to find out what is happening under given conditions, and to observe it more accurately, instruments must be devised. And the technical development of scientific instruments forms a very important part of the history of science, for without these instruments scientific knowledge could not advance. There is a mutual relationship between theory and technology. The more we know about the constitution and laws of motion of material systems, the better the instruments we can devise. The better the instruments we can devise, the more we can advance scientific theory. Advance in theory leads to advance in technology, advance in technology leads to advance in theory, and neither can advance without the other.

In general, then, we find out about the constitution and laws of motion of material processes by bringing about changes in the world. We construct apparatus and instruments such that the character and effects of those changes can be readily perceived and measured by means of the instruments. What scientific theory deals with is then not just the recordings on the instruments, but the changes which are recorded.

For example. We make use of a barometer and thermometer to register changes in pressure and temperature, making use of our knowledge that an increase in the downward thrust of the particles in the atmosphere results in a rise of the mercury column of the barometer (because the instrument is constructed with precisely that end in view), and that an increase in the temperature of the surrounding bodies results in a rise of the mercury column of the thermometer. Thus we can establish that the boiling point of water varies with variations in the atmospheric pressure, and how it varies—a quantitative law. But that law is not just a rule for correlating readings on two scales, but it is a law about the behaviour of water.

A second example. We inject a disease into a guinea pig, and then make use of a microscope in order to see what effect this disease has upon the tissues of the patient. The microscope is constructed according to the laws of the refraction of light in order to produce an image of objects which are not visible to the naked eye. The experiment, however, does not just tell us what happens when we look through a microscope, but it tells us what happens to diseased tissues.

A third example. Rutherford investigated atomic structure as follows. He placed a radio-active substance in front of a very thin piece of metal foil, and behind the foil placed a zinc sulphide screen, with a microscope directed on to the screen. A number of green flashes were observed on the screen (since every time an α-particle emitted by a radio-active substance hits a zinc sulphide screen, it causes a green flash). And from the distribution of the flashes on the screen, Rutherford calculated both the approximate size and the charge of the atomic nucleus of the atoms composing the metal foil.

These green flashes were in fact the data from which Rutherford derived his atomic theory.

Was, then, Rutherford's theory about the size and charge of the atomic nucleus really only a rule about the distribution of flashes on a screen?

No. Because he had devised this apparatus and experiment in such a way that the distribution of the flashes on the screen would record something quite different, namely, something about the properties of the atomic nuclei inside the metal foil. The apparatus was delicately devised in such a way that the effect upon the particles emitted by the radium of their passing through the metal foil would be measured by the distribution of the flashes caused when they hit the screen. Whenever a particle hit an atomic nucleus as it passed through the foil it would be deflected, whereas other particles would go straight through without hitting anything. Thus the number and extent of the deflections suffered by particles registered upon the screen would be an index of the size of the atomic nucleus and its charge. (Clearly the bigger and more massive the nucleus might be, the more particles would be deflected, and the greater would be their deflection.)

These examples show how an apparatus and instruments are constructed, designed to register the results of changes deliberately produced by experiment. Scientific theory is founded, not just on given recorded data, but on the whole activity of producing changes in the world, together with the construction of means to register and record those changes. And the subject matter of scientific theory is not just the recordings, the end-record, but the constitution, properties and laws of the types of objects which are the subject of the experiment.

To understand the significance and the subject matter of science, therefore, it is necessary to premise:

Firstly. That the problems of science have their basis in the problems of social production, of extending our power and control over nature and natural forces.

Secondly. That scientific theory, arising from the need to solve problems of social production, is based, not upon mere observation and recording of experiences or facts, but upon the activity of changing the world.

Thirdly. That in changing things, with the object of gaining knowledge of their properties, constitution and laws, science makes use of an experimental technique—the construction of apparatus and instruments designed to register, record and measure the changes that take place.

Fourthly. That the records thus obtained provide data for the framing and building up of theories, hypotheses and laws—which relate, however, not to the mere readings and other records themselves, but to the objective material things and processes which are being investigated.

But none of these important facts are seriously taken into account by the exponents of the current " logic of science "—or were taken into account, for that matter, by the previous " inductive logic " of such empiricists as J. S. Mill, Venn, and others. On the contrary, they try to present scientific laws and theories simply as inductions from given data. For this reason they cannot grasp the character of science as knowledge of the objective material world. The data are expressed in propositions—protocol statements—and the scientific theories and laws are derived from those propositions by some logical or syntactical rules of inference or construction. But you cannot possibly understand the foundations or significance of science in terms of a " logic " which deals only with the relations between propositions. For that science is objective knowledge can only be understood on the basis of understanding that scientific knowledge is rooted in practical social activity. For we know about the world only from our activity in the world.

3. *Scientific Explanation*

Thus the problems of science arise from social practice, and are problems of determining the constitution and laws of motion of objective material things and processes. And the foundations of scientific knowledge lie in the experimental activity of interrogating nature by changing it. What, then, is the main theoretical outcome of all scientific theory ?

According, for instance, to Carnap's " logic of science," this would appear to be to construct a system of propositions free from contradiction and in accord with the basic protocol.

Of course, scientific theory should be free from contradiction and should accord with the basic observational data. But such a purely formal account of the matter gets us nowhere. For the main theoretical outcome of scientific theory is to *explain* the world in which we live.

A given subject matter may be said to be explained by a theory which states what are the different factors which produce and compose it, and what are their relations and laws of motion.

No explanation is ever complete. But people have always sought for explanatory theories, because we need such theories in our daily lives and for purposes of social production. In so far as things are explained, we know how to act in relation to them, and we know how far we can influence, control or produce them ; whereas we are helpless in relation to that which we cannot explain. And the best test of the correctness of a mode of explanation, of whether it is on the right lines or not, is the extent to which it leads to practical power and control.

Even primitive peoples had explanatory theories. For instance, in relation to the question of rain, they would explain this as being due to the action of the Rain God ; and so, when they needed rain, they would perform that course of action which, according to their theory, would be most likely to induce the Rain God to send it. Their explanation, however, both in theory and in practice was very unsatisfactory, and quite certainly untrue. But we, by means of scientific methods, are still trying to explain things. Science is a method for arriving at more complete and approximately true explanations, which are not mere guesswork or founded on accepted traditions, but are scientifically founded, tested and verified. The scientific explanation of things gives us tremendous power of social production, of handling and altering things in accordance with our particular interests, and of planning our lives.

It is possible to cite very many examples illustrating the meaning of scientific explanation. For instance, medical science is trying at the present day, amongst other things, to explain the nature of cancer. It has succeeded to some extent. It is known that cancers consist in a group of cells that have started to grow independently and out of relation to the rest of the body ; and this knowledge enables cancers to be treated, and sometimes cured. But it is not known why cells should begin to behave like this ; and thus the explanation is very far from complete, and we do not know how to prevent cancers. When medical science finds an explanation which will make it possible to control and prevent cancers, then it will have arrived at a more complete explanation of cancer. For such an explanation will not only explain what cancer is, but how it arises.

Again, modern atomic theory is a theory of extraordinary explanatory power in relation to many phenomena, which enables us to produce things and change things in a way that was not possible without the knowledge provided by this theory. This theory postulates small positive and negative charges as the basic physical constituents of matter, and describes their laws of motion. It explains, for instance, the series of elements, and accounts for their atomic weights. It explains the different states of matter—solids, liquids and gases. It has the most important applications in the electrical and metallurgical industries, and in all processes where we are concerned with transforming matter from one state into another.

It must not be concluded from this, however, that the desire for a direct practical application provides the immediate motive for all explanatory theories.

Indeed, many explanatory theories appear to have no direct practical application at all. For instance, we would like to explain the origin of the solar system, and various theories about it exist. But it does not seem likely that any explanation of the solar system, however perfect, would enable us to control the motions of the sun and planets, or to make another such system for ourselves better than the present one.

The need for such explanations arises not merely from direct practical needs but from the general desirability of extending scientific understanding and getting rid of the unknown and inexplicable.

For instance, when physical philosophers in ancient Greece began to work out physical explanations of thunderstorms, although their explanations were faulty and did not enable them to protect themselves against thunder and lightning, they marked a tremendous advance for human thought. For they began to get rid of superstition and fear of the supernatural, by showing that the thunder was not due to the wrath of Zeus but had a natural origin.

In the same way we still need to explain the origin of the solar system, of the earth, the stars, etc., not because this will have any direct practical application, but because it will banish superstition and advance natural knowledge.

At the same time, it may often turn out that explanations which appear to have no practical application at the time they are first put forward, may turn out later to be of great practical importance. For instance, knowledge of the composition and laws of development of the heavenly bodies, which appears to be knowledge for its own sake, may contribute to knowledge of the sub-atomic properties of matter, whose practical application is very important and immediate indeed.

It should be further noted incidentally, that many such explanations can never be directly verified, and their status must therefore remain a very provisional one, depending on their probability in relation to more general theories.

Thus Jeans' theory that the solar system originated by a star once coming rather close to the sun, and pulling pieces out of the sun by gravitational attraction, is an improbable explanation ; because from what we know of the motions of stars it would be very improbable that such a collision should take place. On the other hand, Haldane's recent theory that the solar system originated through a very energetic photon of light having collided with the sun would be a highly probable explanation, if further evidence should justify the view that the properties of matter change with time in such a way that a long time ago photons of light would have possessed much more energy than is the case at the present stage.

Science does not in fact consist in the statement of scientific laws only, but in terms of those laws it consists in the statement of explanatory theories. An explanatory theory is not the same as a general law. A general law is a statement of the form : "If . . . then . . ." ; but an explanatory theory says : "These *are* the factors which operate, and they operate like this : . . ." Clearly the explanatory theory uses the law, but is not the same as a law. And in terms of the explanatory theory we can recognise and understand the forces operating in the world, and, under certain conditions, change them, control them, and use them for our own purposes.

Failure to grasp that science explains, leads to some queer and puzzling results.

For example, many writers who philosophise about science, in particular about physical science, seem quite unable to relate the theories of science to the facts of common knowledge. They duplicate the world, and write as though there were two worlds—the world of common experience, of the things and processes which we perceive and encounter in our ordinary lives, on the one hand, and the world of physics on the other hand. Thus in his *Nature of the Physical World*, Eddington had something to say about tables, and made out that there are always two tables : the ordinary table, which we see and touch and have our tea on ; and the scientific table, which is studied by physics. The two tables are quite different, for the ordinary one is solid, whereas the scientific table is nearly all empty space. He cannot relate the table as described by physics to the table encountered in ordinary life.[1]

An exactly similar duplication is made by such philosophers as Carnap or Wittgenstein, though they consider themselves and are generally considered as far superior to Eddington in philosophical ability and logical acumen. For them, too, a scientific statement about a table does not relate to the same objects as an ordinary statement about a table. The ordinary statement relates to our ordinary perceptions ; the scientific statement relates to the pointer-readings, flashes on screens, etc., etc., which turn up under the specialised conditions of a physical laboratory.

But the truth is, that the scientific theory of the table explains the characteristics and properties of the ordinary table. There is only one world, one table. Scientific theory relates to exactly the same material world, and to the same table, as is perceived and encountered in ordinary life. For example, the scientific theory which presents the table as nearly all empty space, explains how and why the table is solid. Thus the table is solid, that is to say, it resists pressure ; when I put the teapot on the table it stands there, and does not fall through. Why ? Because when the teapot is put on the

[1] Cf. L. S. Stebbing, *Philosophy and the Physicists*, ch. 3.

table the small objects of which the table is composed keep hitting against those which compose the teapot, and thus cause the teapot to stand on the table and not to fall through. Hence it is explained why the table is solid in relation to such things as teapots—whereas, on the other hand, other things will go right through it ; for example, cosmic rays will go right through the table, because there is nothing to stop them.

This explanation, incidentally, of why bodies, such as tables, are solid, and of what constitutes their solidity, is of very great practical importance. We can, for example, make use of this knowledge if, instead of cutting wood for tables, we set out to make plastic tables out of plastic materials. In that case it is very important to know what conditions bring about solidity, and this scientific knowledge can lead to the construction of tables far more serviceable and far easier to make than the traditional wooden tables.

Thus scientific theory explains the properties of the familiar material world. It does not invent or discover another duplicate world of science.

It can be seen, too, that the denial that scientific theory explains the world is in its tendency entirely reactionary and obscurantist. If the explanatory aim of science is understood, then it can be seen how the advance of scientific explanation advances our power of controlling nature and of organising production for the common welfare of mankind. On the other hand, the denial of the explanatory power of science covers up the potentiality of the use of science for improving human life. If scientific theory is not related to the real material world, but a duplication is invented of the ordinary world and the world of science, then the world we live in and our life in it is presented as something strange and inexplicable.

Lastly, it is worth noting briefly, that logicians and philosophers, in writing about science, often seem to confine their " analysis " to the " exact " sciences, such as physics, chemistry, bio-chemistry, etc., and sometimes even to physics only. But there are other sciences, the historical and social sciences, whose methods are in many respects different, because of the different nature of their subject matter, but which none the less produce scientific explanatory theories.

For instance, the science of history is a science, which can explain the movement of history. But its methods are very different indeed from those of physics. Thus, for instance, the historian can perform no experiments, and the data on which he bases his theories are not the records of experiments, but are the records of the various historical events. But the science of history does explain history. It shows the factors at work. Thus it shows how the chief governing factor is the method of social production; how on this basis classes arise; how the development of social production and the consequent struggle of classes conditions the course of events. In this way it can give a more and more complete explanation, which also enables us in practice to recognise the historical factors at work now, how they operate, and therefore to be able, if we wish, to map out the course of action which is most likely to advance the interests and well-being of the people.

If, then, it is recognised that the aim of science is to formulate explanatory theories, which will give a picture of the different real forces at work in the objective world, and how they operate, so that we can in terms of such theories better control objective forces for our own purposes—then it can be recognised how greatly Carnap's "logic of science," and similar "logical" and "scientific" theories, have misrepresented the character and aim of science.

4. *Scientific Objects*

Science, then, deals with the objective world outside us. It deals with the properties and laws of objective things. As E. Meyerson said: "Science needs the concept of 'thing.'"[1] But nevertheless many doubts are raised as to whether the objects which science studies do really exist. I want in this section to deal with what may be called the status of scientific objects.

Certain types of objects are familiar to us in everyday life—namely, those whose size, constitution and relationship to our senses makes it possible for us to handle and to perceive many of their properties without the use of any special technique.

But such things as the stars, for example, which are very big in relation to our own size, and are a long way away, are shown by science to be very different from what they seem.

[1] Meyerson: *On Explanation in the Sciences*, ch. I.

We perceive them as little points of light, but investigation assures us that they are in reality bodies of enormous size. And again, other objects are revealed on a smaller scale, whose very existence was never thought of prior to scientific investigation.

In general, things of the same order of size as ourselves are familiar. But science introduces other objects, on the one hand very big ones, on the other hand very small ones. By so doing science explains the properties and behaviour of familiar objects, and helps us to transform and to use them. Such explanation involves, on the one hand, the exploration of the outer environment of the universe within which our life on the earth's surface takes place ; on the other hand, the exploration of the inner " microscopic " make-up of material things.

According to the modern " logic of science," such scientific objects are fictions, and nothing corresponding to the scientific description of them exists. To speak of such objects is only a way of speaking of something else—the order of our experiences, or the data presented in the basic protocols, etc. But yet, if science represents knowledge and explanation of the objective material world, then evidently such scientific objects must be held to exist just as surely and objectively as more familiar objects exist.

For example. We know that the earth is a large spherical body, but rather flattened at the poles, with a diameter of 25,000 miles at the equator. The earth and the other planets all rotate on their axes, and travel in elliptical orbits round the sun, which is very big as well as very hot. The Greek scientist Anaxagoras caused a sensation in the age of Pericles by teaching that the sun was in fact bigger than the whole of Greece : that was only his guess, and recent research has proved that it is enormously bigger than the earth.

These statements are not mere rules for predicting experiences, nor generalisations from certain protocols, but are well-established statements descriptive of the objective world in which we live. They are clear, unambiguous and well-verified statements about the sizes, shapes, and relative motions and distances of the bodies composing the solar system, on the surface of one of which we live our lives.

Moreover, by means of improved astronomical methods, we possess not only considerable knowledge of the solar system, but of the lay-out of the stellar universe of which the solar system itself is a part. Thousands of stars have been charted, not visible to the naked eye, and a considerable body of knowledge established about the relative sizes and distances of the stars, as well as about their general character and composition. It is established that our solar system is a part of one island universe—the system of stars composing the Milky Way; and that there are many other island universes, appearing to us in the form of spiral nebulæ, the farthest one so far visible being about 140,000,000 light-years away.

All this gives a picture—fairly reliable, though obviously very abstract and incomplete—of our environment in space. It represents a description of the objective material universe in its spatial extension; not a mere summary of what we may expect to see if we look through telescopes. Our idea of the past history of the universe in time, on the other hand, and of its probable future, is far more incomplete and uncertain; though a good deal of reliable knowledge has been accumulated as regards the past history of the earth.

Now in passing, it is perhaps interesting to note that when Copernicus, just over four hundred years ago, first put forward his famous hypothesis about the solar system, on which our present astronomical knowledge is based, there was even then some misunderstanding about its significance, similar to the misunderstandings which are being propagated today. Copernicus' *De Revolutionibus* was published after its author's death, and a certain clergyman called Osiander undertook to write a preface. He was afraid that the theory would offend the Church, and therefore he explained in his preface that Copernicus did not mean at all that the earth *really* moved round the sun; on the contrary, all Copernicus was doing was to invent a system of rules for predicting the apparent motions of the planets more accurately than was done by the previous planetary tables.[1] Osiander anticipated the "logic" of Wittgenstein and Carnap by four hundred years. But in fact this was not what Copernicus was doing; for the

[1] See A. Wolfe: *History of Science, Technology and Philosophy in the 16th and 17th Centuries*, p. 14.

Copernician theory was a theory which laid the foundations for an entirely new picture of the universe, which did come into violent conflict with the picture previously drawn up and accepted by the Church. Nor was the Church deceived; for the Pope soon put Copernicus' book on the banned list, Later on, Galileo was tortured for writing that the earth moved round the sun; but had Galileo only had time to study "logic," he might have kept himself out of trouble.

Besides gaining scientific knowledge of the universe around us, of the sort of bodies that it contains and of their mutual relations, we also gain scientific knowledge of the internal constitution and motions of things; and this is particularly important for explaining how things work, for controlling them, altering them, etc.

For example, we have gained considerable scientific knowledge of our own bodies, and how they work. Of fundamental importance was the discovery of the cell structure of organic substances, and of the laws of cellular growth through the division and multiplication of cells. Further investigation led to discoveries about the internal structure of cells themselves. Again, the discovery of nerve-cells (neurons), and the investigation of their structure and relationships, and of the way in which they transmit impulses, is of tremendous importance for the explanation of the behaviour of animals; especially of such animals as ourselves, with a highly developed and complicated central nervous system.

The cells of which the body is composed exist just as surely as the body does. Their existence is very well verified. We see them through microscopes, can observe and modify their growth, can influence their behaviour experimentally and observe the results, etc. Though like all scientific knowledge, this knowledge, too, remains extremely incomplete.

It was the development of chemistry which gave rise to the distinction of chemical compounds and elements. On the basis of that distinction, quantitative research began on the ways in which elements combine together to form chemical compounds. It was established that that combination always takes place in fixed numerical ratios. Thus was engendered the atomic hypothesis, according to which all chemical substances consist of very small atoms, different sorts of atoms corresponding to the different elements, and the atoms combining together in definite ways to form chemical molecules.

This was to start with no more than a working hypothesis. (To the nature and significance of working hypotheses I will return briefly later in this section.) Thus the question was agitated, did atoms really exist, or was their existence merely a convenient fiction or manner of speaking? Positivist philosophers in the latter half of the last century, such as Mach and Compte, were extremely scornful of anyone who was so credulous as to think that the atoms really existed. They explained that to talk of atoms was merely a convenient way of formulating the quantitative rules of chemical combination. As for such things as atoms existing, that was ridiculous metaphysics, and could never be capable of verification.

Nevertheless, the atomic hypothesis, originally introduced as a result of chemical discoveries, developed great explanatory power. For instance, it was possible to explain the nature of heat, and to account in an exact manner for many unexplained phenomena of heat, on the hypothesis that heat consisted in the movement of the atoms and molecules of which matter was composed. This led further to the explanation of the solid, liquid and gaseous states of matter. In the solid state, the individual atoms lie very close together, and their movements are not sufficient to counteract the forces that hold them together. If the atomic movements increase, the atoms break away, and the substance enters first into a liquid state, and then becomes a gas. Moreover, further quantitative investigations made it possible to specify fairly exactly what the size and weight of atoms must be, and the number of atoms contained in a given quantity of any substance. (There are $6 \cdot 10^{23}$ atoms in a gramme of hydrogen; the weight of each atom is $1 \cdot 6 \times 10^{-24}$ grammes, and its diameter 10^{-8} cm.)

If the results just mentioned were such as to create an increasing presumption that such things as atoms really existed, their existence has by now become definitely established as a result of the further development of atomic physics—verified experimentally and through the use of technique.

The first full verification of the atomic hypothesis came

through the investigation of radio-active substances. This meant that instead of merely postulating the existence of atoms as an explanatory hypothesis—a hypothesis to which all the more weight could be attached because of the wide field of phenomena it was able to explain—it became possible to study individual atomic processes, and the transformation of atoms of one element into those of another. Moreover, the striking experimental confirmation of the existence of atoms, revealed at the same time the divisibility of atoms, and that the atom was a structure composed of more elementary objects—the atomic nucleus and its accompanying electrons. It became possible to determine with great exactness the size and weight of atoms, to formulate the laws of atomic transformation, to indicate the atomic structure of the atoms of different elements, and to specify the size, charge and weight of atomic nuclei and of the electron. Moreover, all this confirmed the previous quantitative results secured by other methods previously on the basis of the atomic hypothesis.

More recently, the cloud-chamber technique invented by C. T. R. Wilson enables photographs to be taken of the paths traversed by individual atomic nuclei and by other components of atoms, set free by atomic transformations. This technique depends on making water vapour condense around the path of electrically charged particles inside the cloud-chamber; and a photographic apparatus then records on a photographic plate the streaks formed by the condensed water vapour. By means of cloud-chamber technique, not only were electrons and protons identified, but also other types of "elementary particles," positrons and neutrons, whose existence had already been suggested as a hypothesis by certain theoretical developments of atomic physics. In this way the existence of atoms and their various sub-atomic components is established with fully as much certainty as the existence, for example, of distant stars; that is to say, by photographic records.

Moreover, the techniques being developed by physics enable us, not merely to observe and photograph these sorts of objects, but to produce them and influence their motions and effects. Hence their existence must be regarded as very substantially verified.

It was just after I had drafted the above lines, that the

news was announced of the production of the atomic bomb ; namely, that a technique had been invented for utilising the process of the nuclear fission of uranium for definite ends—in the first place, for blowing up cities. This brilliant technical development will inevitably lead to other applications, for the purposes of peace. Naturally, it confirms beyond doubt the existence of the sub-atomic objects and processes, which are no longer put forward as a hypothesis, but are produced and used ; although very much still remains to be learned of their nature and laws. It has also brought forward in a startling and urgent way the philosophical truth, that science is knowledge of objective nature, which is equivalent to power over nature ; and that it behoves us to understand this, and to organise the use of that power for the progress and well-being of mankind.

It must be remarked in these examples how the development of scientific theory proceeds from hypothesis to knowledge. When a subject is under investigation, the explanation of the facts observed is usually in the first place advanced in the form of a working hypothesis. Such a hypothesis suggests further lines of investigation—further results which will be forthcoming if the hypothesis corresponds with the reality. By pressing forward such investigations, the working hypothesis is either shown to be erroneous ; in which case some alternative line of theoretical explanation has to be sought ; or else it is confirmed, and in the process of confirmation the hypothesis becomes knowledge. In the process of confirmation or verification, moreover, the hypothesis itself is generally modified, developed and corrected. And it is also necessary to premise that when we can claim to have scientific knowledge, such knowledge itself cannot be absolute, but is incomplete and provisional.

A very clear example of the confirmation of working hypothesis is sometimes given from the study of the planets. New planets have been discovered as a result of the observation of unexplained irregularities in the motions of known planets. Thus a hundred years ago, irregularities were observed in the motion of Uranus ; and to account for these it was suggested that there must be another planet whose orbit was outside that of Uranus. This was a working hypothesis. On the basis of such hypothesis telescopes were directed upon the position where such an unknown planet was expected to be found, and the result was the discovery of the planet Neptune. The observation of Neptune confirmed the working hypothesis. The existence of Neptune became a matter of knowledge, not of hypothesis. Later on, study of the movement of Neptune revealed more unexplained irregularities, and the hypothesis was advanced that there was yet another planet outside Neptune. This again was observed in 1930, the new planet being named Pluto, its observed period, perihelion, etc., agreeing remarkably well with the predictions made by the working hypothesis.

In this example it seems to be abundantly clear that the working hypothesis is the hypothesis of the existence, objectively in external space, of an object having certain recognisable properties—namely, of a planet. The hypothesis is not just a system of scientific statements giving a rule for where points of light will be observed through telescopes ; but it is a statement to the effect that something exists externally, namely, a planet. When the hypothesis is verified, then, instead of conjecturing the existence of such a planet, we can say that we know that it exists.

The development of scientific knowledge can be likened to the charting of an unexplored, or only partly explored, territory. The territory exists objectively ; whether we have charted them or not, the various mountains and plains, rivers, bays, etc., exist. Suppose the explorers are charting a particular river. They have been up it for 100 miles, and so they can fill in the course of the river for 100 miles on their map. Past that point they are not yet sure ; but they think the river may rise in some mountains another 100 miles in the interior. So on their map they mark the rest of the conjectured course of the river by a dotted line. These explorers will have to be constantly altering their map. Parts of it will be full of dotted lines, other lines will be firmly drawn, but even with regards to some of these they must take care not to use indelible pencil, for they may have to alter them in certain respects.

It of course frequently happens in the development of science that hypotheses are put forward which are not borne out.

For instance, in the 17th and 18th centuries it was generally presumed that the movements of animals were governed by the motions of what were called "the animal spirits." The body was supposed to be full of little channels, along which flowed the animal spirits. This hypothesis was, for instance, taken as gospel by the late Mr. Tristram Shandy, when he wrote in the first chapter of his *Life and Opinions*: "You have all, I dare say, heard of the animal spirits. . . . Well, you may take my word, that nine parts in ten of a man's sense or his nonsense, his successes and miscarriages in this world, depend upon their motions and activity, and the different tracks and trains you put them into." This hypothesis was given up with the development of the cell theory of organic substances, and with the discovery of the nature and functions of nerve cells and of the central nervous system. The hypothesis of the animal spirits was superseded by knowledge of the transmission of impulses through nerve cells. At the same time, it is clear, on the one hand, that the animal spirits hypothesis was not, as we should say, entirely wrong, but it did contain a partial correspondence to the truth; and on the other hand, that our present knowledge of the central nervous system is intermixed with what still remains a great deal of conjecture and hypothesis.

The principal mark of scientific genius is the ability to advance a bold and fruitful working hypothesis, combined with the technical ability to carry out the investigations and experiments indicated by that hypothesis. This ability was possessed, for example, in a most pre-eminent degree by Rutherford. It was Rutherford who advanced, as a working hypothesis to explain the phenomena of radio-activity, the theory that what was taking place in radio-activity was the transformation of elements, and that the atom was divisible. It was this hypothesis which determined the whole subsequent brilliant development of atomic physics; and Rutherford's technical ability in devising delicate experiments played further a leading part in that development. In the course of these experiments, as has already been indicated, the hypothesis was fully confirmed, and our knowledge of atomic and sub-atomic processes was enlarged and extended in many ways.

But in the sphere of atomic physics, it must once again be stressed that our knowledge is general, abstract, incomplete, and in many respects provisional. The detailed analysis of physics at any stage must distinguish those principles which are established from those which are hypothetical—and the distinction is not always a rigid one. For example, in the "Bohr model" of the atom, the electrons were represented as "particles" revolving round the atomic nucleus, on the model of the solar system. This was a working hypothesis which proved very useful, but which seems not to be turning out to be literally true. The further investigation of sub-atomic processes has shown that electrons exhibit wave-like as well as particle-like effects; and also suggestions are made about the possibilities of the creation and annihilation of such "elementary particles" as electrons. Clearly big and important modifications and developments of sub-atomic theory are taking place and are going to take place. But this does not affect the indubitable objective existence of sub-atomic processes; any more than the fact that there are many obscurities about the way in which our central nervous system works, contradicts the objective existence of the central nervous system and the fact that it does control our behaviour.

In concluding this section, it is useful to add a note about the famous "Principle of Economy" or "Occam's Razor," which is supposed to be a guiding principle for the formulation of scientific theories, and to which, as we have seen, great importance is attached by exponents of "the logical analysis of science." This is the principle which states: "Entities are not to be multiplied beyond necessity."

Those philosophers who teach that scientific theory does not describe and explain the nature of the objective material world, but consists in the formulation of rules of the order in which events turn up in experience, always attach great importance to the Principle of Economy. The principle that "entities are not to be multiplied beyond necessity" means simply that we should formulate such rules in the simplest possible way. Thus Wittgenstein restated the principle in this form: "What is not necessary is meaningless." In formulating scientific rules we should use as few entity-words as possible, and if we introduce additional entity-words which are not necessary for the formulation of the rule, then those additional words have in that context no meaning.

On the other hand, some philosophers, and even exponents of materialism, seem to regard the Principle of Economy as some kind of a-priori first principle, which can therefore be applied in constructing any body of knowledge ; as though it were somehow certain that nature herself did not multiply entities beyond necessity, and therefore we in describing nature should not do so either. Thus Howard Selsam tried to justify materialism on this principle, on the grounds that idealism, by bringing in God, Spirit, etc., multiplied entities beyond necessity, whereas materialism was more "economical."[1] But such a justification of materialism on a-priori principles is entirely anti-materialist ; and for that matter, the most "economical" philosophy of all would be solipsism.

But the Principle of Economy has no such fundamental significance as these philosophers, both positivist and materialist, seem to want to give it. And its significance can be understood only if we correctly understand the development of scientific theory from working hypothesis to knowledge.

In attaining to scientific knowledge, theory posits just those entities, and so many entities, as are known to exist and whose existence is verified—no more and no less. For instance, at a certain stage of sub-atomic knowledge we posit electrons, protons, neutrons and positrons as the known "elementary particles"—not because four is an economical number, but because those are the ones which have actually been discovered. Up to recently, there were only two—electrons and protons. Neutrons and positrons were added because they or their effects were observed in a cloud-chamber photograph. If we do not posit any more, it is because no more have been discovered, and there is no evidence that any more exist.

But let us suppose that a working hypothesis is being thought out to explain some unexplained facts that have come to notice. In framing such a hypothesis it is clear that it must be such as to suggest lines of future research and verification ; and it must suggest just so much as is necessary to explain the facts—any more would not be meaningless, but it would be irrelevant speculation.

---

[1] H. Selsam : *What is Philosophy*.

For instance, take the example already given of the explanation of the unexplained irregularity of the movements of Uranus by the hypothesis of another planet, Neptune, outside the orbit of Uranus. If the astronomers who had advanced this hypothesis had advanced a more complicated theory, to the effect that there was not one but two planets outside Uranus, their hypothesis, far from being meaningless, would in fact have been true. But the irregularities of Uranus were explained by the influence of one planet, Neptune. Anyone who at that time had said that Pluto also existed, would have been speculating ; and the data given by the irregularities of Uranus could not have given any indication as to where to look for the second extra planet.

The correct significance of the Principle of Economy has been well expressed by Eddington—perhaps not very consistently with some other of his philosophical formulations. " I am not satisfied with the view so often expressed that the sole aim of scientific theory is ' economy of thought.' I cannot reject the hope that theory is by slow stages leading us nearer to the truth of things. But unless science is to degenerate into idle guessing, the test of value of any theory must be whether it expresses with as little redundancy as possible the facts which it is intended to cover. Accidental truth of a conclusion is no compensation for erroneous deduction."[1]

Thus in advancing scientific knowledge of the various " entities " or objects which enter into the objective processes of nature, we advance from knowledge of those which are known to knowledge of others previously unknown, by the help of hypotheses which suggest just so much as is necessary for explaining observed facts, and which suggest methods of verification of the existence of the objects which enter into the hypothetical explanation. This is the significance of the Principle of Economy. Failure to conform with this principle would lead, as Eddington said, to idle guessing ; even though in some cases such idle guesses might more fully conform to the truth than a verifiable hypothesis.

5. *Science and Religion*

On the basis of this examination and criticism of some of

[1] Eddington : *Space, Time and Gravitation*, p. 29.

the questions of the interpretation of science, I want briefly to return again to the very fundamental question raised in Chapter 2—the compatibility or incompatibility of science and religion.

The problem of reconciling science and religion is one which has been of key importance in the development of philosophy ever since the beginnings of modern natural science—whether this problem was explicitly formulated, as with George Berkeley, or whether it merely conditioned the theoretical development without being itself explicitly recognised.

It has been contended in this book that the whole development of empiricist philosophy, from the " English Empiricists " to " Logical Analysis " and " Logical Positivism," has consisted in the development of a philosophy to reconcile science with religion ; and that this has involved the complete distortion and misinterpretation of the significance of scientific theory and scientific methods.

In contrast to the theories of pure empiricism and "logical analysis," I have tried to show that science represents knowledge of the objective material world and of our place in it. From this materialistic point of view, it can be seen that religious doctrine is incompatible with scientific knowledge. The scientific standpoint cannot reconcile itself with religion, but must necessarily involve the destructive criticism of religion.

The scientific criticism of religion and theology is not, as the agnostics would pretend, merely to say : " We don't know anything about all that." The criticism is a positive criticism.

To understand this criticism it is necessary to understand that the advance of science is not fully described as the development of a body of propositions. That is only one aspect of it. The advance of science is a social process, which is conditioned by the necessity of solving practical problems of life and society, and which leads to such solutions of those problems as enable men to advance their mode of producing and living.

The root criticism of religion from a scientific materialist point of view is, then, that religion too has its foundation in social processes ; but religion is not an effort to gain verified knowledge of the world in order to change the world in accordance with the material interests of mankind, but is an entirely contrary phenomenon. Religion is rather a system of unverified ideas conditioned by the need to reconcile people with the world as it is.

Religion is essentially an ideology. That is to say, a system or collection of ideas which is not based on knowledge (the discovery of truth and its verification), but which is an illusory system, arising from the need to adopt some mental attitude towards natural and social forces which are not understood, and representing therefore a distorted " fantastic " reflection merely of the real world.

An example of such ideology from a sphere other than religion has already been given in this book. The atomism of Hume's philosophy, which was recently taken up and further systematised in the system of " logical atomism," corresponded in no way with philosophical truth. But it did represent the reflection, in philosophical theory, of the economic position of the individual in capitalist society—a position the real nature of which was not understood, and which was reflected in this fantastic theory of the nature of the world.

The essential feature of religious ideology is animism, belief in the supernatural. " It is animism, the belief in the supernatural, which gives to religion its particular ideological character. . . . Religion is a particular fantastic reflection in the social consciousness of the relations of men between themselves and with nature, arising from the fact that men, in primitive society and then in societies divided into classes (ancient, feudal and capitalist), are under the domination of forces external to them, which they do not understand, and which they can neither dominate nor control."[1]

Thus Engels wrote : " All religion is nothing but the fantastic reflection in men's minds of those external forces which control their daily life, a reflection in which the terrestial forces assume the form of supernatural forces. In the beginnings of history it was the forces of nature which were at first so reflected, and in the course of further evolution they underwent the most manifold and various personifications among the various peoples. . . . But it is not long before, side by side with the forces of nature, social forces begin to be active ; forces which present themselves to man as equally

[1] L. Henri : *Les Origines de la Religion*, ch. 1.

extraneous and at first equally inexplicable, dominating them with the same apparent necessity as the forces of nature themselves. The fantastic personifications, which at first only reflected the mysterious forces of nature, at this point acquire social attributes, become representatives of the forces of history."[1]

Religious ideology has, then, no basis in any mode of knowledge. It does not represent a reflection in consciousness of the real existence of religious objects, but a fantastic reflection of the material world. This religious ideology arises in the first place from the helplessness, ignorance and fear of men, in the face of natural and social forces which they cannot understand or control.

Science, on the other hand, in its social significance, represents a revolutionary force. The advance of science is the advance of knowledge and understanding of the real nature of objective natural and social forces ; placing, therefore, in men's hands the means to transform their lives in accordance with their material interests. How great has already been the development of the productive forces of society, and the consequent social transformation, brought about through the development and application of science, is obvious to everyone. This development inevitably places now upon the order of the day, in the capitalist world, the task of realising full social control over all the means and instruments of production, and ending the division of society into exploiters and exploited which acts as a fetter upon social progress. And in so far as this objective is realised, and we gain full social control over all the means of living, and advance on the road of understanding and therefore of being able to control for our own ends the forces of nature and society, religious ideas lose their whole basis and function, and will in the end inevitably decay and become forgotten.

Between science and religion lies, therefore, the whole difference between knowledge of the world and of our life in it, derived from the effort to understand and control the forces of nature and society and leading to the possibility of the fuller and fuller realisation of such understanding and control ; and a system of fantastic beliefs, founded not on knowledge but on lack of knowledge, and not on the effort to

---

[1] Engels : *Anti-Duhring,* Part III, ch. 5.

secure control over nature and society but on inability to secure such control.

Marx summed up the basis of the scientific materialist criticism of religion as follows :

" The foundation of the criticism of religion is : Man makes religion, religion does not make man. Religion is indeed man's self-consciousness and self-estimation while he has not found his feet in the universe. . . . The struggle against religion is therefore indirectly the struggle against that world whose spiritual aroma is religion. Religious misery is in one mouth the expression of real misery, and in another a protest against real misery. Religion is the moan of the oppressed creature, the sentiment of a heartless world, as it is the spirit of spiritless conditions. It is the opium of the people.

" The abolition of religion, as the illusory happiness of the people, is the demand for their real happiness. The demand to abandon the illusions about their condition, is a demand to abandon a condition which requires illusions. . . . Thus the criticism of heaven transforms itself into the criticism of earth, the criticism of religion into the criticism of right, and the criticism of theology into the criticism of politics."[1]

When the revolutionary implications of the scientific criticism of religion are realised, then it is not surprising to find that many, indeed most, scientists prefer to qualify their science with agnosticism.

Agnostics say that while science establishes a body of knowledge about the material world, nevertheless it does not touch the " great " religious questions of God, the immortality of the soul, etc. God may or may not exist, the soul may or may not be immortal ; we cannot verify it and we do not know anything about it.

Is it the case that, setting aside whatever may be the origins and social functions of religious ideology, yet scientific knowledge is nevertheless compatible with the possible truth of some of the main tenets of religion ?

No, this is not the case.

It may readily be admitted that many beliefs associated with religion, such as angels, devils and the fires of hell, are absolutely obviously incompatible with scientific truth—

[1] Marx : *Critique of Hegel's Philosophy of Right.*

though it is at the same time true that most Christian Churches, though they profess the greatest regard for scientific truth, are still very frequently guilty of teaching the very crudest kinds of superstitions. But even if a lot of these cruder superstitions are given up, it is thought that the main essential religious tenets, those of God and immortality, remain ; and that whether we think there is any basis for believing them or not, they cannot be " refuted " by science.

It is perfectly true that, considering the tenets of God and immortality singly and by themselves, it is very hard to see how they can be either verified or refuted by any methods of science. For they are not scientific theories. But yet we do know, because it is tested and verified, that the body of science does provide knowledge of the objective world—and no longer merely odd scraps of knowledge, but a connected and coherent picture. And this whole picture, incomplete as it still is and always will be, already rules out God and the immortality of the soul.

It is not the case at all that the growing body of scientific truth does not touch the essential tenets of religion. All propositions, whether scientific or not, are about the same objective world ; and at a certain point, traditionally accepted myths and dogmas, whether they deal with devils, angels, heaven, hell, gods, God or our immortal souls, can be seen to be inconsistent and incompatible with scientific truth.

The only way, indeed, of salvaging religious theories and influences, in face of the rising tide of scientific truth and of power for human betterment based on the application of science, is to somehow make out that science does not after all give a picture of the objective world—a picture which is incompatible with the religious picture, and which rubs out and banishes the religious illusions. And this is what philosophers have been trying to do for 200 years, from Berkeley to Russell, Wittgenstein and Carnap.

But science does give a picture of the objective world, a picture which we are constantly extending and verifying. And this picture is incompatible with the picture which religion would paint of the world. There is only one world—the objective material world, which we study and learn to control through the sciences, and a merely fantastic reflection of which is embodied in the supernatural ideology of religion.

CHAPTER 14

CONCLUSION

In this book I have reviewed some of the main developments of modern empirical philosophy, from the 17th century to the present day ; and in particular I have examined in some detail the contemporary " logical " schools of empiricism. I have analysed the main different varieties of " logical analysis," and traced their genesis from the empiricism of the past. I have shown how the most crucial question they deal with is that of the interpretation of science ; and I have examined their " logic of science," and have attempted to show that, in contradiction to such " logic," science has as its subject matter the objective material world.

It remains to form a comprehensive judgment of this philosophy as a whole. Summing up the whole discussion, I would accordingly conclude :

Firstly. The contemporary " logical " schools represent in their essentials only a repetition of the older subjectivist theories, refurbished and disguised merely with new terminology and new phrases and catchwords.

While science enlarges our knowledge of nature and history, and our practical control over natural and social forces, these " logical " schools busy themselves with proving that it really does nothing of the sort, and that our knowledge is restricted to the contents of our own experience. With the advent of " logical positivism," not even this can be said about our knowledge. The whole question of the subject matter of science is dismissed as " metaphysics," and attention is directed solely to the forms of words and tricks of syntax employed in the system of " scientific statements."

Secondly. The upshot of the contemporary " logical " and " scientific " philosophy has been to produce a new scholasticism, as barren and as anti-scientific as the disputes of the schoolmen in the Middle Ages.

The essence of scholasticism was to dispute about certain questions according to certain rules ; and neither the questions nor the rules had any bearing upon the advancement of our knowledge of nature and mankind. The same characterisation holds good of the disputes of the logical philosophers today regarding the method of " analysis," and the terms which " analysis " should employ. Endless disputes and discussions are engendered over theories which never had any scientific foundation.

The " elements," " aspects," " events," " objects," " atomic facts," " sense data," " sensory fields," " experience," " worlds " ; the " elementary propositions," " protocols," and " rules " ; the " logico-analytic method," " principle of verification," " logical syntax," " methodical materialism," " physicalism," " principle of tolerance " ; the " protocol language," " scientific languages," " symbolic languages," " physicalistic language "—all these new philosophical terms and phrases, concerning the meaning and relative merits of which so much discussion has taken place over a period of forty years—they are all so much scholastic make-believe, which bears no relationship to the real world, and to the real problems of life and knowledge. And in their essence they are all one, because their essence is to confuse and deny the objective content of scientific knowledge, by means of some ingenious analysis based on the a-priori principles of a system of pure logic.

Medieval obscurantism in place of science is still the upshot of this sort of theorising today, as it was centuries ago.

Thirdly. The social significance of this philosophy is to be found in the fact that, like its predecessors, it disguises and covers up the really revolutionary character of science.

Science in the modern world gives a method for finding out the truth about the world, and can enlighten the whole human race with knowledge of ourselves, of our life and of the world ; the application of science can mean abundant food, shelter, health, rest, culture and happiness for every human being—the planning of social progress for mankind.

But to masses of the people at the present day it often seems a moot question, whether science is their friend or enemy. They see it not so much as an instrument which the people can use to achieve their material progress, as a means for inventing techniques which put men out of work, and for producing weapons of war for the destruction of whole nations.

The very people who use scientific techniques most commonly remain in ignorance of the principles and social significance of scientific knowledge, and our ideas about the world are guided by anything rather than scientific understanding. What is important is that we should fully grasp and understand that science is knowledge of nature which gives power over nature. And that we should accordingly control the means of using that power, so that it can be used to produce and not to destroy, and to produce for the needs of the people.

But powerful classes and great organisations exist, whose monopolistic interests conflict with the interests of the majority of the people, and which seek to limit the application of science rather to securing private profits and the conquest of commercial and political rivals, than to securing human happiness and the conquest of nature by man. Their interests are protected by means of material force and economic power ; and also by the fostering of ignorance, superstition, doubts and fears amongst the masses. The whole objective social role of theories which deny the objectivity of scientific knowledge is that they obscure the theoretical, practical and social significance of science, and leave the way open for the deception of the masses by religious, idealistic and anti-scientific illusions. By teaching that science only gives rules for expecting further observations ; by teaching that science is only a system of scientific sentences ; by teaching that science is not knowledge of the objective world of nature and society ; and by teaching that pure science exists divorced from life and society ; such a philosophy gives a stab in the back to the fight for the extended application of science and for scientific enlightenment, and so objectively serves the interests of the reactionary classes.

The philosophy of logical analysis, logical positivism, etc., stands revealed as the philosophy of the cautious middle-class "intellectual," of the professional, technical or scientific worker, who genuinely wants as an individual to accept and use science, but who does not want to commit himself on fundamental issues or to be involved in great social controversies.

But such a philosophy is theoretically sterile, and in practice plays into the hands of the enemies of scientific progress and enlightenment.

Fourthly. Finally, in opposition to pure empiricism and to

the various forms of logical analysis which derive from it, stands the philosophy of materialism. Our knowledge relates to the objective material world. It derives from the efforts of socially organised human beings to control and reshape for their own purposes the things about them, and the test and proof of the objective truth of our perceptions and our ideas lies in the resulting ability to understand and to control natural and social forces. Knowledge is not to be gained by a-priori theorising, but by the methods of science.

The great basic idea, indeed, for a philosophy which can comprehend the advances of modern science and answer the problems of the modern world, is the idea that the objective material world exists, that our knowledge is objective knowledge, and that science is the method and sum of objective knowledge.

Philosophy is the attempt to understand the nature of the world, and our place and destiny in it. It is necessary to reinstate this aim of philosophy, and to get over the narrow formalising attitude which dismisses all the great historical problems of philosophy as " pseudo-problems." The advance of science provides the means for the solution of the problems of philosophy ; it does not show that there are no such problems.

From the materialist point of view, there is no philosophy standing above the sciences, and science stands in no need of a-priori logical analysis and interpretation. Philosophy, in the classical sense of the search for knowledge of the nature of the world as a whole and of man's place in it, and natural science, merge into one, as ever fresh domains of knowledge are conquered by scientific methods of inquiry.

Thus today science gives a broad philosophical view of the world. For instance, the theories of physics are of profound philosophical significance. Again, nothing could illustrate more vididly the narrowness of the logical scholasticism and religious mysticism of Wittgenstein, than his statement that " the Darwinian theory has no more to do with philosophy than has any other hypothesis of natural science."[1] For the theory of evolution was a theory of revolutionary significance for philosophy—a great liberating idea, which forms part of the basis of the materialist view of man and of society.

---

[1] Wittgenstein : *Tractatus Logico-Philosophicus*, 4.1122.

In contrast to the narrow formalising aims of logical analysis and logical positivism, scientific materialism aims to comprehend the results of the sciences in the sense of showing :

(*a*) How the sciences establish a connected picture of the world, of universal history, of the complexity and laws of motion of events.

(*b*) What this picture means in relation to the problems of human life and society.

(*c*) At the same time, the incompleteness and limitations of this picture in relation to the given stage of scientific knowledge.

(*d*) The basis and mode of development of scientific knowledge, as revealed by the logical study of scientific method, the laws of thought and the conditions of its validity, the relations between thought and its objects, and the principal categories which scientific thought employs.

This being the task of scientific materialism, there is no theoretical limit to its advance, just as there is no theoretical limit to the advance of the sciences. Where philosophers have usually striven to formulate a system which would be final, and which therefore, if accepted, would put an end to the further development of philosophy, scientific materialism admits of no finality.

The liberation of humanity from poverty, oppression and superstition, is the great task of the present age, leading to the realisation of all the achievements of which free and organised humanity is capable. The task of philosophy cannot be separated from this. Those philosophers whose outlook is to accept the existing state of affairs, or who separate their philosophical ideas from the struggle for progress, will no doubt continue to busy themselves with "logical analysis." But nevertheless the advance of science and of life will leave them behind. As for materialism, it sees no limits to the advance of our knowledge of the world, and therefore to our power of living well and planning our lives with the object of securing the best for everyone, making use of the resources of nature for our own benefit.

Such are the general conclusions arising from this critical examination of the theories of empiricism and logical analysis.

INDEX